The Social Life of Forensic Evidence

The Publisher gratefully acknowledges the generous support
of the Publisher's Circle of the University of California Press
Foundation, whose members are:

Mrs. James McClatchy
Gordon E. & Betty I. Moore
Marjorie Randolph
Thomas J. White

The Social Life of
Forensic Evidence

Corinna Kruse

UNIVERSITY OF CALIFORNIA PRESS

University of California Press, one of the most distinguished university presses in the United States, enriches lives around the world by advancing scholarship in the humanities, social sciences, and natural sciences. Its activities are supported by the UC Press Foundation and by philanthropic contributions from individuals and institutions. For more information, visit www.ucpress.edu.

University of California Press
Oakland, California

Library of Congress Cataloging-in-Publication Data

Kruse, Corinna, 1975– author.
  The social life of forensic evidence / Corinna Kruse.
  pages cm
  Includes bibliographical references and index.
  ISBN 978-0-520-28838-6 (cloth : alk. paper)
  —ISBN 978-0-520-28839-3 (pbk. : alk. paper)
  —ISBN 978-0-520-96333-7 (ebook)
  1. Forensic sciences.   2. Criminal investigation.   I. Title.
  HV8073.K688   2016
  363.25—dc23

                                                    2015031935

24   23   22   21   20   19   18   17   16
10   9   8   7   6   5   4   3   2   1

CONTENTS

ACKNOWLEDGMENTS

This book could never have been written without the help of many individuals in the Swedish criminal justice system who took time out of their busy schedules to open their worlds to me, let me in on their daily work, answer all my questions, and read and comment on my manuscript. I am deeply indebted to all of them.

I am also indebted to the Swedish Research Council, whose grant made it possible to both conduct the research for this book and to write it.

I am grateful to my colleagues, particularly to Ericka Johnson, who has been a wonderful academic sister to me and firmly believed in this book from the beginning. She was also the book's first reader and has given me equally encouraging and demanding comments on the manuscript.

I also want to thank Boel Berner for always being such a careful reader and constructively blunt critic, and for getting me out of the corner I had painted myself into.

The Technology, Practice, Identity group at the Department of Thematic Studies – Technology and Social Change at Linköping University read the book and gave me wonderful feedback. I'd like to give special thanks to Magnus Blondin, who came up with the term "organic objectivity."

I am grateful to my *antroforum* colleagues for honest conversations over the years. I also wish to thank the international colleagues I met at various conferences for contributing advice, comments, and questions—in particular Barbara Prainsack and Ilana Gershon. I am especially grateful to Simon Cole, who has opened many doors and given invaluable advice.

A huge thank you to everyone at the University of California Press—especially to Maura Roessner and Jack Young for their enthusiasm and support, to Dore Brown and Genevieve Thurston for their meticulous work, and to the anonymous reviewers for their invaluable suggestions.

Last, but certainly not least, I want to thank Jens for living with this book—a houseguest not of his choosing, who nonetheless hogged the living room floor and weaseled its way into our conversations. Thank you for your unfailing support!

Parts of this book have pasts as articles. An early version of chapter 2 was published as "Legal Storytelling in Pre-Trial Investigation: Arguing for a Wider Perspective on Forensic Evidence" in *New Genetics and Society* 31, no. 3 (2012): 299–309, available online: www.tandfonline.com/10.1080/1463677 8.2012.687084. A large part of chapter 4 and the seed of chapter 6 was published as "The Bayesian Approach to Forensic Evidence: Evaluating, Communicating, and Distributing Responsibility" in *Social Studies of Science* 43, no. 5 (2013): 657–680.

Introduction

Contrary to the popular portrayal of forensic evidence "speaking for itself," it is not a product only of forensic science laboratories but also of the criminal justice system as a whole—and of the society both the system and the evidence are part of. I will show that the crime scene examination is just as crucial in producing forensic evidence as the laboratory; the plaintiff, witness, and suspect statements elicited by police investigators; and the interpretations that prosecutors and defense lawyers contribute to the evidence.

Consider the following case: two people are killed on a quiet residential street. The killing takes place early on a weekday morning, and there are no witnesses. Among other things, the police find a hat with traces of blood on it discarded a couple of streets away. The hat is sent to the laboratory, where forensic scientists extract a DNA profile, which is matched to one of the two victims, from the blood stain and a different DNA profile from a hair found on the inside of the hat.

So far, the case seems very solvable. However, the second DNA profile—which, according to the police and the prosecutor, is in all probability the killer's—does not match any of those stored in the national forensic databases. So the police ask for the public's assistance in reporting any and all observations in the area, especially those of a light-haired man—as the hair found in the hat was light in color and the DNA profile that of a male.

As I am writing this book, the case is ten years old and still open. The police have conducted hundreds of interviews and collected hundreds of buccal swabs. The DNA profile from the hat has been compared not only to the swabs taken for this specific case, but to all swabs taken from suspects in all cases in Sweden since, to all of the DNA profiles recovered from crime scenes in the country, and, through international exchange treaties that have come into effect in the last few years, also to DNA profiles in other European countries. Each year on the anniversary of the crime, the police ask the public to contact them with any observations they might have made, as insignificant as they may seem, and after these appeals the phone calls increase for a while. However, none of this has led to a solution or a suspect so far.

What this case illustrates is not that the police are inefficient or incompetent but that contributions from the criminal justice system as a whole—as well as from the public—are necessary to produce meaningful and useful forensic evidence. In this case, the laboratory extracted a DNA profile, commonly perceived as very reliable and important evidence, but the profile is not meeting expectations. And it cannot do so by itself. While the forensic laboratory's work is a crucial part of producing forensic evidence, in order for that evidence to become full-fledged forensic evidence, the DNA profile just as crucially requires components that the laboratory cannot provide. In this case, for example, the hat had to be found and recovered in a way that preserved the traces it carried—not only the blood on the outside and the skin cells on the inside, but also the single hair that was tested. This is the work of the police's crime scene technicians. Then, in order for the DNA profile to connect a wearer to the bloodstained hat, it must be compared to a DNA profile from a known source—such samples are provided through buccal swabs taken by the police. What is more, these samples are collected not randomly but rather in accordance with the law, respect for personal integrity, and efficient use of the criminal justice system's resources. The procedure for how to properly take a buccal swab is easy to learn, but knowing whom to swab requires a different competence than that of a forensic scientist.

However, a match with a comparison sample is not enough to turn a DNA profile into useful forensic evidence. Even when—or if—someone's DNA profile can be matched to the one obtained from the hat, the case will be far from closed. The hat might belong to this person, but he might not have worn it to the crime scene; he might have been present at the killing, wearing his hat, but not be the killer; or there might be another person, such as an identical twin, who shares the same DNA profile. These possibilities cannot be worked out in the laboratory. Careful work by the police would be required to investigate these potential scenarios, especially the first two. Police would need to interrogate witnesses (in this case, of observations before and after the killing, since there were no witnesses of the actual act) and the suspect in order to clarify the connections between the hat, the owner, and the killing.

The results turned up by this work then need to be interpreted. Perhaps the suspect says that his hat disappeared prior to the morning in question. Is this true, or does he see this explanation as a possibility of escaping responsibility? Perhaps the suspect has an alibi that disputes the DNA match's importance for the case. Does the alibi hold up? How do the witnesses' accounts tie into the information gleaned from the answers to these questions? This is for the police and prosecutor to investigate, but for the court to settle, as is the question of whether or not the killing was a crime and, if it was, which crime.

This book will show that forensic evidence is neither a fixed entity nor solely material but rather that it is inseparably part of particular legal, social, and technological practices. During its production, the forensic evidence-to-be constantly changes. It starts out, for example, as a bloodstained hat, and then becomes a DNA profile, then a match between two DNA profiles, then a piece of information to be set in relation to others, and, perhaps, ends up as evidence that contributes to proving a person's culpability. The material and the social are inevitably and inextricably entangled in the process of producing legally meaningful forensic evidence. Indeed, as I will show, the production of forensic evidence is not finished until the verdict provides closure to both the case and the evidence. In this process, I argue, forensic evidence can be understood as a form of knowledge—albeit particular (and incomplete) knowledge.

This book is thus a contribution to understanding forensic evidence and its role in the criminal justice system. I will follow the production of forensic evidence backward through the criminal justice system, showing that what may seem straightforward at first glance rests on an accumulation of very diverse knowledge practices. I will start with showing how forensic evidence is presented in district court, the part of the criminal justice system that is public, and then proceed to unravel the production of forensic evidence in the parts of the criminal justice system that work less publicly. From the court, the book will move to discuss how the public prosecution's office, the criminal investigation division, the forensics laboratory, and the crime scene division contribute to making forensic evidence. After that, I will gather the unraveled strands together and look at how the evidence-to-be moves through the criminal justice system as a whole, finishing with the final evaluation of the evidence in court. Looking at forensic evidence in this way makes it possible to discuss it in terms of how the "facts" examined in court originate and who is involved in the process.

While the book deals with forensic evidence in the Swedish criminal justice system, its findings are relevant to other systems as well. There certainly are differences between criminal justice systems—for example, in criminal and procedural law, the professions involved and the division of labor between them, and public attitudes and behavior toward law enforcement—but this book provides a vocabulary with which to think about how such factors are part of the production of forensic evidence in general.

This vocabulary can also be used to think about the production and distribution of other types of knowledge, especially knowledge that is produced in one context in order to be used in another—for example, moving knowledge from one profession to another, as is often necessary in large organizations, or making medical knowledge accessible to patients or other laypersons.

THE LEGAL CHAIN

When explaining the production of forensic evidence, members of the criminal justice system talk about the "legal chain" (*rättskedjan*), evoking—perhaps unintentionally—associations of a cast-iron linkage between crime scenes and convictions; the chain consisting of the police, the laboratory, the prosecution, and the courts.

In its ideal form, the legal chain begins with a police patrol arriving at the scene of the reported crime. Their task is to make sure that there is no danger to anyone and to look for indications of a crime having been committed. The officers will also talk to the plaintiff[1] and possible witnesses, and they may cordon off the area to await the crime scene division. Once they arrive, the crime scene division's actions are informed not only by routines and protocols but also by the decisions made by the leader of the pretrial investigation, who at this stage is most probably a police investigator, unless the crime is obviously severe.

As soon as there is a suspect in a case, a prosecutor is appointed. He or she will lead the pretrial investigation and, as a rule, also serve in a subsequent trial. The investigation is to be impartial; the police and prosecution are obliged to pursue and assemble evidence both against and in favor of a suspect.

The pretrial investigation leader's orders are carried out by the police investigators, called the "inner service," as well as by uniformed police officers, known as the "outer service" or officers "on the street." The pretrial investigation leader also decides whether the crime scene should be examined by the crime scene division and, if so, what the crime scene technicians should focus on. This is the next link in the (idealized) legal chain.

The crime scene technicians will arrive at the scene more or less immediately or on a following day, depending on the kind of crime committed, the type of crime scene, and their current workload. They look for and recover physical traces from the suspected crime, such as fingerprints, bodily fluids, scratch marks, and shoe prints. At the same time, they determine whether there is evidence for a crime actually having been committed at the scene.

The physical traces collected by the crime scene division are then sent on in the legal chain to the Swedish National Laboratory of Forensic Science (SKL, after its Swedish name, Statens kriminaltekniska laboratorium).[2] The pretrial investigation leader, sometimes in conference with a crime scene technician, decides which of the traces to analyze and in which way, and the crime scene division then commissions the analyses.

At the SKL, different forensic specialists perform forensic analyses and evaluate their results. The outcome, in the form of written expert statements, is sent to the police and incorporated into a pretrial investigation report. In this report, the expert statements are brought together with the other evidence the police have assembled, which may consist of, for example, statements from interrogations, surveillance footage, telephone records, or bank statements.

When the prosecutor leading the investigation declares it complete, the police investigators put together the investigation report and send it to him or her, and he or she then presses charges in district court (*tingsrätten*). The legal chain concludes with the final verdict. This is usually the verdict of the district court, although if one of the parties appeals, the case goes to the regional court of appeals (*hovrätten*) or, very rarely, to the Supreme Court (*Högsta domstolen*).

In everyday practice, there are variations in the chain. Not all cases involve forensic evidence; not all crime reports lead to a criminal investigation; some investigations never lead to an indictment; and not all verdicts are appealed. In addition, the various bodies in charge of tasks may vary with the crime. For example, when a serious crime has been committed, the crime scene is always examined by the crime scene division, whereas the examination of common crime scenes may be performed by a police patrol.

There may also be regional variations. At the time of my fieldwork, there were twenty-one regional police authorities under the Swedish National

Police Board, and these authorities differed slightly. For example, in the region where I conducted my fieldwork, the scenes of domestic break-ins were usually examined by the crime scene division, but in other police districts, such examinations were handled by *lokusar* (derived from the word *lokal,* "local"), members of the local police who have undergone more forensic training than "ordinary" police officers but less than crime scene technicians.

PRODUCING KNOWLEDGE

One of the central problems of solving crimes—that is, of determining who can be legally held accountable for what—is uncertainty. At the end of the legal chain, the court must make a decision on something about which the jurors have no direct knowledge. As a district court judge I interviewed put it: "Well, how it really is, only, perhaps, the offender knows." With a laugh, he amended his statement, "The *alleged* offender, and perhaps not always that, either [. . .] One can never be certain about how it really is." For a conviction, however, uncertainty is unacceptable—at least the kind of uncertainty that leaves room for reasonable doubt.

The pretrial investigation is meant to reduce this unacceptable uncertainty, in part through the production of forensic evidence. For example, fingerprint evidence can indicate that someone has touched an object, and shoe print evidence can indicate that someone's shoe has been at a crime scene. Thus, forensic evidence is a part of what becomes known about a contested course of events.

Science and Technology Studies (STS) can provide a framework with which to study everyday practices of producing knowledge. STS is an interdisciplinary field concerned with the interconnections of science, technology, and society, a field that takes the entanglements of the social and the material seriously.[3] Some of the underlying questions of the study of scientific knowledge and its production are highly relevant in criminal justice. For example, how do we know something? What makes this knowledge valid and legitimate? How can we be sure that we know?

STS scholars point out the impossibility of separating nature from society. Commonly, scientific knowledge, at least when it is "correctly" produced, is understood as being about nature—that is, free from human intervention and thus free from the social. However, STS shows that what is considered "correct" scientific practice is very much a social and cultural matter. Similarly, what is defined as a crime and how culpability can and should be conceptualized and proven is just as social and cultural (see Rosen 2006). Just as in criminal justice, where "only, perhaps, the offender knows" what happened, in the production of scientific knowledge, there is no way of knowing whether a piece of knowledge is "correct." One cannot step outside one's frame of understanding. Knowledge is produced—or, more precisely, constructed—within and as part of particular sociocultural contexts (just as forensic evidence is produced within and as part of criminal justice) and according to sociocultural norms and ideals of what good science is and how it should be conducted.

Just for clarity's sake, saying that knowledge and forensic evidence are constructed is not synonymous with saying that they are not real. For example, a car is constructed, but it is nonetheless real (cf. Thompson 2005, 33). That it is "constructed" means that it could be constructed *differently*. A car could use different technologies—for example, it could run on helium instead of gasoline, it could be bigger or smaller, it could be more or less powerful, its steering could be (and sometimes is) on the right side, not the left, and so on. These decisions have to do with sociocultural factors, such as the purpose the car is envisioned to have, on which side of the road it is expected to be driven and by whom, and the kind of infrastructure there is for roads, parking spaces, and gas stations.

This also means that it is not very useful to think about knowledge in terms of absolute correctness or truth. One can, however, think about it in terms of how convincing it is. Facts, asserts anthropologist and philosopher of science Bruno Latour, are the result of closed controversies. In Latour's (1987, 12) tracing of technoscience through society, facts or artifacts do not convince others because they *are* inherently true, but they *become* true precisely because they convince. Latour talks of "the tortuous history" of a knowledge claim as it is used and repeated, going "from hand to hand, everyone transforming it into more of a fact or more of an artefact." In this, "we had to abandon the sufficiency of Nature as our main explanation for the closure of controversies, and we had instead to count the long heterogeneous list of resources and allies that scientists were gathering to make dissent impossible" (Latour 1987, 103).

Thus, science and technology are not about *discovering* preexisting knowledge but about *making* new knowledge. Latour describes this as a manipulative and political process of enrolling others in one's agenda and of making dissent an untenable position. The more allies one has, and the more power-ful these allies, the harder it becomes for others to question a fact or to pro-pose an alternative. The parallel to criminal justice is striking. At least in adversarial criminal justice systems, evidence is produced in a framework of dissent and contestation.

Not surprisingly, there are STS studies of forensic evidence. These studies focus on particular technologies or particular aspects of forensic evidence, such as how fingerprint examiners came to be trusted and used as reliable in court (Cole 2001); how DNA profiling was made a stable, standardized, and legally accepted technology in the United States (Derksen 2000, 2003); and how DNA evidence has come to be regarded as a gold standard or "truth machine" (Lynch et al 2008). STS scholars write about the relationship between science and law in the United States (Caudill and LaRue 2006; Jasanoff 2001, 2006) and the credibility of forensic science in the Netherlands (Bal 2005). They look at laboratory practices in the United States (Daemmrich 1998) and the Netherlands (M'charek 2000) and at the contexts and collec-tives that articulate forensic technologies (M'charek 2008). They point to the importance of how forensic evidence in court is presented (Halfon 1998) and viewed (Jasanoff 1998), how the defense produces uncertainty (Lynch 1998), and under which configurations of expertise and commerce it is produced (Daemmrich 1998).

The scope of this research has also gone beyond the production of forensic evidence and its appearance in court toward forensic data exchange in the European Union (Prainsack and Toom 2010), the ethics and consequences of forensic databases in different countries (Dahl and Sætnan 2009; Duster 2006; Haack 2003; Hindmarsh and Prainsack 2010; Jasanoff 2006; McCartney 2006; Simoncelli 2006), and how practices of inclusion in foren-sic databases create suspect populations (see, for example, Hindmarsh and Prainsack 2010; Williams and Johnson 2008). They also examine Norwegian defense lawyers' (Dahl 2009) and Austrian and Portuguese prisoners' (Machado and Prainsack 2012; Prainsack and Kitzberger 2009) views of forensic evidence, predominantly DNA evidence.

These studies only examine parts or specific sites of the production of forensic evidence—the court, the laboratory, the legal community—but they raise important points. They show the interplay of specific constellations of technologies, law, and society. They show that forensic evidence is not self-evidently useful but must be accepted as a reliable, credible, and admissible type of evidence; that different types of forensic evidence may be treated differently, as practices may differ between criminal justice systems or jurisdictions; and that forensic evidence cannot be understood without considering its context. For example, in jurisdictions where DNA evidence is produced by one of several commercial companies that offer the service (such as in the United States), its examination in court may center on the credibility and authority of the expert witness (Daemmrich 1998). However, when there is only one forensic laboratory available, this may not be an issue, as defense lawyers may find it difficult to obtain the counter-expertise that can destabilize the expert witness's credibility and authority (Dahl 2009). How important these issues are and how they are being negotiated in court has an impact on how forensic evidence is produced and used.

SOCIAL THINGS

STS also emphasizes that "things"—facts and artifacts—are social beings, not least because they can modify other beings' behavior in similar ways as humans can (Johnson 1988). Forensic evidence certainly has that capacity. It contributes, sometimes crucially, to inculpating or exonerating people, thus affecting the people involved in a case.

STS offers several perspectives that lend themselves to studying exactly *how* (arti)facts participate in society. One of these is Actor-Network Theory (ANT; for an introduction to this theory, see Latour 2005). Since its inception in the 1980s, ANT has continuously been modified and nuanced, but one of its central tenets is that "entities take their form and acquire their attributes as a result of their relations with other entities. In this scheme of things, entities have no inherent qualities" (Law 1999, 3). ANT speaks about "actants" (instead of "actors"), to emphasize that both humans and nonhumans are of equal (analytical) importance in these networks of relations. Consequently, ANT focuses on how these networks are assembled and how their configurations bring about facts and artifacts (see Latour 1987).

In her praxiography, Annemarie Mol (2002) shows a multiplicity of atheroscleroses—a condition that affects the blood vessels—in a Dutch hospital. By focusing on how different medical professions see and talk about the "same" atherosclerosis, she discusses how a range of practices—which both include and produce patient bodies, blood pressures, painful legs, hardened arteries, statistics—simultaneously enact a diagnosis and a (manifold) disease.[4]

In her notion of agential realism (Barad 1996, 1998, 2003, 2007), Karen Barad stresses the "inseparability of 'objects' and 'agencies of observation'" (1998, 96), arguing that it is in "intra-action"—one might say, through practice—that both the observer, the observed, and the instruments of observation are shaped and meaning is created. "Nature," Barad states, "is neither a blank slate for the free play of social inscriptions, nor some immediately present, transparently given 'thingness'" (1996, 188). Instead, what is understood as nature or reality is material and cultural at the same time (Barad 1996, 185), produced by both material and human agency. There is no clear distinction between the material and the cultural; phenomena are simultaneously and inseparably material and cultural.

What these theoretical approaches have in common is that they recognize nonhuman participants in social endeavors. ANT in particular has, from its beginning, explicitly called for symmetrical analyses (Callon 1986). Of course, this does not mean to say that *relationships* between humans and nonhumans are necessarily symmetrical. Barad points out that there are inherent asymmetries, since humans "do the representing" (1996, 181)—that is, they have the last word on creating meaning. ANT also traces exactly how inequalities of power are created and utilized.

Just as the STS-informed studies of forensic evidence imply, the focus these approaches share on relations and practices stresses the fluidity of facts and artifacts. They all maintain that when practices and relationships change, so may their outcomes, that is to say, the facts and artifacts as well as the actants they produce.

Both are points that are highly relevant to studying forensic evidence. To understand forensic evidence as inherently cultural is, in essence, the same as viewing it as being produced not by nature but rather by a particular criminal justice system within a particular society. An analysis of the social life of forensic evidence is made easier by recognizing material agency and the possibility that nonhuman actants participate in social relationships

An STS perspective thus makes it possible to see forensic evidence as both material and social and to analyze the sociomaterial practices through which it is produced and made relevant in the different links of the legal chain. It also makes it possible to understand which knowledge practices the seemingly straightforward facts of forensic evidence are constructed through. However, the three approaches do not easily lend themselves to focusing on the chain of transformations that the forensic evidence undergoes between crime scene and courtroom. To analyze how the meaning(s) of and around forensic evidence at the different stages of its production are created, maintained, and transported between contexts and which negotiations and frictions they entail will require a slightly different framework, one that combines an STS perspective with an approach that, while its methodological focus follows the (arti)fact, puts its analytical focus on the human actors in the criminal justice system.

THINGS WITH SOCIAL LIVES

To follow forensic evidence and its production through the criminal justice system, I want to dust off Arjun Appadurai's notion of "the social life of things" (1986), which is built on "the conceit that commodities, like persons, have social lives" (1986, 3). In exchanging commodities, people negotiate the objects' value as well as the exchangers' relationships against a background of appropriateness, morals, taste, and other cultural understandings.

That is not to say that forensic evidence is a commodity—at least not in the Swedish criminal justice system—or that it is construed as having *economic* value.[5] However, it is exchanged, and Appadurai's notion allows for the combining of a theoretical focus on human actors (members of the criminal justice system) with a methodological focus on objects (forensic evidence-to-be) traveling through and connecting different cultural contexts. In his words:

> Even if our own approach to things is conditioned necessarily by the view that things have no meanings apart from those that human transactions, attributions, and motivations endow them with, the anthropological problem is that this formal truth does not illuminate the concrete, historical circulation of things. For that we have to follow the things themselves, for their meanings are inscribed in their forms, their uses, their trajectories. It is only through the analysis of these trajectories that we can interpret the human transactions and calculations that enliven things. (1986, 5)

Such an approach makes it possible not only to follow the objects' paths or trajectories but also to study how objects change in the course of such exchanges. It also makes it possible to think about these objects as participating in different sociocultural contexts—or, in Appadurai's words, in different "cultural systems" (1986, 15)—such as the laboratory or the criminal investigation division, and as being an integral part of different sets of relationships in these contexts.

As Appadurai's "things" spend their social lives in a succession of different places and participate in different sets of relationships, one can speak about them as having "cultural biographies" (Kopytoff 1986). In the case of forensic evidence, this biography can be said to span the links of the legal chain, and it involves plaintiffs, suspects, witnesses, crime scene technicians, forensic scientists, police investigators, prosecutors, defense lawyer, judges, and lay assessors—although not always simultaneously. By being made part of relationships and negotiations, forensic evidence contributes to turning people into victims, suspects, defendants, or convicted criminals or to dismissing them from an investigation.

The framework provided by the notion of the social lives of things thus makes it possible to examine how forensic evidence is a part of the criminal justice system. It also makes it possible to understand how this participation takes different forms in the different parts of the criminal justice system and with what ease or difficulty forensic evidence is moved between them.

ETHNOGRAPHIC FIELDWORK

In order to collect the kind of material that lends itself to the analysis I propose, I conducted ethnographic fieldwork in the various links of the Swedish legal chain.[6] I followed everyday work at three units of the SKL, focusing mainly on DNA, fingerprint, and tool mark evidence. I also observed the day-to-day operations of a public prosecution's office, a criminal investigation division, and a crime scene division, typically spending about a week at every place, sometimes spread out over a few weeks' time. I also observed a number of trials in district court. All of this fieldwork was conducted in urban contexts.

After this I took a second tour of the criminal justice system, this time interviewing forensic scientists, prosecutors, district court judges, defense lawyers, a crime scene technician, and a "regular" police officer.[7] I had met all of them other than the police officer and one of the defense lawyers during my fieldwork and thus often had already established relationships with them.

Given the confidentiality of the information that the criminal justice system handles and the police force's reputation of unwillingness to let in outsiders, I was surprised at the openness with which I was received. My interlocutors did not appear the least unwilling to speak with me at any point in the process, provided they could find the time, although observations in certain parts of the criminal justice system took several meetings to work out the how, when, and where of my research in a way that felt comfortable and nondisruptive to the workplace.

My access to defense lawyers was, however, very limited—I only interviewed two. Their work is not formally part of the criminal justice system (although it is important for the system's functioning), and their time is a commodity that were not able to give freely to me. In addition, concerns for client confidentiality would have made observing their work an impossibility. Similarly, although I tried, I did not manage to gain access to court deliberations after a trial. Apparently, the judges I approached felt my presence would intrude on a very private part of their work.

I complemented the ethnographic data I gathered with documents produced by the criminal justice system for its members as well as for the public, such as the SKL's magazine *Kriminalteknik;*[8] the Public Prosecution Service's (n.d.) leaflet *Prosecutor—A Part of the Legal System,* explaining how prosecutors work; and the Swedish National Courts Administration's (2008) brochure *More Modern Court Proceedings—Video Recording and Playback of Examinations in Court,* about changes in court practices.

I did not try to talk to plaintiffs, witnesses, or suspects about their views on forensic evidence. This was in part because I did not want to intrude on them in a stressful situation. Mainly, though, it was because I explicitly wanted to focus on the criminal justice system as a public institution and how it produces forensic evidence.

I do have regrets. One is not having gained access to the court's deliberations; another is that I never tried to arrange to follow a police patrol to a first response at a crime scene.

The main restriction on the fieldwork was my interlocutors' time. They made room in their very busy schedules to explain things to me or to be interviewed, so it was not always easy or even possible to squeeze more from them. Knowing that there would be only limited time in the field, I focused quite tightly on forensic evidence from the beginning. This made it possible to treat, within a manageable time frame, perhaps not their work, but forensic evidence from a holistic point of view.

While ethnographic fieldwork is typically conducted in unfamiliar cultures, I carried out this fieldwork, in many ways, very much "at home." Although I did not grow up in Sweden, I live there, and I have for quite a number of years. My interlocutors and I share a language and live under the same public administration. It is possible that we watch the same television shows and read the same newspapers, and we might even cross paths in our spare time.

However, in other ways, our worlds are quite different. What were perfectly mundane landscapes or cityscapes to me were, to my interlocutors, places closely intertwined with their work. What were to me just some high-rise apartment buildings, for example, were known as the "murderer buildings" (*mördarhusen*) by the crime scene technicians I met because of a murder that had taken place there several years ago. What made that particular case so special, apparently, was not only that murders are comparatively uncommon in the area and that murder cases (or suspected murder cases) that do not have a clear suspect from the outset are even more uncommon, but also that, as the crime scene technicians told the story, the police had been very compassionate toward the victim's widow, and in the course of the investigation, it turned out that they had been "sitting there and having sandwiches with the murderess."

On closer inspection, it becomes apparent that we sometimes share a language only on a superficial level. I had to learn what "a troublemaker" and "a public" were, what "doing housie" was,[9] and what the difference is between murder and manslaughter and between theft and unlawful disposal. I also had to learn to pay attention to the details in the forensic scientists' careful phrasings—details that I might otherwise not even have noticed in their speech or writing.

Doing fieldwork this close to "home" meant that engagement with my interlocutors did not have a prescribed end, since I never really "left the field." In particular, I had quite frequent contact with the SKL after my initial fieldwork there. I was invited to listen to guest lectures (and give one myself), and I was given the opportunity to sit in on a workshop about the statistical evaluation of fingerprint matches and on the laboratory's in-house training course in the Bayesian approach for forensic scientists.

Some of my interlocutors read drafts of some chapters of this book prior to publication. I asked for their help for a number of reasons: I did not want to violate the confidentiality agreement I had signed upon entering the field; I was apprehensive of having gotten things wrong; and, most of all, I wanted to give them a measure of control over how I wrote about them. Not everyone I approached had the time to read and comment on my work, but those who did often brought up issues other than the ones I had anticipated. Some would point out that I had things wrong, such as the order of interrogation in court or how to properly explain the result of a Bayesian evaluation. Others would explain in which ways they saw the world differently from me, adding further dimensions to my interpretations of their work. Their willingness not only to show me their worlds and their work but also to engage with mine, in the form of reviewing my manuscript, has helped anchor my analysis in the field.

The least I could do to repay their generosity is to prevent their being negatively affected by my research, so I've chosen to protect my interlocutors' anonymity to help ensure their safety. Although members of the criminal justice system hold professional positions of authority that give them the power to rather profoundly impact people's lives, they live in a vulnerable position personally. Police officers, prosecutors, and judges, as well as their homes, get threatened and attacked. I do not want to make their lives more difficult, nor do I wish to spread workplace discord, which could occur if someone took exception to a coworker's comment. Accordingly, there are no names in this book, neither of people nor of places, neither real nor made up. The only exception is the SKL in Linköping, a city in southeastern Sweden. As there is only one such laboratory in the country, trying to keep the site of this part of the fieldwork a secret would be rather pointless.

Some of the workplaces I visited were dominated by one gender (not always the same one), making it relatively easy for people of the minority gender to be identified by their colleagues or others. Thus, I have on occasion changed the genders of the people quoted or described. I have also changed the details of cases.

Although it regretfully entails the loss of certain nuances, I have used one descriptive term for each job title to preserve anonymity further (and to make it easier for readers to keep track of who does what in the criminal justice system). Thus, a member of a criminal investigation division is called a police investigator; an employee of the SKL who works with forensic analyses is called a forensic scientist; a member of a crime scene division is a crime scene technician; and a prosecutor of any type, from an assistant to a chief public prosecutor, is simply called a prosecutor.

Finally, I have changed details about all the plaintiffs, suspects, and witnesses, and I will gloss over their parts in cases as much as possible, both for ethical reasons and because I want to keep the book focused on forensic evidence.

———

CHAPTER ONE

In Court

LEGAL STORIES

Forensic evidence comes into the view of the public for the first time during a trial—that is, during the district court hearing. There, forensic laboratory results must be transformed into legally meaningful evidence, and this transformation is achieved through legal storytelling, a way of simultaneously presenting evidence, making it legally meaningful, and evaluating it. It is through legal stories that (forensic) evidence contributes to answering the salient question—whether the prosecution has proved beyond a reasonable doubt that the defendant is guilty of the crime(s) he or she is indicted for—typically but not exclusively in the form of supportive evidence that is used to strengthen or weaken accounts.

The defense can react to the prosecutor's case in different ways. They can challenge the prosecution's legal story, or parts of it; they can tell a different legal story of their own; or they can do a combination. The evidence the defense brings to court can also affect the prosecution's story, as it becomes part of the whole of the evidence and thus must be taken into account for a legal story to be plausible. However, the indictment, and thus the prosecution's initial legal story, sets the agenda for the trial and consequently for how the evidence is framed.

INTO THE COURTROOM

In Sweden, the district courts are the primary site for adjudication in the criminal justice system.[1] Few verdicts are appealed, and even fewer are brought before the Supreme Court. In 2014, for example, the district courts decided about eighty-four thousand criminal cases, the courts of appeal decided nine thousand (36 percent of which were amended), and the Supreme Court decided just twenty-three (Swedish National Courts Administration 2015). These numbers give an indication of the central role the district courts play in the criminal justice system.

The most noticeable difference from Anglo-Saxon criminal justice systems is that Swedish courts do not rely on juries. Instead, the prosecution and defense make their cases to a committee of judges and what are known as lay assessors (*nämndemän*). In the district courts, this committee consists of one judge and three lay assessors; in the courts of appeal, it consists of three judges and two lay assessors.

Lay assessors are legal laypersons who have been nominated by local political parties and appointed by the municipal council. They serve for ten to twenty days a year, and their votes are equal to those of the judges in determining judgment and sentence. Their role is to bring an everyday perspective to the professional judges' legal expertise and focus, a similar function to that of juries in other criminal justice systems.

In the courtroom, the committee—which is also known as the court—is usually seated behind a long table together with a court secretary. The two parties are seated at tables to either side, the prosecution and the plaintiff(s) with their counsel on one side[2] and the defendant(s) and their lawyer on the other. The witness box forms the fourth side of a rectangle with the other tables, facing the court and often with its back to the audience.

In accordance with the presumption of innocence, the burden of proof is on the prosecution to prove their case beyond a reasonable doubt. Accordingly, the trial's point of departure is the prosecutor's written indictment, which states which crime(s) the defendant is being charged with and on what grounds. This document is submitted to the court and the defense well before the trial itself. At the same time, the prosecutor also submits the pretrial investigation report, which lays out all of its evidence and which becomes a public document at this point.

However, although the court knows the prosecution's position and evidence beforehand, the proceedings are, by law, conducted verbally, and the court must take into account only what has been said during the hearing. Thus, a hearing begins with the prosecutor's opening statement in which she or he outlines the indictment, stating what the defendant is being indicted for, giving an overview of the evidence, and specifying which sanction the prosecution demands. One prosecutor I spoke with explained this opening presentation "as a trellis or a lattice." She continued: "I have to sort of give the time, the place, this is the evidence there is, explain [that] these witnesses will be heard, very concisely what they will be heard on [. . .]³ so that the court has a lattice of information that they then can weave the evidence into when we go through the evidence and hear the witnesses, so that it becomes a complete picture for them."

As the prosecution is under the obligation to retain their impartiality in court, she emphasized caution: "I try not to go all out and claim that it should be obvious that it is in a certain way, but [. . .] I present the facts, well anyway, what facts there are, try to sum them up and make them clear. [. . .] A little bit, though, you have to bring up in advance right away [. . .] otherwise it might be difficult to understand for the court. [. . .] I can ask the court to pay particular attention to [specific] details, because this is an important point."

How a trial is structured has, of course, an impact on its content. As the prosecution bears the burden of proof, their outline and their case is what the hearing revolves around—the question to be answered being whether they have proved their claim about the defendant's guilt. Accordingly, the prosecutor's "lattice" and the "details" he or she points out as central to the case affect the course and the focus of the trial when the evidence is put before the court. The defense will have to take this focus into consideration when they outline their view of the case and the evidence they wish to refer to.

After the opening statements, the full evidence is presented to the court. Unlike in the United States, in the Swedish criminal justice system there is freedom of evidence, that is, the parties are free to present anything they regard as relevant as evidence. The court receives all the evidence presented and, in its private considerations after the hearing, decides which parts are relevant. Therefore the demarcations between admissible and inadmissible evidence that can become important in and around US trials (see, for example, Caudill 2002; Jasanoff 2001, 2006; Lynch 1998) are not relevant in a Swedish context.

After the opening statements, the plaintiff is interrogated, first by the prosecutor and then by the defense lawyer. Next, the defendant is interrogated, first by his or her own lawyer and then by the prosecutor. After that, the parties present their evidence in detail. Witness evidence is presented and examined by an interrogation of the witness(es), first by the party who summoned the witness and then by the other party.

Forensic evidence is presented verbally, with the written evidence, such as expert statements, being summed up or read aloud by the party referring to it. Sometimes forensic evidence is presented by an expert witness. Evidence from the Swedish National Laboratory of Forensic Science (SKL) is usually summarized by the prosecutor; the SKL's forensic scientists are rarely summoned to court to appear as expert witnesses.

Finally, the prosecutor, the plaintiff's legal counsel, and the defense lawyer make their closing statements, summing up what they consider the principal points of the case.

During all this, the judge and lay assessors are expected to listen to the evidence put before them and not slip into an investigative role. The judge may, however, on occasion ask a witness for clarification, point out to a participant in the trial that it is not their turn to speak, or rebuke a noisy audience.

The court is required to be impartial. For the prosecutor, impartiality means presenting all the evidence, both for and against the defendant. For the court, it means considering the defense's version of events at least as seriously as the prosecution's. The only party allowed to be partial in court—or in the criminal justice system as a whole—is the defense lawyer, who is allowed, and indeed obligated, to be on his or her client's side. Unlike the prosecutor, the defense lawyer is allowed to keep evidence from the prosecution and the court if it is to the client's disadvantage.

LEGAL STORYTELLING

In presenting their cases, both the prosecution and the defense tell competing narratives about the defendant(s) and his or her relationships to other people—both to the victims and to others. In those narratives, they connect (or disconnect) people and their actions to (or from) the crime(s). Forensic and other evidence is an integral part of these narratives; the evidence is made understandable and relevant at the same time as it contributes to the narratives' coherence and logic.

Telling such stories is a common part of legal systems. Jerome Bruner, for example, describes "storytelling" as at the heart of legal practice (2002, 37). Similarly, Lance Bennett and Martha Feldman assert that "the criminal trial is organized around storytelling" (1981, 3). Their and other courtroom studies discuss how participants in trials employ everyday practices and strategies of telling (and deciphering) stories in order to connect individual pieces of evidence to a case and thus make them meaningful (see, for example, Huntley and Costanzo 2003; Pennington and Hastie 1986, 1992; Sarat 1993). In Bennett's words, a "story is an elegant symbolic framework in which a large amount of information can be organized, compared, tested, and interpreted to yield a clear judgment about disputed versions of an action" (1979, 311).

According to Bennett (1978, 1979), everyday discursive skills of telling and receiving stories provide a means of presenting and processing potentially confusing and contradictory evidence into judgments. Conversely, the stories told in court must incorporate all the evidence in order to be credible and thus valuable (Bennett 1979, 312). Consider the following two cases.

In one case, a man and his adult son were tried for fraud and unlawful disposal. The case concerned whether the defendants had applied for loans and credit cards in other people's names. Application papers had been ordered and then stolen out of the residents' mailboxes, filled out in their names, and returned. The documents and credit cards subsequently sent by the companies were also taken from the mailboxes (the unlawful disposal part) and, in some of the cases, used. Among other evidence, the defendants' fingerprints (as well as unidentified ones) were recovered from the application forms, and the handwriting on the forms had been matched to samples from the defendants. Additionally, a witness had seen the father rummaging in a stranger's mailbox.

The prosecutor maintained that this was a fraud scheme, contrived and carried out by the defendants. Their fingerprints on several of the application forms showed, according to the prosecutor, their involvement, as did the witness's account. Moreover, the witness said that the father, on making eye contact with her, had let go of the mail, closed the mailbox, and left. This, the prosecution maintained, was the behavior of someone who knew that he was doing something he was not supposed to.

The defense did not question that there had been a series of loan and credit card frauds, nor did they contest that the fingerprints on the applications were those of the defendants. What they did question, however, was their clients' involvement. The defense argued that the frauds had actually been carried out by one of the mother's relatives. They claimed that this person (proof for whose existence the police had been unable to find[4]) came and went in the clients' home at liberty, and the family, although being suspicious of his doings, were intimidated by him and felt an obligation to kin. The defense asserted that he was the one who had generated the fraudulent applications, and, as he had kept the papers in the family's apartment, the father's and son's fingerprints must have gotten onto them when they were lying about. In fact, the defense maintained, the unidentified fingerprints found on the application forms were the relative's. The defense also contended that the witness had observed the father doing something he was hired to do by a third party, and that the father, unaware that this was illegal, was simply glad to have found employment.

The second trial was about a car crash. Two cars had collided in a traffic circle, and the prosecution believed that this crash was not an accident, but that one of the drivers, a man in his late middle age, had deliberately hit the other car, seriously injuring the younger man driving it. The police suspected the crash might not have been a regular accident when the responding officers recognized both men as being on opposing sides of a conflict that had involved restraining orders.

The evidence the prosecution presented was composed of both witness testimonies and forensic evidence. The testimonies—given by the plaintiff, members of his family, and a friend—gave evidence of the younger man's troubled relationship with the older man's daughter. The difficulties had extended into a conflict between the young man and his (at that point, former) girlfriend's family, which had been going on with sometimes more and sometimes less intensity over several years.

In presenting the forensic evidence, which was decidedly nonroutine due to the rarity of cars being used as weapons, the complex circumstances of the traffic circle, and the expertise involved, the prosecutor and an array of expert witnesses recounted the steps taken to collect evidence. The crime scene division, with the help of a consultant from the National Road Administration (Vägverket), had cordoned off the traffic circle, arranged the cars involved in accordance with tire marks on the road surface and indentations and crush marks on the cars, and photographed them from a crane to document their presumable positions at the time of the crash. The consultant had then calculated the two cars' speeds from their positions and the skid marks, which had both been documented after the crash. The plaintiff's car had been hit from the side and pushed almost straight sideways across a safety island and a bicycle lane, all on dry asphalt. The consultant's calculations indicated that, at the time of the impact, the defendant's car had been traveling at a rather high rate of speed, whereas the plaintiff's car had been moving very slowly. In addition, the police measured the average speed of cars passing through the traffic circle and conducted test drives to estimate the maximum speed at which a car could travel through it.

All in all, the prosecution declared, this was not an accident. They claimed that the defendant had been driving at a speed that was well above the average for that traffic circle. In fact, it was at least as high as, if not higher than, the highest speed a police officer who was trained in high-speed driving had managed to reach while still being able to make it through the circle. This speed, it was implied, could only be reached if a driver was not overly concerned about staying inside the circle, which was the conclusion the prosecution also reached after considering the angle at which the cars had collided.

The prosecutor maintained that the collision was therefore to be seen in connection with the difficult relationship between the young man and the older man's daughter. After the defendant had caught sight of the young man speaking to his daughter, the prosecutor argued, he proceeded to run his car into the young man's car, trying to kill him and thus put an end to the conflict. It was extraordinary luck that the plaintiff had been only badly injured.

The defense attorney concurred that there had been a conflict, but said that the defendant's family had moved on, a closure testified to by the defendant's wife, the young woman's mother. Furthermore, the defense disputed the forensic evidence. This, the attorney concluded, was not an attempted manslaughter, but a tragic accident. Distracted by thoughts of his daughter's well-being, the defendant had lost control of his car in a trickily cobbled traffic circle, disastrously crashing into the other car. Consequently, he was as much a victim of the accident as the plaintiff; he had just been luckier in escaping almost unhurt.

Both cases were presented and discussed in court as readily understandable stories, incorporating and presenting the evidence in a way that clearly showed how it proved (or disproved) the defendants' guilt. Such storytelling in trials was examined by Bennett and Feldman, who based their conclusions on ethnographic observations carried out in a US superior court, interviews with participants in the observed trials, and mock juror experiments. They concluded that stories are the "link between everyday analytical and communicational skills and the requirements of formal adjudication procedures" (1981, 10). Stories, Bennett and Feldman argue, provide a structure that makes it possible to arrange information in a way that identifies a central activity, places it in a context, and makes it meaningful. They point out that while jurors do not necessarily perceive court proceedings as storytelling, nor do they consciously analyze storytelling strategies, they certainly are adept at making use of the storytelling structure to assess cases (Bennett and Feldman 1981, 15).

This structure, which is familiar to listeners from everyday communications, makes it possible to assess a story's plausibility and the teller's credibility. A story that does not develop such central features as setting, character, means, or motive remains ambiguous, thus drawing attention to missing information (Bennett and Feldman 1981, 10). Listeners, Bennett and Feldman explain, "must construct inferences about the relationships among the surrounding elements in the story that impinge on the central action" (1981, 41). These connections between story elements—for example, pieces of evidence—are what comprise the context within which to understand the central action; in criminal trials, the indictment hinges on the interpretation of this action.

When assessing stories, "the network of symbolic connections drawn around the central action in a story must be tested for internal consistency and descriptive adequacy or completeness. This simply means that the interpreter must determine that the various inferences that make up a general interpretation for a story are both mutually compatible (in light of what is known about similar episodes in the real world) and sufficiently specified to yield an unequivocal interpretation" (Bennett and Feldman 1981, 41). Listeners use their everyday skills and knowledge (including biases) to determine whether the connections being made between story elements are stringent or leave room for ambiguity. Ambiguous connections make stories less plausible, and thus make the interpretations of the central action less strong.

The work of other scholars sheds further light on how connections between story elements are made or tested. Anthony Amsterdam and Jerome Bruner's notion of "legal storytelling," which is based on analysis of the US Supreme Court's reasoning, consists of assembling cultural "stock scripts"— that is, "familiar characters taking appropriate actions in typical settings"— into "narratives" (2000, 45). These narratives provide templates for telling stories through which people and acts are categorized: "It is through narratives that we come to see people as heroes, villains, tricksters, stooges (and so forth), and that we come to see situations as victories, humiliations, career opportunities, tests of character, menaces to dignity (and so forth)" (Amsterdam and Bruner 2000, 46). To put it differently, those presenting a case associate people's actions with legal categories and consequences by telling legally meaningful stories that are organized with the help of familiar types of narratives and that draw on cultural stock scripts.

This is how the prosecution and defense organized their presentations in the cases of the fraud and the crash. In the fraud case, the prosecutor connected the fingerprints on a form to the act of defrauding a bank by using a stock script of the scheming criminal trying to become rich at the expense of others. The defense disconnected the prints and the act, using a stock script of the victim of family obligations. In the case of the car crash, the prosecution drew on stock scripts of fatherhood and misdirected concern for a daughter to connect the defendant to the act of manslaughter, whereas the defense's legal story was built on a stock script of a father's incapacitating concern leading him to near-fatal distraction.

In this way, the parties created divergent understandings of the defendants' actions, categorizing the defendants either as guilty of a crime or as victims of the circumstances. With these narratives, legal meaning is made; the culturally recognizable patterns of behavior or scripts described by Bruner and Amsterdam serve as aids to make sense of the evidence.

My interlocutors would not necessarily call their practices storytelling. When I asked a prosecutor about this, she explained, "I see it in terms of evidence, what has been proven. [...] I don't see it as a narrative. But [...] I understand what you mean, if you see it from the outside [...] you could perceive it [as a narrative], and it might be. [...] I just don't think about it in these terms." What nevertheless makes the notion of legal storytelling a useful analytic concept is that it can make visible how the interpretation of evidence is an integral part of the presentation of evidence.

Legal stories also are a means of assessing individual pieces of evidence. Evidence is not valuable in itself, nor is there a way of appraising its validity or usability outside of the framework of the legal story. As Bennett points out, "if the tactics through which evidence is introduced in a case are not aimed at establishing the status of the evidence within the overall story, the evidence simply won't make sense. These disruptive credibility tactics also show that evidence can be regarded as credible and 'objective' only through its connections in a story, and not as a result of some sort of independent test" (1979, 321).

As a result, as with all other evidence, forensic evidence requires incorporation into legal stories. As Sheila Jasanoff notes, "science enters the courtroom not in the form of bare facts or claimed truths about the world, but as *evidence*. That is, science must be worked into the particular kinds of propositions, representations, or material objects that the law regards as germane to establishing which party is telling the more plausible story" (2006, 329; italics in original). That is, the results produced through forensic science and technologies must be aligned with the law and be made to deliver answers to the questions that are relevant in court.

When I talked about forensic evidence with judges, prosecutors, and defense lawyers, the first thing that struck me was that they often made a marked distinction between forensic and verbal or witness evidence. One contrast they frequently and consistently emphasized was a difference in reliability between forensic and verbal evidence. For example, a district court judge told me: "Of course there's a difference between forensic evidence and verbal evidence. [...] It varies, of course, but with verbal evidence you always have the problem that people might not tell the truth or that they maybe misremember. Or don't remember anything at all. So there's a sort of doubtfulness. In that way it's different from forensic evidence."

Forensic evidence, he explained, was much less doubtful. Barring measurement errors, a possibility he carefully pointed out, forensic evidence was quite reliable. If an expert statement specified a certain percentage of blood alcohol, "then of course we rely on that [the defendant] had the amount of alcohol in his blood that it says [he did]. In that way, it's almost a hundred percent as evidence." Other interviewees typically talked about DNA evidence when discussing forensic evidence in general.

The judge's view of forensic evidence and its contrast to verbal evidence is not unusual. A prosecutor described the difference this way: "One comes from a human mouth, and the other's still a form of more solid . . . objectively observable phenomenon or circumstance whose evidentiary value is, perhaps, easier to have an opinion about. Well, the presence or not of alcohol in exhaled air or the blood, DNA at a crime scene [...], a bullet [that] has come from a certain revolver. [...] It's almost impossible to object to that result, that piece of evidence, so to speak."

"Human perception" and "memory," the prosecutor went on, always entail "a certain element of uncertainty," whereas the "tangible type of forensic evidence [...] once you've examined it, gives what it gives." What it gives are "basic facts" as opposed to flawed human recollections and descriptions.

Another judge highlighted the same problem with verbal accounts: "One doesn't have to consciously sit there and tell a lie," but people will have "their picture and their version of what happened to them, and that's not necessarily all that nuanced." In contrast, forensic evidence was—explicitly or implicitly—described by most of the people I interviewed as free of human intentions, flawed memory, or human bias, when they talked about it using language like "facts" (the prosecutor), "almost a hundred percent" (the judge), and "independent" (a defense lawyer).

Not surprisingly, forensic evidence was often described as very useful. One defense lawyer told me that it reduced uncertainty and therefore made verdicts more legally secure (*rättssäker*): "You can say that all evidence is important in trial. And [forensic evidence] is of course important—in both directions. It might be something that makes it more probable to be able to convict a person who is guilty, but it may also lead to perhaps someone being acquitted through forensic evidence; the person hasn't committed that specific crime. And the greater certainty you attain in judging, the better."

Judges and prosecutors talked about forensic evidence in similar terms, that is, in terms of potentially being very helpful—as long as it was not overrated, which many accused the media of being responsible for.

The contrast between forensic and verbal evidence is reminiscent of the notion of mechanical objectivity developed by Lorraine Daston and Peter Galison (Daston 1992; Daston and Galison 1992, 2007). In the history of science, they argue, different types of subjectivity have been regarded as dangerous for different reasons, and different types of objectivity have, accordingly, been desired. Mechanical objectivity has come to be associated with science and the advent of photography and automatization, and it "strives to eliminate all forms of human intervention in the observation of nature" (Daston 1995, 19). Verbal evidence, on the other hand, is seen to be affected by human bias and memory. Thus, treating forensic evidence as independent fact may have to do with a reliance on knowledge perceived not only as technoscientific but also as mechanically objective.

Judges, prosecutors, and defense lawyers drew less sharp lines between different types of forensic evidence. The Swedish term for forensic evidence is *teknisk bevisning*—literally, technical evidence—and judges, prosecutors, and defense lawyers sometimes considered everything that could be understood as broadly "technical" to fall into the category of forensic evidence, including medical expert evidence, telephone records, and surveillance footage, to name but a few types. The forensic scientists at the SKL, in contrast, tended to focus on forensic evidence that was produced at the laboratory. Typically, however, forensic evidence was spoken about outside of the laboratory predominantly in terms of DNA evidence, with only occasional remarks that there were, of course, other types of forensic evidence.

Perhaps not surprisingly, forensic evidence is questioned in court only in certain ways. With the fingerprint evidence in the fraud case, for example, there never was any question that the fingerprints came from the defendants. Where the parties' legal stories differed was in how the defendants' fingerprints had been deposited on the forms.

Judging from the trials I observed and my interviews and conversations with members of the criminal justice system, such treatment seems to be the norm, at least when it comes to forensic evidence produced by the SKL. One exception was a high-profile serial shooting trial in 2012 in which the defense brought an expert witness from abroad to challenge the SKL's bullet analyses. The evidence in the car crash case was questioned with the help of counter-expertise, perhaps because it had not been produced by the reputable SKL and so was not perceived to be as "scientific" and routine as the more usual forensic evidence produced by them.[5]

When my interlocutors talked about questioning forensic evidence in court, they often contrasted Swedish practices with those in the United States or sometimes the United Kingdom, saying that "we don't have American conditions"—with an implied or explicit "yet." They usually described these "American conditions" as defense lawyers questioning at length expert witnesses' qualifications, the chains of custody, and laboratory procedures. In contrast, a district court judge explained to me, in Sweden "you don't question DNA profiling, whether the SKL did it right, you don't question that. [. . .] It leads too far to, so to speak, go in[to the lab] and look at their work [. . .] [and] find sources of error in how they handle samples and that sort of thing."

He found it unnecessary to question the SKL's work, and he was not alone with his opinion. One judge was a little critical, however: "We sometimes buy into [forensic evidence] very easily—it happens very rarely that someone questions the SKL's results and their way of doing things. It surprises me a little that the defense doesn't do that." Later, the same interviewee went on to speak of the SKL's "solid workmanship," saying "I don't feel insecure, really, relying on the SKL." Thus, his aforementioned surprise was not a comment on the perceived quality of the forensic evidence, but rather a comment on principle. Forensic scientists sometimes expressed similar astonishment that defense lawyers usually did not question forensic evidence produced by the SKL.

What defense lawyers do question, however, is what forensic evidence means for their clients' culpability: "Whether or not it's that person's DNA, that's often—what can I say?—a non-question. Usually, there's such a high probability that it's that person's DNA that there isn't a lot to discuss—

assuming that the SKL has, so to speak, done a correct analysis, but I think one normally does [assume] that. So it's, 'how did it get there?' That's the question that's discussed." Just as the defense did in the fraud case, this defense lawyer shifts focus from the forensic evidence as a laboratory result to how the result can reasonably be interpreted.

In emic terms, forensic evidence requires "explanation." If, as a district court judge put it, "someone can present some circumstance [. . .] that gives an alternative explanation to this forensic evidence saying that they were there," the evidence's significance may change. Such "alternative explanations" can, for example, in the fraud case, be that the fingerprints had been deposited on the application forms in the course of straightening the apartment. In other cases, alternative explanations may be a result of a person making a so-called legal visit to the crime scene before or after the crime (for example, one can expect to find the fingerprints and DNA of a friend all over one's house) or even someone planting material (for example, someone wishing to frame another individual might leave cigarette ends at the crime scene that contain that person's DNA).

To put the difference between verbal and forensic evidence in terms of legal storytelling, there are a number of stock scripts for why people deliver the narratives they do—they may tell the truth, they may lie, they may misremember—but the stock scripts applicable to forensic evidence are more limited. As a laboratory result, it seems, all that can be said about forensic evidence is that the SKL works correctly and impartially. Stock scripts come into play only when it comes to what the forensic evidence means for the case.

With this understanding of forensic evidence, it may be expected that it would be given a central role in trial. But while forensic evidence—if there is any—can certainly be important in a case, it does not take central stage.

MAIN AND SUPPORTIVE EVIDENCE

Although forensic evidence is regarded as reliable, it is consigned to a supporting role in the trial and subordinated to verbal evidence, the inherent unreliability of which the judges, prosecutors, and defense lawyers I spoke with so readily pointed out. Judges, prosecutors, and defense lawyers alike make this distinction between main evidence and supportive evidence. This is a district court judge's description: "Usually [in trial], there is some kind of main evidence, and then there is different supportive evidence, or different forms of supportive evidence. Take rape cases, where you often have situations in which word is against word, a lot of focus is on the main evidence, which is the plaintiff's statement. But that's not enough. Her[6] statement must be supported by the rest of the investigation [and] by the supportive evidence, and this is when forensic evidence is very rewarding, so to speak."

The distinction this judge makes between main and supportive evidence falls along the line between verbal and forensic evidence, but not as one might expect after hearing descriptions of forensic evidence as being reliable, unflawed, and useful. One use of forensic evidence is to enhance the credibility of verbal evidence. The reliability of a plaintiff's or a witness's statement is affected by the uncertainties created by human memory and bias, not to speak of the ability to tell lies. Since such uncertainty is unacceptable in court, or at least for a conviction, the prosecution attempts to reduce it. This is where forensic evidence comes in. In the words of a judge, it serves as "a good support." He explained that if "what one person says also can be verified in another way, with forensic evidence, [...] that someone has been at the scene, for example, that you can find ... DNA, fingerprints, footprints, what have you, then it of course strengthens that narrative."

In terms of legal storytelling, a connection made between the elements of a legal story based on one (inherently uncertain) verbal statement is tenuous. If it is to hold up, the statement must be supported. Conversely, if the statement is weakened by other evidence, the connection is also weakened.

Although support can come from verbal evidence, the reliability of forensic evidence makes it much stronger supportive evidence. Judges, prosecutors, and defense lawyers use forensic evidence to assess other evidence, first and foremost the statements that make up the main evidence. Unlike with verbal evidence, there is minimal doubt about the veracity of forensic evidence, and thus it can be used to assess other evidence. For instance, one judge gave an example of a person who denied that they were in a place where DNA was found that matched theirs. In the judge's view, in light of the DNA evidence, "the discussion is over, so to speak. [...] We'll have to accept [the denial] there, but it's pointless to continue to reason about that."

In this way, when used as supportive evidence, forensic evidence can become an undisputed fixed point in legal stories. One judge told me: "Rape cases are the most striking [...] because there often is no witness evidence. There is a lot of witness evidence on behavior after ... the event, and that is of great importance as well ... how the plaintiff was perceived afterwards, [if] she has confided in others and told them and so on. But usually, there's no one [who saw] the offense itself. There may be injuries and so on, that's a forensic examination, and if her statement of what's happened is supported by the medical examination, [her] statement becomes more reliable."

The same, he went on, applied to DNA evidence. If the defendant's DNA was found on the plaintiff, "then you have evidence for intercourse. Then the question becomes more . . . [was it] voluntarily or not." Thus, the reliability of forensic evidence—which is the quality that makes it so desirable—is subordinated to the narratives delivered by plaintiffs, witnesses, and defendants.

Forensic evidence was treated as secondary to verbal evidence both in the trials I attended and when members of the Swedish criminal justice system talked about it in general terms. Prosecutors would talk about how "DNA isn't enough by itself" and forensic scientists would say that "a DNA match is not the one and only salvation." Asked whether it would be possible to convict someone on only forensic evidence, one of the judges I interviewed had his doubts. What is more, for him it was difficult to even imagine a scenario involving only forensic evidence. Clearly, the idea was alien to him. "When you have a plaintiff, there's always the plaintiff's statement there, as well," he said and asked me to clarify the question.

His reaction may not have to do only with plaintiffless crimes being the exception, but also with how Sweden's procedural and police laws and practices shape the cases he is used to seeing. As soon as someone is formally a suspect—well before trial—they must be informed about the suspicion and the evidence against them. When the police notify a suspect, they also take a statement from him or her. Thus, even if there is no plaintiff whose statement can make up the main evidence, by the time a case reaches the court, forensic evidence is nonetheless usually accompanied by statements.

This may also explain why the judges I interviewed de-emphasized the importance of forensic evidence. As a district court judge explained to me, "You can't say that DNA solves all problems and if there isn't DNA, there's a problem. That's not how it is. There are lots of other [types of] investigations that may be sufficient. Lots of times we don't have DNA or anything like that."

Another judge stressed, "There are more and more [forensic technologies] and the technology is improved more and more. But in the majority of cases, you don't get forensic evidence, and you don't need forensic evidence, either. There may be witnesses."

Thus, forensic evidence is useful but "not salvation," as another judge put it. All of the judges were careful to point out that there were many cases in which forensic evidence was absent or not of central importance. However, since they were equally careful to point out that forensic evidence certainly was very useful, they did not appear to be expressing a generally skeptical attitude to forensic technologies.

With some prodding, the judges did talk about cases in which the types of accounts that usually make up the main evidence in a trial were absent. Those cases are not necessarily "drastic events," such as murders or the like, a judge told me, but might be ordinary thefts, for example. In those instances, the plaintiff cannot give their version of the crime because they were not present. These are much tougher cases, the judge added: since "you can't really build that much on the defendant's statements, [. . .] there's not a lot there you can [take] as your point of departure."

Still, the judge focused on a narrative—in this case the defendant's— rather than on other possible evidence as the point of departure for the trial. His colleagues took the same approach. "Ordinarily," one of them said, "you have a plaintiff's statement, and that is regarded as the main evidence." He could, however, at least in theory, see forensic evidence as becoming central in a plaintiffless case: "You can imagine a situation where the plaintiff . . . is dead . . . [and] you have witness evidence. It's more of a circumstantial case, [with] different forms of weak, indirect evidence, and there a [piece of] forensic evidence may suddenly become the main evidence, so to speak, in that chain of circumstantial evidence."

He described a hypothetical situation in which witnesses saw someone leaving a house at a crucial time where a dead person was later found. If, he went on, this suspect's DNA was recovered from the crime scene, "the forensic evidence becomes very central."

However, even though this judge could conceive of forensic evidence as being at least part of the main evidence in a trial, he concluded, "But only forensic evidence, that's tough. You need something to build onto."

Another judge talked about how "forensic evidence is great in as far as it can clarify circumstances in a different way." But, he said, "how you then put these circumstances together into a conviction, that's still the same problem as it used to be." He is presumably referring to how things were before the advent of, primarily, DNA evidence.

The problem with using forensic evidence as main evidence is that it requires interpretation in order to answer the questions that are salient in a trial. As one judge explained, "Forensic evidence can actually only show such tiny outward circumstances. You can't look inside people. You need to keep it apart. It proves that DNA has been there [...] but then, the conclusions you draw from that, you'll have to go through the process and see how it turns out."

When the judge talks about "tiny outward circumstances" and not being able to "look inside people," he is probably referring to the fact that forensic evidence is often not able to prove how and when DNA or other traces were deposited at a crime scene. It is not able to prove intent either.

In terms of legal storytelling, the difference between verbal and forensic evidence is one of narrative. People's accounts of an event are narratives. Their narratives may not always be perfectly stringent and plausible, but people usually strive to make them coherent. They make connections between the story elements and the central action—that is, between pieces of evidence and the course of events in question. The witness who saw the defendant rummaging in the mailbox, for example, delivered her testimony in a way that made it clear that she did not consider the defendant's behavior innocent. In her narrative, the defendant's furtive facial expression and body language revealed not only that he had become aware of the witness but also that he was aware of the illegitimacy of his errand. Thus, the witness not only reported on the defendant's action but also connected it to the fraud and thus to the question of the defendant's guilt.

Forensic evidence, on the other hand, does not come in the form of narratives. It can connect objects and bodies to each other—for example, linking the loan applications to a defendant through fingerprint evidence—but it typically does not deliver information on the character of their relationships. In very few cases, the relationship between evidence and a crime is self-evident. For instance, if a defendant's DNA matches that extracted from semen found on someone who clearly cannot legally consent to sexual activity, a very tight connection is created between the defendant and the crime. In most cases, however, more evidence—and interpretation—is needed to delineate how forensic evidence fits into the legal story.

However, forensic evidence is not a blank slate upon which any meaning can be inscribed. The context of the case as a whole circumscribes the possible meanings that can be attributed to the forensic evidence. In the case of the fraud, the other evidence affected how the fingerprints found on loan forms could be made legally meaningful. The defendants' explanation that they touched the forms while they were straightening their relative's effects weakened the prosecutor's claim that the fingerprints connected at least one of the defendants to the fraud. The explanation, however, was in turn weakened by the police's inability to find proof of this relative's existence.

Thus, even though forensic evidence is regarded as very reliable, it is also regarded as unable to stand on its own. It requires other evidence to make its connection to a case unambiguous; as the judge put it, the court must "go through the process and see how it turns out." And, at the end of the "process," the court must decide whether the prosecution has proven a defendant's culpability beyond a reasonable doubt.

EVIDENCE WITH A PAST

The legal storytelling in court is not spontaneous. Well before the trial, both the prosecution and the defense have access to the evidence. Thus, the legal stories told during trial are at the very least prepared, and perhaps also rehearsed. They may be adapted to fit the other party's legal story or emphasis, or modified with, say, a surprising detail from a witness, but their essential features and arguments are decided upon beforehand.

In the same way that legal stories have pasts before they are brought to the courtroom, forensic evidence accumulates a pretrial biography. This biography may be hinted at during trial through witnesses—for example, a testimony from the crime scene technician who has recovered a trace or from the forensic scientist who has analyzed it—and I argue that it not only affects but indeed *forms* the forensic evidence that becomes visible in court and, in consequence, also how it is evaluated and made part of the verdict.

In order to unravel this biography, the following chapter will take a step backward into the past of forensic evidence presented in court and examine how it is made part of legal stories as prosecutors lead pretrial investigations and prepare for trial.

CHAPTER TWO

The Public Prosecution's Office

LEADING INVESTIGATIONS

In most cases in Sweden, the Public Prosecution's Office (Åklagarkammaren) comes into a case long before the pretrial investigation is finished. As soon as there is a suspect, or if the suspected crime is serious, a prosecutor is appointed to lead the investigation, which is conducted by the police. (Exceptions are petty crimes, such as shoplifting, which are led by a police investigator.) In practice, leading such an investigation means that the prosecutor gives orders to the police investigators and receives reports from them. Where I conducted my fieldwork, the prosecutors and the police had their offices on different floors of the same building, and investigators would come into a prosecutor's office to report on their progress in a case and discuss how to proceed. Thus, Swedish prosecutors play a central role in processes that have been described as police work in other criminal justice systems, namely of responding to and "making" crime—that is, of establishing whether or not an event constituted a crime (see, for example, Ericson 1981; Innes 2003).

In their work, prosecutors contribute to the biography of forensic evidence by putting it together with other evidence and working it into a legally meaningful framework to be presented and negotiated in court. They do this by making the evidence part of legal stories—that is, through pretrial legal storytelling. The prosecutors' interpretations and assessments are what make a piece of forensic evidence either legally valuable or dismissible.

Assessing and interpreting evidence is also intertwined with acquiring new evidence. Interviews with witnesses and involved parties lead to more interviews as well as to forensic analyses; the new evidence leads to still more interviews and analyses. New pieces of forensic evidence affect the prosecutors' legal stories as well as their interpretations and assessments of other pieces of evidence. Thus, the prosecutors not only oversee the assembly of evidence, but also its interpretation, simultaneously assembling and assessing evidence and legal stories, fixing multiple possible stories into one during the course of the investigation.

In interpreting evidence, prosecutors draw on the same stock scripts and legal categories that they later use in the trial, assessing the evidence as a whole and organizing it into plausible and reasonable legal stories. Even before the trial, stock scripts are used to make connections between pieces of evidence and people, casting people "as heroes, villains, tricksters, stooges (and so forth)" (Amsterdam and Bruner 2000, 46). In other words, they use stock scripts to classify crimes and categorize people as suspects and presumable victims.

Both the police and the prosecutor are under obligation of impartiality. That means that the pretrial investigation must investigate both sides of the case—in other words, they must look for evidence that implicates as well as exonerates suspects.

The pretrial investigation is thus an important part of transforming traces of suspected crimes into legally meaningful evidence (cf. Jasanoff 2006, 32). Throughout the pretrial investigation, the prosecutor works with the help of multiple tentative pretrial legal stories.

STARTING FROM SCRATCH

"This can go any which way. It can turn out absolutely huge or be an absolute flop." This was the prediction of a prosecutor who had just been told by police investigators about a rape case. As with many cases, this one started with someone contacting the police to report having been the victim of a crime. In this case, as there was a suspect, named by the plaintiff, and the alleged crime is serious, there is no question about involving a prosecutor immediately.

How the investigation proceeds from such a beginning depends, a prosecutor explained, "on how much you have from the start. If you only have maybe very meager information in the police report, you'll have to start by getting more information, and then you have to build on that . . . on what you learn."

In this initial stage, leading an investigation is about making sure that nothing is overlooked or lost. The prosecutor aims to "collect *everything*. You don't know what will be useful, and, you know, you can bet your ass that the one thing you didn't collect, the one thing you didn't photograph, there will be objection about."

Accordingly, the prosecutor sends the police to collect any and all potential evidence. This includes documenting injuries on the plaintiff as well as on the suspect, "if it's that type of crime." Witness reports are collected, as well as the plaintiff's and the suspect's versions of what happened. Blood samples are taken if there is suspicion that one (or both) of the parties was under the influence of drugs or alcohol at the time of the purported crime and if not too much time has passed. If relevant, the clothes the suspect and plaintiff were wearing at the time of the incident are collected, along with cell phones and computers. Photographs of the possible crime scene are taken.

Many of these traces will only be available for a short time. Drugs and alcohol are metabolized rather quickly, injuries heal, clothes may be washed or worn again so that traces on them disappear, people may erase text messages from cell phones and files from computers (or at least try to), and witnesses' memories of the event may fade or change. Not surprisingly, prosecutors are worried about missing something obvious or important that will result in questions remaining unanswered later in the investigation and, consequently, in court. "That's the fear you live in, [. . .] that you get a case, perhaps a quite serious crime, and you forget that one really important measure [. . .] and it turns out later that you should have taken that, it would have been very . . . very crucial, perhaps decisive for whether it will hold up or not."

In deciding what potential evidence to collect, the prosecutor in charge uses stock scripts—hinted at above by the comment, "if it's that type of crime"—to put the scant details that are known about the case in relation to each other. At that point, the prosecutor tells rather generic and thin legal stories to classify the crime, categorizing the course of events as a case of a particular unlawful action and simultaneously deciding which evidence is therefore needed. Much in the same way as prosecutors at a public defender's office in California, described by David Sudnow (1965), did, prosecutors in Sweden draw on stock scripts of "normal crimes"—that is, typical ways of how, by whom, and why particular crimes are usually committed—to interpret actions, or in many cases reported actions, in order to decide whether they can be classified as potential crimes.

Take, for example, a case where the police caught several persons amassing a cache of guns and balaclavas. As the custodees consistently refused to talk, I was surprised to hear a prosecutor speak of "the robbers" and "the preparation to commit robbery." Surely, I thought, this must be a case of illegal possession of firearms. So I asked the prosecutor how he could know that the custodees had been preparing for a robbery, as they had refused to speak and thus certainly had not explained their cache in those terms. He just shrugged and said, "What else were they going to do with all those weapons?" I must have looked puzzled because, smiling, he added, "The only other thing it could possibly be would be preparation to commit murder, and that's a worse crime." In other words, he used a stock script of a normal robbery (and discarded stock scripts of other crimes) to translate the cache into a particular unlawful act.

Early on in any investigation, there are usually several options as to how a particular course of events can be classified. For example, a knife fight might be considered an assault, an attempted murder, or a robbery that escalated. If the fight resulted in a death, it would not necessarily be classified as murder; it might be classified as manslaughter or even involuntary manslaughter, depending on the circumstances.

The interpretation is guided by the law, which defines prerequisites that must be fulfilled for an action to be considered a particular crime. Similar crimes are differentiated by the degree of damage (emotional as well as physical or financial) and the offender's intent. Thus, stealing a truck full of computers is a more serious crime than shoplifting a chocolate bar; breaking into an apartment and thus violating someone's feeling of privacy and security is a more serious crime than breaking into a shed or basement; and intentionally killing someone is a more serious crime than accidentally causing a death.

These interpretations also matter for the pretrial investigation in practical ways. Firstly, the more serious the crime, the more resources can be spent on the investigation and the more intrusive the police can be in collecting evidence. (Prosecutors cannot, for example, obtain court permission to tap telephones on suspicion of petty crimes.) Secondly, the classification makes an impact on the kind of evidence that will be required to prove to the court that the crime's prerequisites have been fulfilled. Classification (i.e., matching evidence to actions and legal categories) is a continuous process that takes place throughout the pretrial investigation. As evidence is collected and evaluated, the prosecutor assesses which classification is reasonable and which evidence they might need for a case to hold up in court.

Because they were concerned with treating suspects fairly, the prosecutors I spent time with started the classification "at the top"—that is, with the most serious crime that can reasonably be suspected. Telling a suspect first that he or she is suspected of a comparatively mild crime and later informing them that the classification has changed to one that is much more serious was not seen as acceptable. One prosecutor said: "It feels [. . .] less appealing to go up, you know: 'Now you're suspected of threat. No, we'll change it to attempted manslaughter.' [. . .] It doesn't feel very appealing to sort of sneak up on people like that." It does not feel appealing either when this happens unintentionally—for example, when the evidence assembled during investigation unexpectedly leads to a more severe classification.[1]

Even though the prosecutor did not put it in these terms, I understood this discomfort as having to do with the prosecution being responsible for and thus having obligations toward suspects. The prosecutors did not only take care to be impartial—in that they did not dismiss suspects' versions of the events in question and had both sides investigated—but were also concerned about not keeping someone in custody unnecessarily.

In some cases, a prosecutor may use a number of possible legal stories to guide the classification of an action and the collection of evidence. For example, one prosecutor told me the story of a suspected burglary case that was underway.[2] At that point in the investigation, it was not even certain whether burglary was the correct classification. So far, there were a number of different avenues of investigation. Blood smears and blood drops had been found on a wall and the floor of a basement that had been broken into. Being prudent with resources, the prosecutor had only one of the smears analyzed. A DNA profile was extracted that gave a cold hit—that is, a match in a forensic database—on a previously convicted burglar. When he was taken into custody, he denied involvement in the break-in and gave his own suggestion as to why his blood was found on the wall. He claimed that he had been in a fight the same night as the burglary and gotten his face mashed, and that the person who had hit him must have gotten his blood on their hands, broken into the house, and smeared it on the wall. So the prosecutor "sicced the medical examiner" on the suspect to inspect him for traces of facial injuries. Simultaneously, however, she had the examiner check the suspect's hands for injuries that might have been acquired from breaking a window. She also had the forensic science laboratory analyze the blood drops from the crime scene, "because it's not so probable that this other person should have, dripping blood [. . .], traveled ten kilometers [from the place where the fight was supposed to have taken place], broken into the house, and then dripped blood around." But, she added, "maybe it will turn out these drops are from someone else. Well, then maybe someone has had a nosebleed after this guy's fight. [. . .] What do I know about that?"[3]

Similarly, tentative and preliminary storytelling was used in a case of someone reporting their ex-partner for neglecting their child. The prosecutor considered the possibility that the case was based on the plaintiff's genuine concern for the child and insight into their ex-partner's situation just as seriously as the possibility that the report was a purely strategic first move in a custody dispute, giving each possibility equal weight.

But prosecutors cannot go to court on multiple and contradictory legal stories. During the pretrial investigation, a prosecutor must gain sufficient certainty that the story they bring to court could reasonably be expected to obtain a conviction. Sometimes, prosecutors put a number on this likelihood, saying, for example, that they should be convinced by at least 51 percent that a suspect will be found guilty. But how do they attain such certainty in the face of multiple and perhaps contradictory stories, statements, and evidence? And how does a prosecutor decide whom and what to believe?

ASSEMBLING AND ASSESSING EVIDENCE

Assembling and assessing evidence are inseparable in the pretrial investigation, whether it involves which traces are submitted to which type of forensic analysis or whom the police are to interrogate and about what. The process involves navigating all the versions of events given by the plaintiff, suspect, and witnesses. But at some point, the prosecutor must have enough certainty to decide whether to indict.

One prosecutor's strategy when going through the versions of events that are part of a case was to not believe anyone. "I don't even believe my own mother," she told me. Because of her experience, she recognized the difficulty in determining truth. "After plenty of classes and lots of cases you know that truth is subjective," she said and went on to explain that, usually, the involved parties and possible witnesses each tell their own story of what they saw. "Sometimes I may say they are lying; it's quite obvious," but, often, people have seen different parts of an incident from different angles and distances, and they see the incident through the filter of their relationships with the involved parties. "They may not be lying at all," she concluded. "They tell it exactly like they think they've seen it, but whose truth is the true truth, I can't know." One of her colleagues explained the phenomenon in terms of perceptions:

Because we perceive reality around us . . . differently, people have different abilities to describe it. We notice different details. So it's more about being able to see what [different people's accounts] have in common in order to understand what they're talking about, that they're not lying or at least haven't overlooked something significant, and that the stories still add up. Because you get that a lot, that someone has seen one part and someone else has seen another. [. . .] And then it's not so difficult. It's more of a problem when you have witnesses that give [. . .] totally diverging statements. Then you have to decide whom to believe.

It turned out that for this prosecutor, deciding whom to believe had nothing to do with believing people either but rather with figuring out how different statements could be related to other pieces of evidence.

Thus, instead of concerning themselves with what "actually" happened, the prosecutors turned to what was attainable, namely the evidence. As one prosecutor told me, "You need to differentiate—and I think people sometimes may find that hard to understand—is this [evidence] enough or not? Yes, sure, someone was badly injured in this fight, but I still can't prove who started it and who defended themselves against whom, even though one was injured much worse than the other one. I feel really bad for the one who was injured, but I can't prove it." And if something can't be proven, a prosecutor cannot indict for it.

In some cases, the evidence is contradictory. Two combatants may each claim the other one started the fight and they were only defending themselves; one person may speak about consensual sex and the other about having been raped; someone pointed out as an assailant may deny having even been near the place of the fight.

So, if prosecutors are skeptical about whom and what to believe, how do they arrive at enough certainty to make an indictment in the face of such contradictions? Sometimes, the diverging accounts agree on at least parts of an event. For example, in the case of a hypothetical fight, a charge could be brought if "several people can at least agree that, in the end, someone's lying on the ground and being perhaps kicked by the other one who's been involved in the fight," a prosecutor explained. "Then perhaps you can prosecute for at least the last part. Because that part is a crime. Even if they all disagree about how the fight started, 'Olle' has gone too far when he keeps at it when 'Kalle' is knocked out on the ground. So, you have to find the bits you can use."

The prosecutor might "feel bad" for fictitious Olle, who might have been injured much worse than equally fictitious Kalle, but that cannot affect his decision. In addition, he conceded, even if Kalle did start the fight in the first place, if there is no evidence to prove it, the prosecutor cannot charge him for it.

Sometimes, the people involved in a case made the types of statements that the prosecutors talked about as being "believable." A suspect who admitted to having been at the scene of the alleged crime, for example, was usually believed, as prosecutors and investigators thought that the suspect had nothing to gain from falsely admitting their presence, especially if they still denied committing the crime itself. The prosecutor would then focus on finding evidence that could contribute to explaining what the suspect had been doing at the crime scene.

Prosecutors may arrive at a decision by using their multiple and tentative legal stories to examine the evidence. These stories make up a "symbolic framework in which a large amount of information can be organized, compared, tested, and interpreted" (Bennett 1979, 311; see also Hald 2011, 78ff.). In his description of Olle and Kalle's fight, the prosecutor not only focused strictly on the evidence but also navigated it by weighing and testing pieces of evidence against each other, corroborating and weakening the different accounts. If witnesses who disagree on just about everything agree on how the fight ended, it is reasonable to conclude that their combined accounts can prove that Olle unlawfully kicked Kalle.

It may also be possible to use forensic analyses to corroborate or weaken statements. "Even if you have two good accounts from [the plaintiff and the suspect] and they disagree," a prosecutor explained, "it's not enough to have the plaintiff's account [to prove the prosecution's version and disprove the suspect's]. There has to be more. There has to be what we call supportive evidence."

The supportive evidence can of course be used to corroborate the account of a suspect or a plaintiff. The prosecutors I met always emphasized their responsibility to be impartial, especially in cases of serious crimes. Likewise, I heard very few stories from other members of the criminal justice system about prosecutors who, in their opinion, had gotten carried away and focused on proving guilt without considering the possibility of innocence.

While prosecutors may have been inclined to believe a suspect's admission that he or she had been at the crime scene, especially if the suspect denied committing the crime itself, they did not easily accept full confessions, especially not when it came to serious crimes. The prosecutors' stock scripts caution that people may admit to crimes they did not commit for any number of reasons—for example, because they are afraid of the police, because they wish to protect someone else, because they have been threatened, or because they are mentally disordered.[4] Thus, confessions also require supportive evidence, not only because they might be retracted at a later point but also, first and foremost, because prosecutors want to ensure against false confessions and prevent miscarriages of justice.

Finding supportive evidence is more difficult in some types of cases than in others. "Domestic violence, or violence or rape [committed] in a closed room, so to speak, without any witnesses, those are really difficult crimes," a prosecutor said. She explained that in those cases, one person's word is typically pitted against the other's. Usually, gathering supportive evidence is a matter of having a medical examiner look at injuries, having the police interview the neighbors, or trying to find someone who might be able to describe the plaintiff's emotional state after the event.

Not all evidence can play this supporting role. Many types of forensic evidence cannot contribute anything new to a case. Fiber evidence, for example, may be helpful in rape cases to establish contact between articles of clothing. But if the suspect and the plaintiff live together, their clothes will show the same "flora of fibers," as forensic scientists call it, and thus it would be impossible in these instances to draw conclusions about the alleged crime from fiber evidence. Likewise, fingerprint and DNA evidence showing that a suspect was present cannot be used to clarify anything if the crime scene is the home he or she shares with the plaintiff.

In some cases, forensic evidence can be used to bring about confessions. As a prosecutor told me, "There are cases of course [. . .] where there has been a huge and extensive forensic investigation of serious crimes, which later turned out to be sort of a complete waste, because the person confessed. And it's not a waste, of course, because, without that investigation, they wouldn't confess."

Prosecutors, police investigators, judges, and even forensic scientists had similar stories. In their experience, suspects often consider themselves already convicted when they learn the results of a forensic investigation. At that point, instead of continuing to deny any involvement in a crime, a suspect will frequently choose to tell their version of the events in question, hoping to be able to influence the charges against them or at least to improve their situation by showing themselves to be cooperative and remorseful.

Sometimes, a prosecutor told me, even an imminent forensic investigation may prompt a confession:

There are different kinds of suspects. I mean, there are those like [a certain recently convicted offender]—he confessed after the committal proceedings, when he'd learned that a knife and a shirt with blood on it were seized at his house. He found that out during proceedings, and when [the police] interrogated him afterward, he admitted to the crime. Well, he . . . never admitted he'd gone out with the intention to kill someone, but he admitted that "it was me who did it." [. . .] The blood hadn't been analyzed yet, but sure, he knew, if he's been watching *CSI,* [laughs] [. . .] that the blood would be there.

And when suspects realize that such forensic evidence will be produced, the prosecutor continued, it is pointless for them to "be difficult about it," although there are some who will not admit to anything, no matter how much evidence they are confronted with.[5]

Once the forensic analyses have been performed (some of them perhaps even before there is a suspect), the main concern becomes determining which interrogation technique to use. Police investigators must decide how much to reveal about the analysis results to the suspect. Disclosing everything to the suspect at once could lead to a credible but possibly false confession. Sharing only part of the results with the suspect makes it possible to assess a possible confession according to how well it is supported by the rest of the evidence. Other evidence may also be used to assess the credibility of the suspect's narrative in terms of how forthcoming they are. A narrative that gives details that are confirmed by evidence the suspect does not yet know about is regarded as more credible than a narrative that sticks closely to the evidence that has been revealed and perhaps even changes with every new piece of information.

Ordering forensic analyses also has its own complexities in a pretrial investigation, one of which is determining priorities. A smear of blood may contain DNA and hold a fingerprint, but extracting DNA from the blood will obliterate the fingerprint, and making the fingerprint visible for comparison will make the blood unsuitable for DNA analysis. Consequently, the prosecutor leading the investigation must decide which forensic analyses are the most relevant to the case, which, of course, has to do with the possible story lines.

Decisions about which evidence is assembled also depend on the evidence that has already been assembled and must be assessed, and the evidence that is being assembled affects the assessment of the other evidence in the case and impacts future avenues of investigation. What decides whether a pretrial investigation is taken to court is whether the prosecutor can settle the multiplicity of pretrial legal storytelling into one sufficiently certain legal story.

Concluding pretrial investigations and settling on one (provable) legal story depends on the prosecutor's ability to match the evidence to the prerequisites for a specific crime. The prosecutors' approach to piecing together evidence depends on a number of factors: the nature of the evidence, the resources available, the seriousness of the crime, the responsibilities prosecutors have to society and individuals, and circumstances such as political overtones. These factors form the context that affects which legal stories can be expected to be successfully told.

In deciding on which legal story to take to court, the prosecutors pieced together evidence in order to attain sufficient certainty to make a conviction more likely than an acquittal. The closest they come to certainty are occasions when, as a prosecutor told me, "someone confesses, puts all their cards on the table and tells it in a way that really corresponds with the witnesses we may have, with all the forensic evidence. There actually are such occasions when you think that, this time, we actually got to know everything." But these cases are rare, and consequently so is certainty. Most cases therefore revolve around reducing uncertainty.

Sometimes the prerequisites for identifying an event as a particular crime are easy to meet. Someone may have been filmed shoplifting by a surveillance camera and the image quality may be good enough to recognize them. Someone may be caught driving a stolen car—which of course does not prove that they actually stole the car. But if they are using a screwdriver in the ignition instead of a key, they must have been aware that the car was stolen and thus the screwdriver can be taken as evidence to prove the suspect was handling stolen goods.

At other times, the prerequisites are difficult to prove. A prosecutor vividly describes the problem of a knife fight, where intent is an important issue:

> Well, it could be an accident. Alright, not [if there were] eight knife stabs, but [...] if you only have a single stab, there is very, very often no point at all to charge for murder, [or] alternatively attempted murder. [...] The defense attorney is only going to say—with a certain justification—"well, my client could have followed through with further stabs [if he meant to kill the other person]," unless there are witnesses who show [the police] how he stabbed once, "and then, when he threw himself at the other, screaming 'You're gonna die, you're gonna die,' we dragged him off."

In this kind of hypothetical case, the witness reports—if deemed credible and reliable—might prove the intent to kill. But, as the prosecutor points out, it is much more usual that two people involved in a stabbing would be alone, and the intent behind a single knife stab could be anything from an accident to an attempted murder.

The availability of resources was one factor that determined how much effort the prosecutor would expend to try to attain sufficient certainty. While the prosecution does not pay directly for the police investigators' time or for laboratory analyses, they are aware that there is a limited budget for law enforcement and that resources must therefore be used prudently. One of these resources is time; time spent on investigating one case cannot be spent on another.

As a prosecutor explained, the seriousness of a suspected crime is typically a factor to be considered in connection with spending resources: "By rights, all crimes should perhaps be investigated to the same extent, but you just can't spend as much resources on a breach of domiciliary peace as on a murder. So if it's a rape or murder or a serious robbery, then you might really turn every stone, do things that you might be quite sure won't amount to anything, but we'll do it anyway, just to be on the safe side. But if it's a breach of domiciliary peace, you maybe just do what's absolutely necessary to see if it holds up."

To illustrate what "turning every stone" meant, she told the story of a colleague's murder investigation in another city. The police could not find the gun that was suspected to have been used, so the colleague decided to have a river emptied to look for the gun on the bottom, although "they didn't even have a witness who saw [the suspect] walk in that direction or saw someone throw something from a bridge. They had nothing. [The victim] lived nearby, they couldn't find a gun, could he perhaps have walked off in that direction and chucked it into [the river]?"

The police did not find the gun on the river bottom—it was found later in an attic—but "if you can take such measures, just on an off-chance, well, then you can do just about anything." The story became the prosecutor's touchstone for the lengths to which one can go in investigating crimes, although she reiterated that a crime has to be serious in order to justify such tactics: "you don't empty [a river] for a petty theft."

The measures taken in that particular case were extraordinary, but the desire to leave no avenue unexplored when investigating what might be a serious crime is not. Generally speaking, investigations of serious crimes tend to assemble more evidence than less serious ones, both because such cases tend to be more complicated and because there are more avenues of investigation and more resources to pursue them. Prosecutors also seem to aim for a stronger certainty of getting a conviction before pressing serious charges.

How much evidence is needed to take a case to court depends on the circumstances of the case itself. Additional corroborating evidence is needed for notoriously difficult cases, such as those in which ex-partners report each other to the police, especially if they are in the middle of a custody dispute. Prosecutors consider these kinds of circumstances a "warning sign." In such cases, the prosecutors examined the evidence—typically interviews with both parties and people close to them—very critically, considering different possibilities of how to interpret the statements. For example, if a mother reports her ex-partner or the ex-partner's new partner for hitting her child while the child spent time with them, caution is advised. "If you go to court with a case like that, then of course the defense attorney will say that the mother may have put the words into the child's mouth to improve her own position in the custody dispute." Accordingly, "you have to keep that in mind when you assess the evidence. [. . .] You might need better evidence for something really having happened."[6]

Similarly, a case with political overtones may require more or "better" evidence than one without them. A prosecutor described a situation that involved a feud between left- and right-wing extremists and their followers: "They reported each other for just about everything, and quite certainly things did happen, but it was knives in doors and just about everything. Sometimes we'd even have a suspect, often it was just, you know, reports to the police that didn't amount to anything. You didn't know who had done something. And it was assault and battery, and it was threats, and it was criminal damage and what have you."

Against this backdrop, a case of suspected assault was dismissed by the court, even though the prosecutor told me, "I kind of thought the evidence was good enough—ordinarily, it should have been enough—but the court wrote something like, 'taking into consideration the different ideological sympathies and the conflict [between them], their testimonies must be regarded with particular care.' And they dismissed it." The prosecutor concluded, "I got even more support for my assessment that a little extra evidence is needed in these cases."

When the prerequisites for a certain crime cannot be met and sufficient certainty cannot be attained, investigations are often closed without being taken to court. This happens not because the prosecutor or the police decide to believe the suspects and not the plaintiffs, but because the prosecutor assesses, based on the evidence and the circumstances, that an acquittal is the most likely outcome and there are no more avenues of investigation to pursue. In some cases, however, a lesser classification will be used to lay a charge.

In terms of legal storytelling, this demonstrates that not all legal stories are equipotent. In all investigations, the suspect's account is given precedence over the prosecution's legal stories, because the latter—due to the legal principle of the presumption of innocence—must be proven. But in some cases, the burden of proof is heavier, as the accounts foreground stock scripts that cannot readily be ignored, such as those of adversaries—political or personal—reporting each other to the police with the intention of making the other's life more difficult.

Even in investigations with less fraught contexts, sufficient certainty cannot always be arrived at. Sometimes, it is a case of one person's word against another's, and it is impossible to find supportive evidence. In accordance with the presumption of innocence, the court will therefore acquit in these situations; thus, there is no point in wasting public resources on a trial. Another option may be to lower the severity of the initial classification of the crime. The prosecutor might not be able to attain adequate certainty that the suspect was, for example, trying to intentionally murder the plaintiff with the one knife stab, but she might be able to attain it for charges of assault or involuntary manslaughter.

However, cases of serious crimes, especially of suspected murders, are closed only after all possible lines of investigation have been exhausted, and even then only reluctantly.[7] Prosecutors are willing to expend many resources and much effort on solving these cases, even against slim odds—they will do things such as emptying a river to look for a gun, for example—and they are reluctant to give up. It seems that this persistence has to do primarily with upholding an obligation to society to solve such cases and not wanting to upset the public. No one should be allowed to get away with murder, and closing an investigation without being able to produce a suspect, preferably one who will subsequently be convicted, would mean failing to do one's job and letting society down.

On occasion, both the public and the police have accused prosecutors of erring too much on the side of caution in order to avoid losing prestige. However, one prosecutor assured me that she felt no such loss of prestige in losing a case. Her attitude—which was shared by many of her colleagues—was that most cases are tragedies, and she added that although she condemned the deed, she would never condemn the person. "In fact," she continued, "there really aren't any winners," and thus she did not feel like she had "won" a case when a defendant had been convicted. In addition, she explained, being impartial means that prosecutors should not regard themselves as pitched against the defendant.

What she—and most of her colleagues—did dislike was seeing a defendant acquitted because a prosecutor had left a "hole" in the evidence. Considering that prosecutors sometimes discuss cases in terms of "should someone like that be out [in society]?" this dislike may be as much due to wanting to fulfill an obligation to society as to maintaining a sense of professional pride.

The discussion that I heard prosecutors once having about what they called their "safety margins" can be seen in connection with the issue of prestige versus an obligation to society. The prosecutors discussed the width of these margins predominantly in terms of their suggesting the severity of sentences when it came to moving for sanctions, but also in connection with efficiency statistics.[8] Always getting what one demands, they said, means that "you have too much of a safety margin." That is, if the court always agrees to the sentence the prosecutor suggests, there is the possibility that the sentence in at least some of these cases would have been stricter if the prosecutor had moved for a more severe sanction. Similarly, they said, not having any cases dismissed would be a sign of too wide a safety margin when pressing charges. The ratio of dismissed cases to convictions could be taken as an indication of whether the prosecution is cautious to a fault or whether it drops charges too freely and could thus fulfill their obligations better than it currently does.

Still, a lack of sufficient evidence does not always mean that a case does not get taken to court. Prosecutors may decide to press charges on what they perceive as rather weak cases when they deem them to be of legal interest. In other words, they may take cases to court when they want the court to examine a point of principle so they can obtain a precedent and thus a future reference for how to interpret a particular point of the law.

In order to indict and take a case to court, a prosecutor must prepare their legal story.

PREPARING A LEGAL STORY

When preparing for trial, the prosecutors carefully orchestrated the legal stories they were going to tell, aiming to strengthen the presentation of their interpretations and assessments of the evidence before the court. Because they shape which forensic evidence is assembled and what other evidence it is juxtaposed with, prosecutors play a crucial role in the criminal justice system's production of forensic evidence. They also set the agenda of legal stories told and reacted to in court.

Once the prosecutor works out what story to tell during a trial, they write it up in a summons application that will be sent to the court. In the summons application, the prosecutor specifies who is charged for which crime and on what evidence. Together with the police's pretrial investigation report, which contains all of the evidence they have assembled, the summons application is submitted to the court and the defense.[9]

Many of the issues that are crucial during an investigation are still important when the summons application is being written. One is classification. The prosecutor must press charges for a particular crime, and to do that he or she must be able to prove that the prerequisites for that crime are fulfilled. Accordingly, just as during the investigation, the evidence must be translated into the legal classification of a crime. Again, the central issue is not what may have actually happened but what the prosecution can prove.

As the classification process starts "from the top," it is not uncommon for a suspect to be charged in court with a less serious crime than the one they were initially suspected of. In addition, if the prosecutor decides that there is a risk the evidence is too weak to support charges for a serious crime, they might include a less serious variant of the crime as an alternative in the indictment. This prevents the case from ending in an acquittal if the court were to dismiss the more serious charge.

When writing a summons application, there are also other issues to consider. One is that a prosecutor must balance the aspiration to include all potential crimes (or instances of the same crime) with their assessment of the strength of the evidence and the possible effect of outside circumstances. For example, in a prominent fraud case that had received local media attention, the prosecutor decided only to press charges on the instances that had been reported to the police before the newspaper published a story about the case. Even though the prosecutor was certain the same suspects were responsible for the later incidences of fraud as well, she and her colleagues agreed that the defense lawyer was going to claim that the later reports could have been made by people who had seen the newspaper story and were hoping to line their pockets by falsely claiming that they had been defrauded. As having a few more or a few less plaintiffs was not going to make much of a difference for the outcome of the trial, the prosecution agreed it was not worth opening up their case to argument.

The prosecutors also worked out *how* to tell the story in court. An important part of that is deciding whom to summon as a witness. This is not only a question of *what* the person can contribute to the case, but also a question of *how* the person can contribute. As discussed in the previous chapter, in Swedish courts the spoken word is what counts during a trial. Along with the defense, judges and lay assessors receive the police's complete pretrial report well before the hearing, but in making their verdict, they must only take into account what is said (or read aloud) in the courtroom. Thus, witnesses' and plaintiffs' firsthand testimonies are important, and prosecutors want to know beforehand what kind of person they are dealing with.

However, since the prosecutors did not usually know the people involved in their cases in person, they had to rely mainly on the police investigators to tell them how "good" a witness or plaintiff was—in other words, how well they could be expected to perform in court. So when police investigators reported to prosecutors, they intertwined what people said with how they said it.

According to one of the prosecutors I interviewed, the established legal practice in court is to take coherence as a sign of authenticity and reliability, even though research in witness psychology suggested to him that coherence was not necessarily of central importance. This legal practice is established through the ruling of the Supreme Court; even though Sweden does not rely on case law (as, for example, Britain does), the written law is complemented by precedents that exemplify how to interpret the law. And "if that's how the Supreme Court rules [on witness credibility]," the prosecutor shrugged, "then the other courts will do the same, and then we have to deal with it, too. We have to make the same assessment because we know, sure, we can go to court with anything—if we want it dismissed." By setting standards—in this instance of how to assess the credibility of a witness testimony—the Supreme Court shapes legal usage in the other courts, which, in turn, has bearing on a prosecution's assessment of their case or witness.

The prosecutors also wanted witnesses who would not lose their calm and become incoherent under the defense's questioning. They did not want a witness who looked "good on paper" but turned out to be less than articulate. Nor did they want a witness who would give a rehearsed story that sounded as if it had been put into his or her mouth by the prosecution. And finally, they did not want a confused and disoriented witness whose story would be difficult, if not impossible, to understand. In one case, for example, the prosecution's low-water mark, so to speak, was a defendant who had been caught driving his car on the left side of the road because he had forgotten that Sweden switched to driving on the right in the 1960s. Such confusion is certainly undesirable in witnesses.

That the prosecution did this type of analysis does not mean that they saw witnesses and plaintiffs only as props in their legal stories. They did empathize with the victims of crime. They discussed the stories of victims and witnesses with the police investigators who had met them, and, if injuries had been documented, they saw the photographs and read the medical reports. They empathized with what people had presumably been through and with the difficulties they faced when they had to meet their assailants in court and then got questioned and perhaps discredited by the defense attorney. One prosecutor told me she always arrived in court early so as to have time to speak to the plaintiff and to try to reassure them.

When it came to expert witnesses, there was never a question that they would give their statements calmly, cohesively, and understandably; the question was rather *what* they could contribute to a trial. In one case, for example, a fairly new prosecutor wavered over whether to summon a forensic scientist to court as an expert witness in a particular case. While the forensic scientist could explain the evidence in person, the expert statement already contained all the important points, and, as one of her colleagues observed, the defense and the court "should trust that." What eventually resolved the discussion were two points in favor of summoning the forensic scientist. Firstly, the laboratory was not accredited for the particular forensic method that was being used, and the prosecutor in charge did not want the defense lawyer to spring this on the court in his closing statement. Secondly, the defense lawyer apparently had said he would summon the expert if the prosecutor did not. The prosecutor would then lose some control over the situation because she would be the second one to ask questions, and the defense would therefore have the chance to set the agenda for the piece of evidence in question.

The prosecution's pretrial legal storytelling both anticipates and affects the subsequent legal storytelling in court. Their contribution to the biography of forensic evidence is not only to instigate crime scene examinations and laboratory analyses, but also to set it in relation to other evidence, as well as to the law. In playing their role in making forensic evidence, prosecutors also depend on police investigators' investigations. The investigators provide the evidence that the prosecutor requests, and they meet plaintiffs, witnesses, and suspects. In addition, their work contributes personal knowledge of these plaintiffs, suspects, and witnesses to the social life of forensic evidence, giving it another dimension.

CHAPTER THREE

The Criminal Investigation Division

PEOPLE

From the vantage point of the prosecutor's office, it might seem that police investigators primarily carry out prosecutors' orders and that their contribution to the biography of forensic evidence thus does not differ significantly from that of the prosecutors. The police investigators frequently visited the prosecutor's office. They provided a part of the evidence that the prosecutors translated into legally meaningful stories—most notably accounts from plaintiffs, witnesses, and suspects, which make up the main evidence in most cases. What is more, they participated in the prosecutors' pretrial legal storytelling.

However, from the vantage point of the criminal investigation division, it becomes clear that this impression is due to the investigators' work being a *result* in the prosecutor's office. The details and circumstances of that work were not very visible; when talking to the prosecutors, the police investigators spoke very little about *how* they assembled the evidence. They occasionally talked about whether an interviewee came across as articulate or how different statements fit or did not fit together, but they typically only reported their conclusions, summing up in just a few sentences an interrogation that may have taken quite some time.

This chapter aims to show how the investigators produced these results and how forensic evidence fits into the police investigators' work. I argue that the criminal investigation division, which is made up of police officers and civilian investigators, is a different epistemic culture (Knorr Cetina 1999) than the prosecution's office; that is, the two have different ways of producing and recognizing knowledge.

The chapter will show how the police investigators relied on personal and sometimes close knowledge of particular people. The investigators acquired personal knowledge about plaintiffs, witnesses, and, primarily, suspects from their own interrogations, from shared stories (cf. Orr 1996), and from databases. They built relationships with people so as to gain their cooperation, and they used these relationships to bring a personal dimension into the investigation and, therefore, into the production of forensic evidence.

Investigators not only provide the statements and other information that is used to interpret forensic evidence, they also instigate forensic analyses in the context of what they know about the people involved. These forensic analyses can be used as a tool to help elicit statements—that is, to help steer interrogations or to influence people's decisions on their participation in investigations. As a result, the contribution investigators make to the biographies of pieces of forensic evidence centers on personal knowledge about the people involved in each case.

Investigators are often constrained by the pressures of time, for the most part because they cannot hold people for an unlimited amount of time. Holding someone for more than twenty-four hours requires that a prosecutor issue a warrant, and after three days, a suspect must be either released or placed under formal arrest by a judge. The latter is done through committal proceedings; a prosecutor puts the evidence against the suspect that has been collected up to that point before the judge in a public hearing, and the suspect and their lawyer give their view. The judge then decides whether the evidence is sufficient to place the suspect under formal arrest and whether the crimes and the state of the investigation justify formal arrest or if he or she should be released.

Mondays are often busy for criminal investigation divisions, especially if the weekend has been preceded by a payday,[1] which means that people have both time and money on their hands. For someone taken into custody on a Friday night—perhaps because they were caught assaulting someone or driving a stolen car—the initial three-day holding period runs out on the following Monday. Since criminal investigation divisions are lightly staffed on the weekends, investigators coming in for Monday-morning shifts can find themselves facing full holding cells and with very little time to interrogate the suspects or collect other evidence in their cases. In addition, some suspects might be under investigation for other offenses, so the investigators may want to take the chance to interrogate them about these cases as well while they are easily accessible.

Although the rest of the week is often a bit calmer, the time pressure never goes away. After a suspect has been placed under formal arrest by the court, the prosecutor has two weeks to bring in an indictment or have the arrest renewed through a new committal hearing. This means that, within this period, investigators have to either produce the evidence needed for an indictment or make enough progress that the court will rule to recommit the suspect.

The investigators I met also worked on cases in which a suspect had not been found or in which either the evidence or the classification of the crime did not suffice for taking the suspect into custody. These cases had different time pressures. Producing evidence becomes more difficult as time elapses, and thus it is important to investigate as speedily as possible. It is important, for example, to question people early on because time affects memory and emotions. The impression witnesses and plaintiffs give immediately after an event may be considerably different than the one they give once they have recovered and straightened out their stories. In some cases, the investigators were concerned about offenders committing more crimes—for example, when a fraud or break-in was suspected to be part of a series. In these situations, time pressure was about solving crimes before more damage is done. The investigators were also very aware of the often-voiced public opinion that the police worked much too slowly and inefficiently.

The investigators were also aware of pressures other than time. Public debate in Sweden recurrently contrasts the gathering of forensic evidence, and especially "swabbing" for DNA evidence[2] on a larger scale, to "real police work" or "good old-fashioned police work." The implication is that substituting "real police work" with gathering DNA samples will lead to inferior results. The reason seems to be that extensive swabbing—although forensic evidence is otherwise described as very desirable and reliable—is perceived as a shortcut favored by the intellectually lazy. If extensive swabbing leads to a DNA match and thus a suspect, it is considered a lucky coincidence, whereas it is believed that proper police work should regularly and dependably produce results. This contrast also implies that the two somehow exclude each other.

At first, what I heard from police investigators seemed to echo these implicit values. For example, they talked in a tongue-in-cheek manner about how extensive swabbing was going to solve a murder that had occurred several years ago. In that case, DNA had been recovered that was believed to be the offender's, but no suspect had been apprehended. The investigators jokingly predicted that the murderer was going to walk into their hands any day now after being swabbed because of a speeding offense. (The police do not have the authority to swab speeders.) But such jokes notwithstanding, this chapter will show that the professional skills of the investigators—the "real" police work—are needed to bring meaning to forensic material.

The criminal investigation division is brought into cases after the salient events have occurred, which means that the investigators start with limited information and a high level of uncertainty. They must, through their investigation, bring clarity to and produce evidence about the events.

I will use two very different cases to illustrate the work of the criminal investigation division. Both of the cases were in their early stages when I was told about them, and a prosecutor had not gotten involved in either one at that point.

The first case demonstrates the uncertainty inherent in investigators' work and also hints at their dependence on people's cooperation. A man had been reported missing to the police by a very worried family member. The only certainty was that the man was gone, but apart from that, there was no certainty about anything.[3]

The investigators explained that they did not usually investigate adult missing persons, but in this case there were circumstances that, as one of them said, felt "wrong." Among other things, the man's car had been found parked improperly in another city, unlocked and with the keys in the ignition. There were also similarities to cases in other parts of the country, in which several missing persons had eventually been found dead. Consequently, the investigators worked on finding out where the man might be and whether he had left voluntarily. They talked to his family about the last time they had seen him, had the tax office check his assets and debts, and, with the help of his family, searched his home and office for his passport and possible notes. They requested data from the missing man's cell phone company, justifying the measure with the sentiment, "what's that [cost] compared to a life?"

They also had a long discussion with the crime scene division about what to do with the car. Should one of the investigators and one of the local crime scene technicians make the trip to examine the car, or could the examination be delegated to the crime scene division in whose jurisdiction the car had been found? What kind of traces might be found in the car, and which questions should a possible request to the other crime scene division contain?

The investigators did not find a passport, but no one in his family knew whether the disappeared person had even possessed one. The wife had said that their relationship had been very frank and that they had been able to talk about anything, thus she believed that he would have confided any worries to her. Of course, the investigators pointed out, that was only her perception of the relationship.

As the investigators discussed the little evidence they had, they tried out different theories (or different potential stories) of what might have happened. The man might have committed suicide—but why drive to another city to do that? He might have gotten tired of his life and just up and left; he might have borrowed money from the wrong people and gotten into trouble; or, if there indeed was a connection to the other missing persons cases mentioned above, he could be in danger or even dead. There simply was not enough evidence to decide, which was a bit frustrating. "I'm so curious! I want the answer *now!*" one of the investigators said, moving his hands as though he were leafing to the back of a crime novel. But of course, there was no final chapter to leaf to where everything would be explained.

This was certainly not a routine case, and it was given quite a lot of attention and resources. One investigator described it as "a little fun—or perhaps I shouldn't say that when someone has disappeared and there's a family who are worried or miserable, but it *is* interesting." Although the case was unusual, the uncertainty at its core was not. Nor was it unusual that the investigators relied on the potential victim's family and friends to supply information and facilitate the investigation.

The second case, which was as mundane as the first was unusual, illustrates the importance of personal knowledge of people and how that knowledge can lead to producing forensic evidence. On my first morning, one of the investigators gave me a fresh report from the patrol police to read as an introduction to the criminal investigation division's everyday work. Winking as he left the room, he said he would be back soon to test me on what I thought they should do.

The report recounted that the alarm system of a business in an industrial park had alerted the police in the middle of the night. The patrol that had been dispatched had found the wire fence around the property cut and the premises broken into. The report went on to state that shortly afterward the police patrol had encountered two people bicycling near the site of the suspected burglary. They searched them and seized a pair of pliers and a sum of money that corresponded to half of the—rather modest—amount that had been looted from the business. The patrol also reported that the now-suspects had claimed they had found the bicycles and were on their way to turn them in to the police.

I was fairly sure that the investigator wanted me to say something about whether to send the pliers to the Swedish National Laboratory of Forensic

Science (SKL), but what puzzled me most was the explanation about the bicycles. To be sure, someone explaining in the middle of the night that they were about to turn in bicycles to the police seemed a bit strange—but why talk about the bicycles in the first place? Had the police patrol asked about them? But why would they ask about the bicycles of two people in a city full of bicycles and bicycle lanes?

The investigator patiently explained to me, a civilian, that the reason the police patrol had stopped the suspects in the first place was that the officers had recognized them from having been involved in similar break-ins. Their reputation as "troublemakers"[4] had caused the police officers to ask about the bicycles and had also made their subsequent bicycle story less than credible. While "Svensson" (the Swedish average Joe or Jane) might have been able to believably claim to be about to hand over lost bicycles to the police in the middle of the night, petty criminals well known for stealing could not. The investigator went on to talk about having sent the pliers, together with samples of the cut wires in the fence, to the SKL. He did not think that the forensic scientists would be able to do much with such small surfaces as the diameter of the wire but said one could always hope.

I asked (naively, in retrospect) whether ordering a forensic analysis of the pliers and the cut fence wires was not a lot of trouble for a crime that had yielded the offenders a relatively modest loot. The investigator raised his eyebrows and said politely, "Well, one might think that." It was a consideration to factor in, he told me, but the business owner had not only suffered the loss of the money, they had also suffered damage to their property and had to spend time having that damage repaired and dealing with the authorities. Besides, he added, the suspects kept committing crimes like this one. So, he concluded, while one could consider them "crappy crimes" (*skitbrott*), the suspects made a living that way and they should not be allowed to do so.

Together, these two cases illustrate the core of the criminal investigation division's work. They also suggest that the "real" or "good old-fashioned" police work is very much about people.

BUILDING (ON) PERSONAL RELATIONSHIPS

While the investigators did draw on general stock scripts in their legal storytelling (Amsterdam and Bruner 2000), they also drew on their knowledge of individuals and of the prior activities of these individuals, as the second case I described above especially shows. The professional relationships the investigators formed with the people involved in their cases were of central importance, albeit in different ways. In the first case, the investigators relied heavily on the willingness of the missing person's family to talk to them. Their accounts were used both to shed light on the disappearance and to figure out what other evidence to look for.

In the second case, the investigators relied on the police patrol having recognized "known troublemakers"—people that frequently were involved in crimes. This was not exceptional; the investigators I spoke with relied on their local police's personal knowledge of troublemakers to help them in various ways. For example, some would ask officers who were known to be "good at recognizing troublemakers" to look at surveillance videos or read witness descriptions to see if they could match them with a name.

The investigators themselves also had personal knowledge of some troublemakers because they had had repeated interactions with them during the course of interrogations and investigations and so had come to know them as individuals. Most of my fieldwork at the crime investigation division was with a theft squad, which handles property crimes—in other words, burglaries, thefts, and dealing with stolen goods. These are regarded as the types of crime where repeat offenders are especially common.[5] Thus, the theft investigators had so-called regular customers, whom they met repeatedly over the course of several years. One investigator, for example, showed me a fat pile of papers concerning one person, and explained that these were the things she "had to discuss with him" as soon as she got hold of him.

Investigators also develop relationships with various people while investigating other types of crimes as well. In bigger, more complicated cases, for example, they meet the same people during repeated interrogations. They often need to build rapport to induce people to want to cooperate with them. Without such cooperation, an investigation becomes extremely difficult at best.

The police investigators' professional relationships with people seemed to give them a more people-centered perspective to the investigations than the prosecutors tended to have. One consequence of such a perspective among the investigators that I met was that they often expressed a concern for and a sense of obligation to the people caught up in investigations. The investigators' concern was personal, whereas the prosecutors described a rather distant and abstract obligation to plaintiffs. In the case of the man who disappeared, for example, the investigators decided not to let me sit in on interviews with the distressed family, so as not to stress them further. Their personal concern was also reflected in the stories they told me about other ongoing cases. One was a case of domestic violence where someone had assaulted his "possibly future live-in partner." The investigator commented that the victim would hopefully have second thoughts about moving in with a man who had assaulted her. In a tone that put him firmly on the plaintiff's side, he went on to explain that the woman had defended herself by throwing a heavy object at the man and that the police had had to take him to the emergency room before taking him into custody.

Investigators also expressed concern about suspects, especially about juveniles ruining their futures. Not all of their relationships with suspects were conciliatory, though, especially not those with known offenders. One example of this was the investigator who believed that habitual criminals, as a matter of principle, should not be allowed to get away with break-ins, even if an investigation might cost more than the damage caused by the crime.

Another consequence of personal knowledge and relationships was the frequent frustration investigators expressed of knowing that someone had committed a crime but not being able to prove it. At times, the evidence and circumstances of a case, together with personal knowledge of the people involved, is enough to satisfy investigators that they have solved the crime. However, they might not necessarily have enough evidence for the case to hold up in court, and so investigations are closed or suspects acquitted. In police jargon, such cases are called "police solved" (*polisiärt uppklarat*).[6] This is a contrast to the attitude of the prosecutors, who emphasized that it was impossible to truly know what had happened during a crime.

This difference in perspective led to investigators getting occasionally exasperated with prosecutors who they felt were being overly cautious. This happened in a case where someone had been taken into custody for driving a stolen car. The investigator was sure the custodee had not only driven the car but also stolen it. He based this assumption on the custodee having said in a police interview a few months earlier that the particular brand of the car in question was easy to steal. (According to the investigators, most car thieves have favorite car brands or even models they "specialize in.") The investigator wanted the custodee placed under formal arrest by the court, a procedure that has to be initiated by a prosecutor. Accordingly, we paid a visit to the prosecutor's office. On the way there, I learned that the investigator thought some prosecutors were more "difficult" than others, and that the one we were going to see was one of them.

"What can he be tied to?" the prosecutor asked, and the investigator launched into the case. The suspect had only admitted to driving a stolen car, something that was impossible to deny with any credibility, as there had been a screwdriver in the ignition instead of keys. But he denied having stolen the car, claiming that he had borrowed it from an unnamed friend. A knife had also been found in the car, but he claimed that it had already been there when he got in and was not his, which the car's owner later confirmed.[7] The owner, the investigator added, had never had anything to do with the police, which made the confirmation credible. The investigator concluded his case for having the custodee arraigned with pointing out that he was, after all, "very active." He had previous convictions for similar offenses and would presumably go right back to these activities upon being released.

The prosecutor, however, shook his head. He agreed that the custodee probably should not be "out there," but he was not convinced that the case would hold up for car theft and thus be sufficient for a formal arraignment. Instead, he asked the investigator to look through the other cases open on the suspect to glean more evidence.

On the way back to his office, the investigator grumbled that this particular prosecutor was always like that: "He's being completely impossible. Completely impossible!" Of course the suspect had stolen the car, he said.

It took some digging through the suspect's previous encounters with the police to turn up evidence that, after some discussion, satisfied the prosecutor enough to be willing to attempt an arraignment. When the investigators talked about the case during their afternoon coffee break, their tones of voice and their comments made it clear that they were in agreement that the prosecutor had been unnecessarily cautious. As one of the investigators exclaimed, "if one doesn't get arraigned for *this*, I don't know what one has to do [to get arraigned]!"

One might try to explain this clash by claiming that (some) investigators are lazy and have no understanding of what a court hearing requires or that (some) prosecutors are overly cautious and do not like to lose in court. But I think it was a clash not so much of individual opinions and personalities over a case but of what Karin Knorr Cetina calls "epistemic cultures" (1999), or in other words, cultures of knowledge. That is, the police investigator and the prosecutor disagreed on the issue of *how* they could know that the custodee had been involved in a crime that was serious enough to make a successful arraignment likely.

In Knorr Cetina's words, epistemic cultures are "amalgams of arrangements and mechanisms—bonded through affinity, necessity, and historical coincidence—which, in a given field, make up *how we know what we know.* Epistemic cultures are cultures that create and warrant knowledge" (1999, 1; italics in original).

Knorr Cetina develops and explores the concept through comparative analysis of two sciences, particle physics and molecular biology, but she considers it applicable to other sciences and to nonscientific expert cultures (1999, 246). The concept's focus is on the "strategies and policies of knowing that are not codified in textbooks but do inform expert practice" and the "complex texture of knowledge as practiced in the deep social spaces of modern institutions" (1999, 2). In other words, Knorr Cetina emphasizes the informality and sociality of how groups of people make knowledge, and, more importantly, how they make and maintain "the machineries of knowledge construction" (1999, 3).

Although prosecutors and police investigators make very different knowledge than scientists, it is fruitful to consider them as having epistemic cultures as well. Prosecutors and police investigators each have their own ways of contributing to the knowledge—that is, the evidence—in a case. Prosecutors are, among other things, specialized in legally *assessing* evidence. As discussed in the previous chapter, they translate evidence into law by means of pretrial legal storytelling, focusing only on the evidence and how it can be interpreted to prove or disprove a suspect's guilt in a crime. Investigators are, among other things, specialists in interrogation—that is to say, in *assembling* evidence. They rely on personal and sometimes close knowledge of particular people. So, given the prosecutors' and investigators' different epistemic cultures, it would perhaps be strange if they were never at odds.[8]

MAINTAINING THE MACHINERY OF KNOWLEDGE
CONSTRUCTION THROUGH STORIES

Personal relationships may seem a strange base for an epistemic culture. After all, culture is a collective enterprise, whereas relationships, even professional ones, are formed and maintained between individuals.

However, while the relationships police investigators formed with people involved in their cases were personal, the knowledge gained through them was shared. The police investigators I met frequently discussed cases and people with each other. For example, they talked about what a certain suspect taken into custody looked like and whether they thought he had been involved in certain other, apparently well-known, crimes in the past. They also told (or perhaps retold) each other a story about someone who had stolen jewelry from a pawnshop and had been filmed in the act by the shop's security system; it was not the first time he had gotten caught either. "He must be the worst thief in the world," one of the investigators remarked.

It was clear that the storytellers deliberately used amusing turns of phrase such as "took care of" instead of "stole," or having "unexpected visitors" instead of a break-in (alluding to a long-running catchphrase from a coffee brand that advertises itself as the means of extending hospitality to unexpected visitors). Listeners visibly appreciated the entertainment value of the stories and were validated by their outcomes—inevitably, the offenders always get caught in the end.[9]

These stories may seem like idle gossip, and they were certainly meant to be entertaining, but they also created shared knowledge. Julian Orr (1996) analyzed similar storytelling in another professional community: that of photocopier technicians. He argues that the technicians use narratives about photocopiers to simultaneously diagnose malfunctioning machines and to trade their personal experiences with one another. Orr discusses how these stories allow their tellers to "make claims of membership or seniority within the community" and to "amuse, instruct, and celebrate the tellers' identity" (1996, 126). The stories become artifacts that can be circulated among members of the community, thus turning an individual's experiences into a shared body of knowledge.

Even though the technicians were talking about machines and the investigators were talking about people, there are distinct parallels that can be drawn between the two groups. Both technicians and investigators come into the situations that form the basis of these stories after a problem has occurred, after either machines or relationships between people have broken down. Both have only limited information available regarding the situations, resulting in uncertainty (Orr 1996, 2). This is how Orr describes the technicians' situation:

> There is an inherent uncertainty in the situation of diagnosis. In difficult diagnoses the technicians are contending with the limits of their knowledge. The known weaknesses of their sources of information suggest that they may be presumed to have an incomplete set of facts about the machine; they lack the perspective of understanding which would integrate those facts into a coherent representation, which might or might not indicate the need for

additional facts. This is a double-edged coherence, requiring both coherence of story and connectivity of the facts. Without coherence, the technicians cannot know whether they have all the facts they need. They do not know whether they have overlooked something, whether there are more facts to gather, or whether this is a new problem that is completely beyond their experience and understanding. They do not know whether they lack a fact or an interpretation. (1996, 127)

Both technicians and investigators must attain understanding—in the form of diagnoses or of pretrial legal stories—despite the limitations of their knowledge. Moreover, their narratives must be coherent and must take into consideration all of the known facts or evidence, which is precisely what Bennett (1979) points out applies to legitimate legal stories. Just as the technicians' narratives swung between war stories and diagnoses, the investigators' moved between legal storytelling that made sense of a case at hand, sharing experience and knowledge, maintaining and reinforcing identity, and providing entertainment. Similarly, Innes (2002) discusses how overlapping and interlocking police discourses shape the world of police investigators and make investigations meaningful within it.

What Orr calls "the social distribution of experiential knowledge through community interaction" (1996, 2) served at the criminal investigation division as a means of sustaining individual and group identity. It was also a means of maintaining a shared, but not necessarily codified, body of knowledge about particular people.

Knorr Cetina calls stories a "memory organ that preserves experience" (1999, 106). Telling and retelling stories about past cases kept them and the lessons to be learned from them fresher in investigators' memories. The stories also make personal knowledge collective. The investigator who had had the "worst thief in the world" for a "customer," for example, may have known the most about him, but if her colleagues encounter him in the future, they will know his criminal history and what kind of person he is. Likewise, the discussion of what the suspect in custody looked like will help investigators recognize him should they meet him. Such knowledge can be important; if a suspect is known to be violent, for instance, investigators can take precautions when questioning him or her. Thus, these stories form and maintain the investigators' epistemic culture.

The investigators also gained knowledge about suspects and their history (albeit less personal and detailed) from databases. In order to draw on more than their personal knowledge of individuals, investigators looked up convictions in the national General Criminal Register and their own police authority's database of suspects. The latter also contained open cases and information on suspicions related to investigations that were closed or suspended and on cases in which plaintiffs have dropped charges. There are limitations to these databases, however. At the time of my fieldwork, only the General Criminal Register was a national database. Each of the then twenty-one county police authorities in the country had its own database, accessible only to the police of that county, on open investigations and suspects. This system, an investigator explained, had been the problem in a much-discussed case a few years earlier, in which the police had caught a murderer only after several years and after he had killed a second victim, a ten-year-old. He had worked as a truck driver, traveling all over the country, and although he did not have any prior convictions, it turned out that he had been under suspicion for a number of crimes in several counties for quite some time. Like many of his colleagues, the investigator thought that the difficulty of exchanging information had hampered the investigation and, ultimately, had made the second murder possible.[10]

Thus, knowledge of and about people was at the center of the police investigators' epistemic culture. It was acquired through personal professional relationships, formed during the personal contact of interrogations, and shared and thus made collective through stories and databases. To paraphrase Knorr Cetina, this collectivized personal knowledge is an integral part of the police investigators' machinery of creating and warranting knowledge about potential crimes and offenders. Just as the photocopier technicians shared their knowledge about malfunctioning machines through stories, the police investigators shared their knowledge about people and cases through stories, and these stories informed their investigations and their practices of pretrial legal storytelling. The personal knowledge that the police rely on makes some people more ready suspects than others[11] and also facilitates investigations. Without this personal knowledge, for example, the police may not have found the pliers that were suspected to have been used to cut open the wire fence at the site of the burglary mentioned above.

CONNECTING PERSONAL KNOWLEDGE
AND FORENSIC EVIDENCE

So far, it may seem that the investigators' work was only about people and had very little to do with forensic evidence, but their professional relationships with people included the production of forensic evidence. For one, police investigators contribute to the production of evidence by providing material from known sources. A DNA profile recovered from a crime scene is not particularly useful by itself; in order for a laboratory analysis to produce forensic evidence, a trace from a crime scene must be compared to one or several known sources.[12] Police investigators provide these known sources when they take DNA samples from suspects.

The production of comparison samples from potential suspects is informed by the investigators' experience with and knowledge of people. The investigators I met ascribed their eagerness to swab to a superior who had made extensive sample taking a priority. But their swabbing was not simply a matter of following orders; they underscored that they had managed to swab most of the "professional troublemakers" in their district in the few years that had passed since a new DNA law extending the police's powers had come into force.[13] This meant that the DNA profiles were now stored in the national forensic DNA database and were therefore automatically compared to DNA profiles obtained from crime scenes all over the country. This made these troublemakers much more likely to get caught, and thus the investigators felt that swabbing made their work easier.

However, they also talked about when it was pointless to swab, or more precisely, which people it was pointless to swab. For example, one of the investigators told me, if hypothetical eighty-two-year-old Agda were caught shoplifting a tub of yogurt, she would be in no danger of having her DNA profile put on the database. "Agda" is an age that normally connotes being the victim of crime rather than an offender, and she is the bearer of a name that evokes little old ladyhood, but more importantly, she has committed the proverbial petty and easily solved crime. She illustrates a harmless person who has committed a fairly harmless and simple crime, and therefore her DNA profile would not be expected to help solve any ongoing or future cases.

Conversely, the investigators might take samples from some suspects as a preventive measure. Taking DNA samples or fingerprints from juvenile suspects, for instance, even though it was not necessary in the investigation, was sometimes described as "sending a signal." The investigators reasoned that if suspects knew that their DNA profile was on file, they might be afraid of getting caught and therefore might "behave" in the future. This could be interpreted as a way of investigators trying to make their jobs easier, but it could also be seen as investigators taking preemptive action. By also giving these suspects a stern talking-to, describing in detail the consequences of committing crimes, and reminding them of the futures they are ruining, they are helping to prevent repeat offenses as well as trying to steer the juveniles toward a better future.

These examples illustrate that the investigators' epistemic culture intertwined the production of forensic evidence with the interpretation of situations and the understanding and categorization of people. Some people are, for different reasons, regarded as more useful to swab than others.

The police also contribute to the production of forensic evidence by conducting interrogations and extracting statements from suspects. Interviews with plaintiffs, suspects, and witnesses are an integral part of making forensic evidence usable and useful in court. The police investigators produce, through their interrogations, the main evidence, to which the forensic evidence will be related by pretrial legal storytelling and, later, through legal storytelling in court. The police investigators are the ones to notify suspects of the suspicions and the evidence against them. In connection with that, they take the suspect's statement (or record that the suspect has declined to make one).

Forensic evidence is also, conversely, a useful tool for getting suspects to confess. According to the investigators I talked with, the vast majority of suspects admit to having committed a crime when confronted with forensic evidence. They "lie down flat on their backs," as one investigator put it, mimicking a submissive dog's paws by drawing his hands up against his chest. "Professional criminals" may "deny and deny," but they realize when "the game is over," that is, when the evidence has become so overwhelming that the only sensible thing left to do is to confess.

In some cases, even just the possibility that forensic evidence could be produced was enough to motivate suspects to make statements. The investigators told me about cases in which suspects had started to talk when the interviewer brought up the police's intention to have forensic analyses performed. Even though those forensic analyses might not yield any results in the end, the possibilities they evoked affect the statements produced in the interrogation.

Investigators cannot use forensic evidence equally well on all interviewees, however. According to them, students, people with higher educations, and "the younger generation" were "used to calling things into question. 'Why is that?' 'Why should I confess?'" Their stubbornness was unfavorably compared to the "professional" criminals' knowing when denying was sensible and when it was not.

The degree of usefulness of forensic evidence also changes in cases involving "regular customers." Because the repeat offenders know the "trade," the investigators explained, they do not admit to anything needlessly. On top of that, the investigators said that the more suspects and defense lawyers educate themselves about forensic evidence, the harder it becomes to prove someone's involvement in a crime. Where a fingerprint on the outside of a homemade caltrop (a device used to stop pursuing police cars) may once have elicited a confession, for example, the defense had learned to argue that the defendant might have touched it when passing by, and so it did not necessarily prove the defendant's involvement in the robbery in which it had been used. But touching caltrops lying in the street in the middle of a robbery? "Who the hell does that?" the investigator exclaimed.

How investigators use forensic analysis results is of crucial importance to the investigation. Just as a piece of evidence needs an explanation, a statement needs corroboration from other evidence. How well a statement corresponds to the available evidence as a whole gives an indication of its credibility, in particular how well a statement corresponds to the evidence *before* the interrogator has informed the interviewee about it. Consequently, the investigators were careful to ask interviewees to describe their version of what happened before disclosing what others had said or what forensic investigations had produced. They were also careful to ask about things that could later be corroborated or refuted, such as asking a suspect whether a plaintiff had ever been in their apartment. If the suspect denied the plaintiff's presence, forensic evidence or the plaintiff's detailed description of the apartment could then be taken as an indication that the suspect had lied at least about this one thing.

The way forensic evidence was woven into the criminal investigation division's epistemic culture—how forensic analysis results shape interrogations, how they are used to elicit useful statements, and how the investigators contribute both their interpretation and their instigation—suggests that the contrast being made between forensic technologies and "real police work" does not describe the police's investigative work very well. Forensic evidence requires quite a lot of "real police work" in order to become legally meaningful. The investigators' use of forensic evidence shows that it does not replace police investigation but can be (and is) productively incorporated into it.

The contrast being made between forensic technologies and police work may thus, rather than reflecting work practices, be a variation of "identity work"—that is to say, of constructing and negotiating professional identities (see Snow and Anderson 1987). When the police investigators made wry jokes about catching a murderer by swabbing speeders, they made fun of and thus invalidated popular discourse that emphasizes forensic evidence over other types of evidence and thus de-emphasizes investigators' work. Public belief that the police swab instead of pursuing real police work might, on the other hand, be seen in connection with other forms of criticism of what is perceived as police inefficiency or laziness, perhaps due to most of the criminal investigation division's work being performed out of sight of the public.[14] Believing that the police are seeking a technological quick fix and therefore prefer swabbing for DNA to doing diligent, time-consuming work fits quite well into familiar discourses.

The criminal investigation division's epistemic culture, with its focus on people, brought together the forensic and the personal in a mutually constituting relationship. The investigators produced knowledge and contributed to the biography of forensic evidence based on (professional) personal relationships: relationships with all sorts of people—not only suspects, witnesses, and plaintiffs but also people with very different social, educational, and cultural backgrounds.

The forensic analyses the investigators instigated and whose results they used were performed within a very different epistemic culture, again, namely the epistemic culture of the forensic science laboratory.

CHAPTER FOUR

In the Laboratory

QUANTIFICATION AND ORGANIC OBJECTIVITY

When the Swedish National Laboratory of Forensic Science—or SKL, after its Swedish name, Statens kriminaltekniska laboratorium[1]—analyzes traces, its contribution to the biography of forensic evidence is to turn the material form of the traces sent to them into a meaningful symbolical form.

From watching popular portrayals of forensic evidence in the media, one might think that a forensic science laboratory trades in truth and certainty. The television series *Crime Scene Investigation* (*CSI*), for example, depicts forensic evidence as being able to speak for itself and, what is more, always speak the truth (Kruse 2010). By the end of a *CSI* episode, there is absolute certainty about who has committed the crime of the week, which is usually a murder, and this certainty is so strong and so all-encompassing that a trial is not necessary. In the series, forensic evidence reveals an absolute truth about which there is no doubt that it is, to borrow the expression of one of the prosecutors from chapter 2, "the true truth."

In contrast, the forensic scientists who work at the SKL manage uncertainty. More precisely, they manage particular forms of uncertainty: firstly, the uncertainty associated with the production of forensic evidence (for example, possible contamination, mistakes, or mix-ups); secondly, the uncertainty about what counts as "the same" and what does not (for example, two fibers, two marks, or a partial and a perfect fingerprint); and thirdly, the uncertainty of limited knowledge (for example, not knowing the "populations" of shoes, tools, or fibers—that is, how common a particular sole pattern, tool model, or fiber is). The SKL makes some of these inherent uncertainties manageable. It is impossible to attain absolute certainty about the source of a trace, but it is possible to provide a probability figure that allows conclusions to be drawn about the relationship of a trace and its suspected source.

The SKL is the only forensic science laboratory in Sweden.[2] It is funded by the state and falls under the authority of the Swedish National Police Board, but it is independent from the police force itself.[3] Accordingly, although its employees are technically employed by the police, they are not police officers. Their backgrounds vary, although staff typically come to the laboratory with training and experience in natural sciences or technical fields and then receive additional in-house training in forensic science.

The SKL's forensic scientists are organized into different departments: the Biology Unit, which performs DNA analyses and manages the DNA databases; the Chemistry and Technology Unit, which handles materials as diverse as fingerprints, fibers, shoe and tool marks, ballistics, fire debris, explosives, and glass; the Forensic Document and Information Technology Unit, which examines handwriting and suspected forgeries as well as computers; the Drug Analysis Unit, which identifies suspected drugs; and the Administration Unit, which handles registrations and archives, among other things. Most of my fieldwork at the SKL took place in the Biology Unit and the Chemistry and Technology Unit. I focused mainly, but not exclusively, on practices related to DNA, fingerprint, and tool mark evidence.

COMPARING SAMPLES

In the process of analyzing traces, the forensic scientists at the SKL transform the material into the symbolic. In other words, they turn physical traces into writing, in the form of work sheets, laboratory notes, and ultimately expert statements, which, in STS terms, are called "inscriptions" (see Latour and Woolgar 1986 [1979]; Latour 1987, 1999). Moreover, they do not turn only *one* trace into an inscription but combine several pieces of information into a symbolic form that is meaningful for the investigation and, eventually, a possible trial.

Uncertainty is a concern for the SKL from the moment a sample enters the building. The laboratory must prevent contamination, both cross-contamination between traces and contamination by the forensic scientists themselves. They must also prevent mix-ups between cases—one cotton swab or cigarette end looks very much like the next one, and so do the crowbars and screwdrivers and pliers that come in for tool mark analysis. Contamination or mix-ups would mean that there was uncertainty about whether the result really originated from the trace the paperwork says it does and thus whether the laboratory's expert statement is really relevant to the case.

Such uncertainty is unacceptable at the SKL. It would undermine trust in the laboratory and, ultimately, in the criminal justice system as a whole. The forensic scientists I met were also aware that their statements affected real people's lives: depending on the results the laboratory produces, people may be dismissed from consideration in investigations or become suspects, defendants, and later even inmates.

The forensic scientists, however, did not refer to this as "uncertainty" but talked about preventing contamination and mix-ups in terms of managing and eliminating risks, risks that can be minimized by logistics and routines. For example, tracking at the SKL is extensive. Many cases[4] pass through the SKL—about 105,000 in 2012 and about 96,000 in 2013 (Swedish National Laboratory of Forensic Science 2014)—and many are subjected to several subsequent analyses and thus travel between groups or even units. At the units, packages from different cases are unpacked separately. Each material is given its own case number, and they and their numbers are meticulously kept track of through, among other things, work sheets that are both signed and countersigned. In addition, every case is treated in exactly the same way within a unit (although, for example, the Chemistry and Technology Unit of course treats fingerprint traces differently from how the Biology Unit treats DNA traces), and important steps in the analysis are overseen or reviewed by a second forensic scientist.

Typically, forensic analyses compare a trace recovered during an investigation to a sample from a known source.[5] For instance, they might compare DNA from bodily fluids collected from a crime scene with known DNA profiles; a mark on a forced lock with a screwdriver that had been found in a suspect's home; a shoe print with a suspect's shoe; fibers recovered from a crime scene with a piece of clothing that belongs to a suspect; a glass fragment found on or in a suspect's clothes to a smashed window pane at the site of a burglary.

Doing comparisons presupposes that there are known sources. The samples of cut fence that the police had sent to the SKL, for example, described in the previous chapter, would have been useless without the pair of pliers to compare them to. The same applies to any other isolated trace.

When there is no suspect from whom to take a comparison sample, forensic databases become important. In Sweden, there is a national forensic fingerprint database maintained by the Swedish National Police Board that catalogs fingerprints from suspects and convicted offenders. In addition, the SKL maintains three[6] forensic DNA databases: the trace register, containing DNA profiles recovered from the scenes of unsolved crimes; the investigation register, containing DNA profiles from people suspected of crimes that can lead to a prison sentence; and the national DNA register, containing the DNA profiles of convicts.[7]

How the forensic scientists perform comparisons differs between specializations. DNA analysis, for example, is quite automated. Once DNA has been extracted from the medium that carried it to the laboratory—cigarette ends, cotton swabs, pieces of fabric, a jar of urine—machines and computers turn the sample into a DNA profile. In other words, they turn it into a string of numbers (at the time of my fieldwork, profiles were based on ten loci[8] and a sex marker; since then, the SKL has switched to a European standard that uses fifteen loci). These profiles are then uploaded into the databases, and the databases are automatically compared against each other after every working day.

Other forensic analyses require more work "by hand." Fingerprints, for example, were first developed, that is, made visible by chemical means, and photographed. Then they were identified, that is, compared to known fingerprints on a computer screen. These known fingerprints were typically retrieved from the national database, either directly, using the suspect's personal identification number,[9] or through a computerized database search. For the latter, the forensic scientists used software to mark out peculiarities in the fingerprint on their screens—lines that stopped or bifurcated, types of patterns—and then had the software compare the print against those in the database. Minutes or hours later, they received a number of suggested matches. Many of these they could dismiss immediately. Others they enlarged on the screen alongside the fingerprint from the crime scene for closer comparison. What makes fingerprint comparison difficult, according to the fingerprint examiners, is that fingers are soft and so are some surfaces. Thus, while fingerprints are considered unique, the pattern made up by the ridges in the skin transfers a little differently each time it touches something. In a distorted fingerprint, the distances between the lines in the pattern look different than in a fingerprint made under ideal circumstances, and it can be difficult to decide whether a print that on first glance looks quite different was actually made by the same finger.

Fiber analysis consists of different judgments. It takes into account the premise that "on all clothes, there is a whole carpet of fibers that you have to dismiss"—for example, fibers from other clothes that got transferred in the washing machine. The fiber specialist needs to know what that fiber carpet can be expected look like because the "flora" of fibers differs from household to household, and therefore which fibers may be significant for comparison varies also. Having picked out the relevant fibers, the forensic scientists then compare them under different microscopes in different kinds of light to determine if and which fibers are "the same" (which is not a trivial question; see Martin and Lynch 2009; Cole 2009). To do this, they need to know how fibers' appearances are affected by magnification, light, moisture, and dirt in order to determine which details are relevant and which are not, what is "there" and what is an artifact, and whether a similarity (or difference) is caused by "sameness" (or, respectively, "differentness") or other factors.

Examining tool marks is tricky in yet another way. The forensic scientists specialized in these analyses have to work with marks that are layered over each other, impressions as well as scrapes, and in some cases very small surfaces. On a piece of cut wire, for example, there is not very much space for marks and thus not much material to work with. A window frame, on the other hand, can be forced open in a number of ways (and it may take several attempts), which means there are a number of places where, for example, a crowbar may have left marks. In addition, if these marks are on top of each other, a scrape could obliterate part of an impression or an impression could distort a scrape. One of the scientists explained the difficulty:

> A crowbar has a lot more than two ends, let me tell you. Good heavens, and the ways you can pry open a window with a crowbar! [...] I had a case where I said, "It can't be that crowb—it's not even the same width!" [...] "Yes, but have you thought of this?" [a colleague said.] And it turned out that I had looked in the wrong place, because the window was here, but then there is a windowsill, and that [windowsill] was where the cast was from. And that's decimeters from the end [of the crowbar when it is applied to the window frame]—of course the width is different there. I was so embarrassed!

Not surprisingly, the tool mark examiners I spent time with frequently stopped to have a look at the doors in their laboratory to imagine how they would force them open. They also tried to find different ways of prying open imaginary windows with a suspected tool in their hands, all in order not to overlook a potential source of the traces in question.

In all of the analyses, the forensic scientists had to deal with the messiness of materiality, which contributed uncertainty of its own to the question of sameness. Unlike known samples, traces from crime scenes often are indistinct. When fingerprinting or swabbing someone, a police officer can redo the procedure until the results are satisfactory. Similarly, a forensic scientist can make a clear comparison print of a shoe sole or a comparison mark with a screwdriver. Traces at a crime scene, on the other hand, are not necessarily left under ideal circumstances or on ideal surfaces, and comparison can therefore be difficult. Fingerprints can be partial or blurry; there might only be a very small amount of a bodily fluid left there or it might be contaminated; a shoe mark might have been found on a piece of stretchy or crumpled fabric. In addition, traces may have deteriorated over time or during recovery.

According to my interlocutors, the ability to make these comparisons—the ability to *see*—takes several years to acquire under the tutelage of one's colleagues. Thus forensic scientists saw no point in including photographs of their findings in expert statements or in bringing them to court; "they wouldn't see the picture in the same way," a tool mark specialist said.

In theoretical terms, forensic scientists acquire what Charles Goodwin calls "professional vision" (1994, 1995), a way of seeing and understanding that is connected to belonging to a profession. In Goodwin's words, professions and their practitioners rely on "socially organized ways of seeing and understanding events that are answerable to the distinctive interests of a particular social group" (1994, 606). Based on very detailed observations of communicative situations, Goodwin discusses how members of a profession transform what they see into "objects of knowledge" (1994, 606) through specific practices of drawing attention to and classifying features of relevance.

Goodwin emphasizes the collective dimension of professional vision: "The ability to see a meaningful event is not a transparent, psychological process but instead a socially situated activity accomplished through the deployment of a range of historically constituted discursive practices. [...] All vision is perspectival and lodged within endogenous communities of practice" (1994, 606). Forensic scientists within the same specialization share frames of reference and discussions and, through them, develop shared practices of seeing. These could be explicit or more tacit, as encountered by a forensic scientist who, at the time she is referring to in the following quote, had only been examining tool marks for a few years: "We had a discussion about how small an area there actually can be for a +4.[10] [...] I was a little skeptical [because the area was so small], but the others who know this stuff said, 'It's a +4, don't you see that?' 'Yes, I see that there's lots of detail there, but it's such a terribly tiny area if you look at it without a microscope.' [And they said,] 'Yeah, but that's enough. We've got this [detail] and this [one] and this [one].'" In discussions like this, forensic scientists referred to the objects under the microscope, showing features to each other and changing magnification and angles of light. Professional vision is, as in this account, developed through discussions similar to the "talking science" observed in research laboratories, in which interpretations are established from more or less ambiguous data (Lynch 1985b, 155ff.).

At the SKL, such discussions occur in teaching situations, but they are also a routine part of work. Cases are always assigned to two forensic scientists, who each perform the same work as independently as possible and then disclose their results to one another. They are expected to arrive at the same result or at least to be able to find and resolve the cause for their disagreement. If they do not, a third forensic scientist is consulted—although this is apparently a very rare occurrence.

While this practice is meant to catch possible errors and misjudgments (as well as to prevent forensic scientists from feeling individually responsible for the results), it also contributes to a specialization's professional vision, both through necessitating discussions about results and through checking an individual forensic scientist's professional vision against that of the collective. In addition, the shared analyses advance the standardization that the SKL strives for; the goal is that it should "not matter who is assigned which case, the result should be the same." Thus, while comparison in many cases depends heavily on a forensic scientist's individual abilities, skill, and assessments, this individual dimension is anchored in and monitored by a professional collective.

However, the forensic scientists at the SKL very carefully pointed out that they could not know anything about the "truth." They could only examine the traces before them, and they could only speak about the results of their examinations, not about the events that had produced the traces. In the event of a match, "it's not for us to guarantee that they belonged together, because we can't through analysis arrive at the conclusion that they belonged together." They could only be reasonably certain when they found discrepancies. A discrepancy might come in the form of a number where the DNA profile from a trace differs from the suspect's DNA, or a detail where a suspected shoe sole differs from a shoe mark found at a crime scene; these are both indications that the trace and the sample had not "belonged together."

In STS terms, the work of forensic scientists revolves around reducing and managing uncertainty. In the forensic scientists' terms, they anchor individual assessments and decisions in the collective and thus counteract the hazard of undiscovered mistakes. By the end of a comparison, the forensic scientists have no doubt about the results they have produced. Either the trace and the sample match or they do not (or the result is inconclusive), but the accuracy of the analyses is not in question. What is in question, or more accurately what the next question is, is what a match means.

EVALUATING RESULTS

In crime fiction, a match between the suspect or their possessions and the crime scene is often treated as indicating indubitable identification and, by extension, indubitable guilt. Nonfictional criminal justice, however, must assess a match: The known source might match the trace from the crime scene because it has made the trace, but the match might also be coincidental. In other words, a match must be evaluated.

Thus, after analyzing the traces, the SKL's forensic scientists evaluate the results of these analyses in order to be able to convey in their expert statements what the result is "worth," a step that, according to its staff, distinguishes the SKL "from just any analysis lab."

Take, for example, a glass fragment possibly carried off during a burglary. The forensic scientist might examine the thickness, refraction, and chemical composition of both the fragment and the windowpane. If the two differ in even just one of these characteristics, the forensic scientist can—barring errors and mix-ups—rule out the possibility that the fragment was carried off from the crime scene. Conversely, a match does not inevitably mean that the fragment once was a part of the particular windowpane in question. Window glass is mass-produced, and thus there could be numerous windowpanes and perhaps even other objects that might match the fragment equally well. Thus, at the core of this evaluation is the forensic scientists' recognition that, even if the trace and its suspected source match, one cannot be certain that the trace indeed originated from that source: "A match isn't automatically something terrific, [. . .] but what's good and what we want to point to is that we know what it usually looks like and that the result we got is unusually similar . . . which we hadn't expected. It's so unusual that we hadn't expected it, not even once in a million analyses." It is not particularly "terrific" if a suspect's boots match shoe prints in pattern and size at a crime scene on a military base—so, presumably, would quite a number of other soldiers' boots. The same match might be more "terrific," however, if the crime scene were in a residential area, where military boots are unusual. Similarly, a match, chemically as well as in thickness and refraction, between a fragment of glass and a broken window pane does not mean as much as if the fragment could also be fitted together, jigsaw-style, with the pieces from the window. That would be unexpected and thus valuable.

In order to do justice to these complexities, the SKL's forensic scientists not only produce laboratory results but also establish what these results mean, (i.e., they evaluate the results of their comparisons). With the exception of fingerprints—which, due to convention and membership in international organizations, are reported as "match," "non-match," or "inconclusive"—this evaluation is done with a Bayesian approach[11] (see, for example, Robertson and Vignaux 1995; Cook et al. 1998a; for a critical discussion see Lawless and Williams 2010). According to the forensic scientists at the SKL, this approach is a way of reasoning as much as a way of calculating.

The philosophy underlying the Bayesian approach is that, while it is impossible to achieve certainty that a trace comes from a specific source, it is possible to make inferences from the analysis results. In the words of a forensic scientist, "There are only two possibilities. Either it comes from that window or it doesn't [. . .] and I don't know which is . . . the truth. And I can never find out, either, through my analyses; the only thing I can do is to analyze these in all possible conceivable ways, and then I can give an opinion on how strongly my results support one or the other." In Bayesian terms, this evaluation produces a likelihood ratio: the likelihood of obtaining the analysis result (e.g., a match), given that one proposition is true (e.g., the fragment of glass comes from the window at the crime scene), compared to the likelihood of obtaining the same result, given that the alternative proposition is true (e.g., the fragment of glass comes from some other glass object). Formally:

$$\text{Likelihood ratio} = \frac{\text{Probability of the result if proposition 1 is true}}{\text{Probability of the result if proposition 2 is true}}$$

The likelihood ratio expresses how strongly the results support one proposition over the other. Applied to the example of the glass, the probability of obtaining the match if the fragment came from the window in question is divided by the probability of obtaining the match if it did not. For example, it is very probable that the glass matches, given that the fragment was carried off from the crime scene, so the numerator will be close to 1. The denominator depends on how common the type of glass is. With a commonplace type of glass, a random match would be much more probable than with a rare type of glass. Thus, the denominator will be smaller for a rare type, resulting in a large quotient—the likelihood ratio. A high likelihood ratio would indicate stronger support for the first proposition (in this case, the fragment coming from the window at the crime scene) than a low likelihood ratio would. That is, the likelihood ratio expresses the weight of the evidence, not its accuracy. In this example, the match between trace and suspected source is assumed to have been determined without error.

The SKL expresses the likelihood ratio through a scale of nine grades, from -4 to +4, with an associated verbal scale, each grade corresponding to an interval of likelihood ratios and +4 expressing the strongest support (see Nordgaard et al. 2012 for an "insider" discussion of the scale). A grade is supposed to express the same value, or strength of support, regardless of whether it is applied to shoe print, DNA, or glass evidence. The SKL's forensic scientists underscored that one of the benefits of using a common scale for all types of results was that it made different pieces of evidence commensurable and combinable.

Ideally, the propositions are developed by the police or the prosecution: proposition 1 is typically linked to the prosecution's version of the events in question and proposition 2 to the defense's. The forensic scientists are, however—especially in complex cases—sometimes asked for advice on which propositions could be fruitful.

The propositions can be stated at different levels, such as the "source," "activity," and "offense" levels (see Cook et al. 1998b). Propositions on the source level revolve around the question of a trace's origin—for example, whether a glass fragment came from a specific window or a bloodstain from a specific person. On the activity level, the propositions concern the activity that left the trace—for example, whether a specific suspect broke the window at the crime scene or injured the plaintiff. The offense level concerns whether the trace was left during a *criminal* activity—that is, whether the suspect is guilty of, for example, breaking and entering or attempting homicide.

Often, the propositions that the SKL's forensic scientists consider involve the source level. Usually, only a few types of analysis yield results at the activity level—for example, fiber analysis. Others might reach the activity level through the circumstances of the case or by combining several pieces of evidence. For example, examining a knife for fingerprints as well as for traces of blood could provide results that allow propositions about whether a particular person used the knife to stab another person. The SKL's forensic scientists emphasized, however, that the offense level—which indicates whether a suspect has committed a crime—was always solely the court's province.

It is important to note that, in the Bayesian approach as used by the SKL, the forensic scientists do not give an expert opinion on the propositions. For example, they would not declare whether the fragment of glass came from the smashed window. They restrict their opinions to their calculations of how strongly their analysis results support one proposition over the other. The difference may seem trivial from the outside, and perhaps even unnecessarily complicating, but it is very important to the forensic scientists because as a result the decision on the propositions is left to the court. By stating the likelihood ratio, the forensic scientists deliver information that the court can use, together with the other evidence in the case, for making the decision about the facts of the case.

According to the forensic scientists, this distribution of responsibility also gives them more latitude: "I think [forensic scientists] have refrained from strong statements sometimes, because they think you have to be so very certain that it's like this. [. . .] You're not saying how certain you are that it's like this, what you're saying is that your result indicates it. But if you do another analysis, it may indicate something else—that's something you have no idea about. You don't have to take responsibility for how it is." As long as the decision on—and with it the responsibility for—a proposition lies with the court, forensic scientists also feel able to deliver uncertain evidence. As a consequence, the body of evidence in a given case could become larger as well as more nuanced.

The Bayesian approach is not the only possible way to evaluate a match, and nor is it uncontroversial. There is (sometimes vehement) disagreement on how best to present probabilistic evidence (see, for example, Koehler 1996; Lindsey et al. 2003; Schklar and Diamond 1999). While the Bayesian approach is widely used in Europe, for example by forensic science laboratories in England, Wales, Ireland, and the Netherlands, the standard practice in the United States, at least for DNA evidence, is to use random match probabilities.[12] In addition, different forensic science institutions that use a Bayesian approach sometimes use different intervals as well as different verbal expressions, and they do not all necessarily use a numerical scale (see, for example, Jackson 2009).

While it may seem that making a Bayesian evaluation is a simple matter of plugging the right numbers into the right slots, figuring out what the right numbers are and how to arrive at them is not an easy task—this is another form of uncertainty inherent in forensic evidence practices in the laboratory.

One question to consider is what reference "population" should be used for a comparison. In the case of the glass fragment, for example, when calculating the probability of the result if the fragment did not come from the smashed window, should one consider all glass objects in the world? Or only windowpanes? If only windows, should one consider only the ones in the neighborhood? Or the town? Or the country? These questions are not trivial—a type of glass, a shoe sole pattern, or a DNA marker may be common in one context and uncommon in another, and thus different reference populations can lead to different likelihood ratios and thus different grades on the scale. As a result, the reference population the forensic scientist chooses has significance for the evidence and the conclusions that the court can draw from it. Amade M'charek (2000) discusses such "practices of population" and looks at how evidence's value changes when a different reference population is used for DNA evidence in the Netherlands.

Secondly, the forensic scientist needs information about the reference population. For DNA evidence, for example, the SKL's forensic scientists can use a reference database of a few hundred DNA profiles[13] for their calculation, but for other types of evidence, comparable statistical information was not available. It would be very hard, for example, to know exactly how many pairs of shoes with a particular sole pattern and of a particular size are in circulation at a given time. What is more, unlike the distribution of genes in the human population, this number is subject to constant change. New models are made and sold continually and old pairs of shoes are thrown away. In the words of a forensic scientist: "And that's different for different types of cases—how . . . quickly, so to speak, the market changes. Flammable liquids, for example, there are new products all the time, and [. . .] we need to know at all times what kinds of products are there on the market, what kinds of flammables they are, what they look like. If we're talking about shoe prints, we need to have an idea about [. . .] new models, and now they've made up new sole patterns and [laughs] [. . .] it changes all the time."

The forensic scientists do have reference material that can help them assign an interval of likelihood ratios and thus a grade on the scale. Such material is not understood and used in the same fashion as the reference DNA database, but as an extension of the forensic scientists' personal experience. The reference material can be, for example, old cases, samples of fibers stored in file binders, or local databases. The forensic scientists also build up their experience by taking field trips to tool factories, by testing different tools and techniques for prying open doors and windows, and by conducting small-scale studies. A study of sole patterns, for example, which was conducted by students in a forensics course held jointly by the SKL and the local university, was received with keen interest by forensic scientists:

> And well, that's a study that, I think, that gave many an aha moment about the variation of patterns on shoe soles, and that's terrific. [. . .] It gives us an idea [laughs] about how much variation there actually is. Then again, it doesn't give us the whole truth because it's a limited study; it was done in a few shopping malls in Linköping,[14] and it was a particular year, so you need to keep that in mind. [. . .] But it still is a tremendous help. And that's how it is with almost all databases we've got. However we build it, it has its limitations.

These limitations have to do with both the ever-changing "markets" of the products in question and practicalities: "You try to build up databases that are as up-to-date and as good as absolutely possible—but that's also a resource issue. [. . .] The, well, how to put this . . . the . . . absolute database, the one that'd give us . . . the truth, that doesn't exist, and it can't be made, either."

Thus, limited knowledge made a precise calculation of a likelihood ratio impossible with most types of forensic evidence. And, strictly speaking, the foundation for the likelihood ratio for DNA evidence is also incomplete, as the reference database does not contain all of the relevant population. (In addition, full profile matches are routinely assumed to pass the likelihood ratio threshold required for the grade +4.)

What the forensic scientists do, however, is use their experience and the reference material to estimate a likelihood ratio. The match between the glass fragment and the windowpane at the crime scene, for example, might be given a +2 based on thickness, composition, and refraction alone, but if it could be pieced together with other fragments from the windowpane, it would be graded higher.

In fiber analysis, the intervals of likelihood ratios have been translated into rough guidelines. A fiber specialist described examining whether a particular shirt had been in contact[15] with a particular chair like this:

Let's say we find a few fibers, four or five of them, that might tip it toward a +1. We find a lot of fibers of the same type, hundreds of them, but they're just one type from one shirt. A +2? Roughly speaking. For a +3 we need crosswise: I need fibers from the chair on my shirt [and] shirt fibers on the chair [...] then we think it's strong enough for a grade +3.[16] And +4 ... well, in theory we'd be able to reach that, but [...] by the time we'd done all that, the trial would be over already, so we stop at grade +3, that is quite strong after all. [...] But these different grades, [...] we know how much a fiber attaches itself, for how long it stays on, how common it is and how easy it is to find it by coincidence.

The negative side of the scale seemed to be regarded as more difficult than the positive side. The fiber specialist—who was by no means the only forensic scientist who held such a view—put it like this:

The negative side is difficult. [...] To say that I'm -2 certain that they haven't been in contact, why am I -2, not -3 or -4? That's really hard. [...] because it's difficult to say [...] that it's a hundred times more likely to get these results if it isn't this way than if it is some other way [...] to be negatively certain, so to speak [laughs]. Well, if I find more and more [fibers], that's one thing, then I get more and more certain, but if I've already found nothing, how certain am I that it's nothing? I don't have fewer and fewer results, I still haven't got any fibers. [...] If I'm to be on the negative [side], I almost need to know the details of how everything happened, you know, time-wise, what were they wearing, was he wearing anything else, are there other clothes around that might look the same. [...] Because on the positive side, I'd find more and more, [but on the negative side] I don't find less and less—it's really difficult.

The assessment the forensic scientist talks about is thus based on professional vision and on what she knows about the circumstances of the case[17] (how long since the alleged contact, what happened to the shirt and the chair afterwards, etc.) and about the fabric types involved. Very few chair fibers found on the shirt mean something different if the chair sheds many adhesive fibers and both shirt and chair were collected and sealed within minutes of the alleged contact than if the chair fabric sheds few fibers or if the shirt had been washed.

In tool mark analyses, comparing and grading were similarly inseparable. When the forensic scientists were comparing scrape marks, for example, it did not seem to be difficult for them to find similar gouges in the two samples. The difficult part seemed to be whether these similarities were coincidental and thus to be expected or whether their number and placement made such a coincidence unlikely. As a forensic scientist explained, marks that matched "a little bit everywhere" did not mean very much. As a rule, a +4 did not match at all except for the one (sufficiently large) area that matched perfectly, a match that became clearer and clearer with increased magnification. Deciding whether marks from a crime scene and marks made in the laboratory were "the same" thus inseparably included deciding how *much* they were the same.

Thus, the Bayesian evaluation, while producing comparable and commensurable results, could rest on a conglomeration of different practices and skills. As limitations of knowledge made it in many cases impossible to calculate a precise likelihood ratio, the forensic scientists estimated an interval of likelihood ratios and expressed them through the graded scale.

This does not mean to say that employing a Bayesian approach and delivering quantified forensic evidence is somehow cheating. Rather, the SKL's forensic scientists described and used the Bayesian approach as a way of combining professional experience with the statistics that were (and could reasonably be) available, thereby balancing the impossibility of knowing for certain against the desire to aid criminal justice. Some things (such as the exact number of shoes with a particular sole pattern currently in use) cannot be known, much less at a reasonable cost, but the forensic scientists could estimate an interval of likelihood ratios and thus a grade on their scale.

QUANTIFICATION—MECHANICAL OBJECTIVITY AND MORE

From an STS point of view, the Bayesian approach can be seen as an instance of trust in—or rather, through—numbers (see Porter 1992a, 1992b, 1995; Daston 1992, 1995; Daston and Galison 2007). For instance, numbers suggest accuracy. Lynch and his colleagues, for example, note that "the apparently precise measures of uncertainty provided by probability figures [for DNA evidence] became a source of credibility. Then, with the multiplication of markers in currently used STR systems, random match probabilities approached a vanishing point, and match declarations effectively implied certainty" (2008, 345).[18]

Secondly, numbers produced by quantification can be associated with mechanical objectivity, one of the concepts of objectivity that Lorraine Daston and Peter Galison (Daston 1992; Daston and Galison 1992, 2007) have traced in the history of science. Daston describes it as "the form of objec-

tivity that strives to eliminate all forms of human intervention in the observation of nature, either by using machines, such as self-inscription devices or
the camera, or by mechanizing scientific procedures, as in deploying statistical techniques to choose the best of a set of observations" (Daston 1995, 19).

Daston and Galison argue that ideals of objectivity are an expression of
the dangers perceived in subjectivity and of "how, why, and when various
forms of subjectivity came to be seen as *dangerously* subjective" (1992, 82;
italics in original). The "dangerous" subjectivity in forensic science consists
of the forensic scientists' personal, individual idiosyncrasies as well as their
choices and judgments (cf. Daston and Galison 1992, 82ff.), as they might be
biased.

Mechanical objectivity through quantification associates forensic science
and its results with impartiality—the counterpart to forensic science's most
dangerous subjectivity—by removing the risk of making a potentially subjective and thus a potentially partial decision: "A decision made by the numbers
(or by explicit rules of some other sort) has at least the appearance of being
fair and impersonal. Scientific objectivity thus provides an answer to a moral
demand for impartiality and fairness. Quantification is a way of making decisions without seeming to decide" (Porter 1995, 9).

Quantification is perceived as objective (in the sense of being fair and
impartial) because it produces knowledge by following rules instead of personal (i.e., subjective and thus potentially biased) judgment. Thus, as
Theodore Porter points out, quantification also establishes authority: "The
impersonality of numbers [. . .] is at least as crucial for their authority as is the
plausibility of their claims to truth" (Porter 1992b, 20).

A personal judgment, potentially biased and flawed, is replaced with the
impersonal result from calculations, which is devoid of subjective flaws and
idiosyncrasies. Moreover, an impersonal result associates forensic science
with impartiality—there is no subject involved that can take sides.[19] Porter
also draws parallels to making judgments in court, emphasizing an association with morality: "In most contexts, objectivity means fairness and impartiality. Someone who 'isn't objective' has allowed prejudice or self-interest to
distort a judgment. The credibility of courts depends on an ability to elude
such charges. [. . .] Rules should rule, that professional as well as personal
judgment should be held in check. They point to the alliance of objectivity as
an ideal of knowing and objectivity as a moral value" (1995, 4–5).

A quantitative approach in forensic science could thus disassociate the
evidence it produces from partiality, bias, and subjectivity. This can be seen

in connection with criticism of aspects of forensic science as unscientific. That is, an evaluation based on an impersonal and thus impartial calculation makes it possible to address some of the issues identified as problematic in forensic science. Some of these issues are, for example, bias (Ghoshray 2007) and forensic science's foundation in personal judgment and professional agreement (discussed in, for example, Cole 2009). A quantitative approach does not automatically do more, however, than conceptually disassociate forensic science from these issues. A British forensic science consultant interviewed and quoted by Christopher Lawless and Robin Williams describes the Bayesian approach as window dressing: "It's giving a scientific coating to what basically is a human judgment about the belief in something" 2010, 748).

In Sweden, where forensic science and the SKL seem to enjoy considerable trust not only from the criminal justice system but also from the media and the public, the turn toward the Bayesian approach[20] could be seen as a move to conserve this trust. It may be seen as a form of credibility work, demonstrating affiliation with scientific values and, even more importantly, loyalty to results and their evaluation. Without it, the SKL might appear to side with one of the parties in a case. As the forensic scientists emphatically do not give opinions on the propositions, and the propositions are developed by the prosecution and often also consider the defense's position,[21] the scientists cannot be accused of compromising their impartiality.

However, the SKL's use of the Bayesian approach does more than make a contribution to establishing the credibility of its forensic science. The introduction of the Bayesian approach has also affected laboratory practices. For the scale to be truly uniform for all analyses, grading must be consistent throughout the laboratory. Within the same specialization, consistency is brought about with the standardized seeing of professional vision. Uniformity between different specializations requires additional effort, as professional vision is not shared across specializations. This wider uniformity is aimed for through "calibration talks," during which laboratory members from different specializations discuss and compare their work, particularly more "knotty" cases that have been given low grades:

> We have these calibration talks. [. . .] I for instance just had one with a girl who develops fingerprints. That's developing, and they don't grade, [. . .] so I thought, what are we going to talk about? But it was really interesting. [. . .] They need to know lots of things. And there we sit, and she's given me a case

and I've given her a case and we sit and discuss each other's cases. It's fantastic. It's really interesting to see how other units think about the scale [...] and their explanations, what's behind it, it's really interesting—super good in fact.

Fingerprints are developed (made visible by chemical means) by one set of specialists and then identified (compared with other fingerprints) by another set of specialists. The person the interviewee is referring to above belongs to the first group. The scale is not used for fingerprints, but if it were, it would be used by the second set of specialists, so the interviewee's initial hesitation was twofold. However, according to this interviewee, calibration talks enabled him to see "how other units think" and "what's behind it"—that is, to understand how other units translated the intervals of likelihood ratios into guidelines and criteria that were relevant for their analyses.

Similarly, other forensic scientists mentioned that calibration talks were very helpful for achieving transparency and consistency when grading across specializations. Some of them warned, however, against conflating agreement and accuracy. "We calibrate against each other," one of them said, meaning that, by talking to each other, they establish and calibrate against shared standards, "so it's not so odd that we arrive at the same numbers—which does not mean that they are correct."

These calibration talks could be understood as a version of mechanical objectivity. As a lot of forensic science is performed "by hand" rather than by machines, following explicit and transparent rules makes it less personal and idiosyncratic. Meeting subjectivity with rules—that is, with quantification— can achieve mechanical objectivity by excluding judgment (Porter 1992a, 639). Also, the SKL's use of the term "calibration talks" evokes mechanical objectivity. The term "calibration" suggests that if tasks that are imperiled by subjectivity cannot be delegated to machines, at least people can be disciplined to behave in a machinelike fashion and turn out uniform assessments. The equating of a scientist's body and mind to an instrument has been noted before: "The science laboratory [...] takes possession of the scientist's body and employs it—in a disciplined manner—in order to pursue particular purposes" (Knorr-Cetina et al. 1988, 97; my translation). To push the metaphor, calibrating forensic scientists like instruments suggests that the results produced by them are as reliable and impartial as results produced by machines.

There is more to the calibration talks than evoking mechanical objectivity, however. For one, the forensic scientists are expected to calibrate themselves, and they are expected to do so not only by learning rules but also by widening their perspectives by discussing cases outside of the immediate scope of their expertise, such as the fiber specialist learning about the fingerprint developer's cases and vice versa.

Secondly, long-time experience, and particularly experience in several specializations, was described as valuable to the laboratory and as a crucial part of producing solid forensic evidence. People with such experience and skill were often mentioned in discussions and typically described as important resources. For example, the forensic scientist quoted above mentioned that she had consulted "the others who know this stuff."

These points indicate that the SKL does not strive for nonintervention, which would be impossible, considering that forensic analyses require judgments and decisions. Rather, it strives for restrained and disciplined intervention—a nonsubjective standardized intervention, so to speak. Human subjectivity in the form of personal judgment is balanced by combining the desired human experience and skill with machinelike self-restraint. This self-restraint is supported and enforced by practices such as professional vision, "calibration talks," transparency, and the assignment of two forensic scientists to do crucial parts of each analysis. While the outcome sought is similar to that achieved through relying on machines and their mechanical objectivity, both the means and their implications are different.

Thus, the objectivity performed in the SKL's forensic practices of quantification is an objectivity of divided and shared decisions as well as of collective practices of uniformity and restraint. Rather than eliminating subjectivity through mechanical use of rules (Daston and Galison 1992, 83ff.), the forensic scientists strive to move away from undesirable subjectivity by reaching toward intersubjectivity. This is not an intersubjectivity in the Popperian sense of one person testing or reproducing someone else's results (Popper 1972 [1959], 44), but an intersubjectivity of counterbalancing subjectivity with shared decisions and perspectives. Inspired by Émile Durkheim's distinction of mechanical and organic solidarity in society, it could also be called organic objectivity. Division of labor and diversified specializations, Durkheim (1984 [1893]) argues, engender organic solidarity based on difference rather than similarity.

I certainly do not wish to invoke the cultural evolutionism inherent in Durkheim's argument; however, it seems that the intersubjectivity in the forensic laboratory that is used to counter the subjectivity of bias, limited perspective, and mistakes is correspondingly based on division of labor along different specializations. Different experts work together and calibrate themselves to turn out expert opinions that strive both toward uniformity and standardization and toward personal experience and skill.

Analogous to the discussions that take place within specializations, the calibration talks oblige forensic scientists to make their thinking explicit. Thus, while the talks may not develop a shared professional vision throughout the laboratory, they contribute to shared reasoning. In addition, they contribute to the SKL achieving its aspirations for transparency by establishing that laboratory practices are open for discussion. The Bayesian approach's effect on the SKL thus appears to be making practices of analyzing and grading more visible and transparent within the laboratory. It appears to be an important factor in shaping and maintaining the laboratory's epistemic culture (Knorr Cetina 1999).

It is, of course, conceivable that transparency and organic objectivity could be arrived at with other tools. Moreover, the use of a Bayesian approach does not guarantee organic objectivity. It might also have other implications. Lawless and Williams (2010), for example, connect the Bayesian approach to economic values, showing how the transparency of following explicit rules enabled the now-closed British Forensic Science Service to assess the expected value of an analysis and thus provide a basis for the customers' decisions on whether to commission it. As the SKL's "customers" do not pay directly for its services—like other publicly run functions, the SKL operates on a set annual budget—this aspect of the Bayesian approach is not an issue. For the SKL, the Bayesian approach seems to have enabled forensic scientists to make their practices transparent to themselves, each other, and eventually their "customers."[22] Other evaluation tools that necessitate similar standardization across specializations might bring about similar organic objectivity.

MAKING UNCERTAINTY TRACTABLE

The forensic scientists' contribution to the biography of forensic evidence is thus to make some of its inherent uncertainties manageable. It is impossible to attain absolute certainty about the source of a trace, but what is possible is to produce a figure that allows conclusions about the relationship of a trace and its suspected source and that makes the results' value knowable, manageable, and communicable.[23]

The uncertainty (or perhaps ambiguity) of what a piece of forensic evidence means for a defendant's culpability—to use Lynch and his collaborators' phrasing, the "field of possibilities" of "how to make sense of the evidence" (2008, 345)—is emphatically not an issue at the SKL. In the forensic scientists' terms, this uncertainty—which they did describe as "uncertainty"—is at the offense level and thus not in the laboratory's sphere but in the court's.

The forensic scientists' contribution to forensic evidence is thus contingent on the court making the final decision and settling the issue. But it is also contingent on other members of the criminal justice system. While the forensic evidence that the scientists produce is important in the criminal investigation division's work and the pretrial investigation, the police investigators' work of producing suspects (and having them "swabbed" and fingerprinted) is, in turn, important for making the laboratory's comparisons possible. Equally important, of course, is the work of the police's crime scene division, whose technicians recover the traces that the forensic scientists analyze.

CHAPTER FIVE

The Crime Scene Division

TRACES

The first crime scene I was taken along to was as mundane as they come: a rather unfashionable suburb[1] where a crime scene technician looked at some burned-out cars. While he walked, camera in hand, around the first one, which was not much more than a charred skeleton cordoned off from the parking lot with blue-and-white police tape, he pointed out various details: the windows that had melted in the heat of the fire, the badly burned place behind the driver's seat, and the lock missing from one of the doors. He picked up an oil canister from under the car, had a look at it, and discarded it. It did not necessarily have to have anything to with the fire, he explained, and anyway, "the car has been like this since Sunday morning," sitting in the parking lot with its windows melted away, only protected by police tape. No one in their right mind would believe that there had not been spectators and that the tape had prevented anyone from touching the car since it had been on fire. Anything could have been taken away from or added to the scene. If one were to be serious about it, he said, the car would have to have been guarded by the police until the crime scene division arrived.

Then he pointed to a cigarette end, fairly clean and lying on top of the rubble. Many uniformed police officers would collect that and have it analyzed for DNA, he said, shaking his head. "If you get a hit on that, what is that going to mean?" He went on to explain that there was no point in looking for gasoline in a car fire, as one would do after an apartment fire; in cars, gasoline was only to be expected. But cars did not spontaneously burst into flames, at least not in the summertime, so something must have happened.

And something must have also happened to another car that was sitting in another parking lot on the other side of the same suburb. One of the tires was singed, the technician pointed out, and he showed me the two places

91

where he thought the fire had started. "But to prove that, that's a totally different question." A car this old might be set on fire by its owner, in the hope of an insurance payment toward a new one. But, he amended, people usually drive their cars out into the forest to do that.

It was clear that the burned-out cars held a lot more meanings for him than for me. He had been able to decide which of all the objects and traces[2] at the crime scene had the relevance and the potential to help solve the crime. And he turned messy crime scenes such as this one into the neat and comprehensible reports I had seen at the criminal investigation division and in the prosecutor's office.

In terms of the biography of forensic evidence, the crime scene technicians abstract the traces—the evidence-to-be—that they assess to be relevant to the crime based on their professional vision (Goodwin 1994, 1995). This abstraction (Latour 1999, 48ff.) transforms the material to the symbolic, the messy to the ordered. It is also an interpretation that draws on the technicians' skill and experience and joins their observations at the crime scene with other information, such as laboratory results and witnesses' or plaintiffs' accounts.

The crime scene technicians play an intermediary role in multiple ways. They mediate between the material and the symbolic as well as between disparate epistemic cultures (Knorr Cetina 1999). They are the vanguard of the forensic science laboratory at the crime scene, laying the groundwork for the forensic scientists' analyses; they mediate between the laboratory and the police and prosecution; and they make the world of law enforcement accessible to plaintiffs. The crime scene reports—inscriptions (Latour and Woolgar 1986 [1979]; Latour 1987, 1990, 1999)—they produce are meant to be read without professional vision by people who lack the technicians' expertise.

CRIME SCENES AND CRIME SCENE REPORTS: MAKING INSCRIPTIONS

In Sweden, crime scenes—or at this stage of the investigation, potential crime scenes—are examined by the police. Very "simple" crime scenes, such as break-ins into basements or cars, are typically handled by the patrol police. These crimes have not usually caused much damage to the victims' property, bodies, or psyches, and traces are expected to be scant and easy to find. More complicated cases and the types of crimes that police management feels affect victims significantly are handled by specialists—crime scene technicians with the police's crime scene divisions. In very complicated cases and severe crimes, the technicians may consult with forensic scientists from the Swedish National Laboratory of Forensic Science (SKL).

Crime scene technicians are police officers who have received specialized training in forensics and crime scene investigation.[3] Their police background shows in their uniform sweaters and pants, in the police coveralls they sometimes wear, in the service weapons they carry when they leave the office, and in their radio contact with the police's communications center. In their daily work, they have as much contact with the SKL and the prosecutor's office as they have with the police officers at the criminal investigation division. They have very little contact with the patrol police.

Like other crime scene divisions, the one I visited had a small laboratory of its own. There, the crime scene technicians performed some routine analyses, lifted fingerprints from objects to be sent for comparison, and pre-examined material before sending it to the SKL in order to assess whether laboratory analysis was likely to yield a result.

Literally, the division's Swedish name (*tekniska roteln*) translates as "technical division," and the crime scene technicians I met often grumbled that anything that could be construed as remotely technical would be dumped on them, such as extracting information from cell phones and fingerprinting suspects taken into custody. In one case, a technician was asked to open a letter that someone had brought in to the police and that the police investigator felt apprehensive about. The problem with this, according to the crime scene technicians, was that they spent less and less time doing what they should be doing (i.e., examining the scenes of crimes, especially serious crimes).

Not surprisingly, the cases the crime scene technicians showed me as examples of their work and talked about with pride were cases in which they had played an important role in producing the forensic evidence that had solved the crime. One was a robbery and murder in which the crime scene technician had found the crucial tiny specks of the victim's blood on the offender's sleeve, on a fabric that made it very hard to see them. In another case, the crime scene technicians had helped catch a suspected serial burglar by applying a fluorescent powder to his bicycle. The same powder was found in a burgled apartment a few days later, and a search of the suspect's house yielded the stolen goods.

Of course, the crime scene division's central contribution to these and other cases does not become clear until the verdict. The immediate result of the crime scene division's work and their contribution to the pretrial investigation are not solved crimes but written crime scene reports. These reports document—in writing as well as in photographs—the crime scene (or car or set of clothing) as a whole as well as the details of the traces found and recovered.

In most cases, these reports are all that will be left of the crime scene. Exceptions include material that crime scene divisions store while awaiting the pretrial investigation leader's decision (in unsolved cases, material may be saved for years). Leftover material is also stored by the SKL for a set period of time after analysis, unless it is to be restored to its owners. But the crime scene as a whole will be gone; after the crime scene examination, the police tape will be removed and restrictions lifted. Even if it were to remain closed off, it would degrade over time. In addition, a crime scene examination removes objects and traces and leaves traces of its own.

In Science and Technology Studies (STS) terms, the crime scene technicians turn the physical, material crime scene into inscriptions (Latour and Woolgar 1986 [1979]; Latour 1987, 1999), that is, into written traces. Inscriptions can be looked at, treated, and combined in a way that would not have been possible with the matter from which they were obtained (Latour and Woolgar 1986 [1979], 50ff.; Latour 1987, 65ff.). Just as importantly, they simplify matter into something that is "easily readable and presentable" (Latour 1990, 39).

In scientific research, making inscriptions means that researchers turn matter into symbolic forms like graphs, diagrams, and lists. The result of such an abstraction (Latour 1999, 48ff.) is much easier to manage than the material it has been abstracted from. Instead of looking at cages of rats or a large area of forest floor, for example, researchers can place diagrams side by side and look for patterns. Inscriptions also make it easier to show one's result to others in order to convince them of discoveries. (Latour portrays science as being very much about convincing and enrolling others.) Instead of using the actual rats and forest floors to demonstrate their points, scientists use representations, like "a tiny set of figures" (Latour 1990, 39) extracted from them, because "nothing can be said about the rats, but a great deal can be said about the figures" (Latour 1990, 39).

Just as figures can be used in a way the phenomena they represent cannot, so can crime scene reports. The reports conserve as well as simplify the crime scene by focusing on what is important for the investigation, namely the traces the crime scene technicians have found and will remove for possible future analysis after photographs have been taken. They incorporate the forensic laboratory's expert statements on the traces that have been sent for analysis and also include the crime scene technicians' conclusions, their so-called crime scene analysis—for example, conclusions about how a burglar broke into a house, where and how a fire started, or whether a reported crime could possibly have taken place at an indicated location.

Through their reports, the crime scene technicians make it possible to "look at" a crime scene a long time after the examination (and without changes accumulating over time). They also make it possible to "look at" a crime scene while in a different place (for example, in a courtroom or a prosecutor's office) and within a different analytical time frame (i.e., after the forensic analyses and the technicians' conclusions). Thus, they turn a messy, complicated, and deteriorating potential crime scene into a report that fits smoothly and efficiently into the criminal justice system's work.[4]

Latour points out "the dialectic of gain and loss" (1999, 70) inherent in transforming matter into representations. On the one hand, there is reduction in "locality, particularity, materiality, multiplicity, and continuity," but on the other hand, there is amplification, as "much greater compatibility, standardization, text, calculation, circulation, and relative universality" are gained and make the connection to previous knowledge and the creation of understanding possible (Latour 1999, 70–71). As Michael Lynch notes, such representations do not only simplify but also limit their use: "Material media, in addition to the coded sounds or marks of verbal and written language, already define, to an indefinite degree, what becomes 'knowable' or 'repeatable' in linguistic or conceptual terms. Intelligibility is built into the visible form of materials in the way they are brought under scrutiny" (1985a, 52).

Both Lynch and Latour talk about scientific research instead of forensic evidence. The two, while certainly related, differ in a fundamental aspect: scientific knowledge aims at the general and universal, while forensic science strives to produce knowledge about the particular (i.e., forensic evidence).[5] Thus, crime scene reports are not meant to contribute to a growing body of generalized knowledge but are rather meant to contribute to the evidence in a particular case, to a specific question about an individual's culpability. But the same principle of gain and loss still applies. When a report replaces a crime scene, the crime scene becomes more understandable through the interpretation the crime scene technicians have made, but it also becomes more limited. The details that have not been documented are lost with the crime scene, and the report shapes how the readers understand the crime scene and thus the forensic evidence.

How, then, do crime scene technicians transform potential crime scenes into reports?

INVESTIGATING A BREAK-IN

During my fieldwork, a suspected break-in had been reported to the police by residents who had come home to a house emptied of valuables. A patrol was sent to the scene, and it confirmed the possible burglary and cordoned off the house. The residents spent the night with family, and in the morning, the crime scene technician gave them a call to meet us with the keys.

On the way, he explained that it was a good thing that the residents had a place to stay the night because now he would be able to examine the crime scene in daylight. In other cases, I had seen the crime scene technicians shake their heads about investigation leaders letting residents go to a lot of trouble to find a place to stay instead of having the technician on call come in the same evening or night. So, apparently, the decision of when to examine a crime scene is a balance between the best conditions (daylight instead of flashlights in the dark) and concern for the residents and presumptive victims. As I learned later, another concern was not giving offenders time to get rid of evidence—for example, by selling stolen property.

When we arrived at the house, the residents were waiting in the driveway. The crime scene technician let them show us around the outside of the house, stopping from time to time to have a closer look at a window or a flower bed, only half listening to their descriptions of what was missing and how they had found the terrace door open and the cat gone when they had come home from work. After that, we went inside. Standing in the hallway, the crime scene technician craned his head to look through doorways. He had the residents point to where things were missing and where they walked with the police patrol. He also had them show him things that were out of place, which thus had probably been touched by the burglar or burglars.

Then he asked the residents to wait outside as he got his camera out of his bag and took pictures of the house's exterior and interior. He could not find any points of forced entry, not on the doors on the ground floor, not on the windows, not even on a tilt window that had been left slightly ajar. Maybe the residents had left a door open, he mused, but then again, they were probably very careful about that because of the cat.

Later, in the car on our way back, he would explain that he is always rather curt to begin with at a crime scene. Of course one should talk to the residents, but he prefers to do so when he is done. He does not like them looking over his shoulder while he works. Apart from wanting to work in peace, he does not want them there when he might need to discuss something suspicious with a colleague. On the other hand, he would never venture into a house or apartment on his own, to avoid a situation where it would be his word against someone else's that he did not break anything. If he were not working with a colleague (or taking me along, as he had that day), a patrol would have to come along as witnesses, in which case they could also talk to the residents.

For the moment, though, I was too busy watching him to think about why he had the residents wait outside. Tilting his head and looking along the wooden living room floor, he showed me a shoe print in a spot where the police patrol had not stepped.[6] He fetched his bag and took out a roll of electrostatic dust lifting foil, which he rolled out over the trace. When he applied electricity, the foil clung to the floor. The idea is, he explained, that it will electrostatically pick up any dust—the medium of the print.

As he flattened out a few air bubbles trapped under the foil, he told me, "It's always like this with the police patrols." They walk all over the place although they really should know better. Most of the time, he assumed, they do so out of pure curiosity, although perhaps also out of hope that they will find the clue that will catch the offender. But really, he said, all they need to do is to ascertain that there has been a break-in and something is gone. A missing TV set would do just fine; the rest "can be filled in later." Of course they also need to make sure that the burglars are not still there, but that does not require them to walk all over the place. If they just want to show that the police care, he concluded, they could do that just as well by explaining that it is better to wait for the crime scene division to arrive.

The foil did not pick up the shoe print, only a couple of cat hairs. He rubbed the edge of the print a little with a finger, wondering whether it might be under the lacquer on the floorboards, but it came off. Shrugging, he tried to lift it with a different foil, this one not electrostatic but instead backed with sticky gelatin. He did not seem particularly enthusiastic about the result, but he put it in his bag, saying, "We'll take it with us and have a proper look in the lab later."

Then he turned his attention to a carton that, according to the residents, had been moved from the back of a cabinet to the kitchen table. He carried it to the sink and busied himself with a brush and fine black fingerprint powder. Using the sink would make it easier for the residents to clean up later, he remarked as he examined his work with a flashlight and found something that could be a partial print. He recovered it with adhesive film and put it into his bag with the shoe print.

In another room of the house, which looked like a study, he turned his attention to a bunch of papers and foreign currency notes lying on a chair. People do not usually keep their things on chairs, he said, and fetched the residents. They explained that the papers and money had been in a drawer, and the technician wondered whether the bills were very valuable. "No, no, no," the owners said, and besides, they added, "that's the last thing you need to take into consideration."

The technician explained that he could take the bills into the laboratory and examine them for fingerprints there, but warned that this would ruin the notes, possibly making it difficult to have them exchanged afterward. But before he put them into his bag, he took them into the kitchen and tried the fingerprint powder. Apparently, there is a chance of finding really fresh prints on paper in this less destructive way.

After packing up, he decided to take another look at the windows from outside, as he still did not know how the burglars got into the house. He asked the residents whether they were really sure that the doors had been locked. Nodding, he listened to their explanations of why they were particularly certain that the back door—the one that neighbors told the police had been wide open—had been locked.[7] He went inside with them because they wanted to show him the tilt window a second time. This time, he explained in detail and with no sign of impatience that no one could have entered through it without leaving marks.

During the conversation, he found out that the residents had moved to the house only a couple of months ago, and they mentioned that they had several keys to the front door, but only one to the back door, and that they had not changed the locks yet. They also felt a little uncomfortable about the previous owners, who might perhaps have had shady acquaintances. But, they said, they felt equally uncomfortable insinuating anything, and without waiting for a response to their discomfort, they asked whether he had found anything.

Not much, he said, and went on to explain that this was not unusual. Generally speaking, he said, burglars touch only the things they take, with the possible exception of window frames and the like, which they touch when they climb into a house. He also explained the residents' next course of action. First, they needed to change the locks—"that's what you should do when you move into a new place"—and then they needed to make a list of the missing items, describing them as closely as possible. This would give them a chance of getting their possessions back, he told them, because it would give the police a chance of seizing them from a suspect. An item that cannot be tied to an owner's detailed description has to be returned to the thief. Finally, the technician gave them advice on how to clean up the fingerprint powder in the sink.

Back at the office, the crime scene technician decided that the partial fingerprint from the carton—a "borderline case"—should be sent off in the hope that it might be identifiable. Although he was familiar with the previous owners and their "shady" acquaintances, he decided not to point them out as potential suspects merely on the grounds of the residents' vague mention.

The gelatin film turned out to have captured a rather blurry partial shoe print, and after examination, the technician decided that it was worthless and probably left over from when the residents' moved into the house. "They must have missed that spot" when cleaning, he concluded, and showed me similar gelatin films with much clearer complete shoe prints. Still, he said, it was strange that he had not found any footprints at all, but perhaps the burglars had not walked on that part of the floor.

He then called the police investigator in charge of the case (as there was no suspect, a prosecutor had not been involved) and told him that the crime scene examination had not turned up anything in particular and that there was no need for the house to be cordoned off any longer. They chatted about the fingerprint and the investigator agreed with the technician's assessment. Before he rang off, the technician took the opportunity to complain about the patrol's having walked all over the house "as usual." I recognized his tone of voice from a coffee break a couple of days earlier, when the crime scene technicians had rolled their eyes at a police patrol's detailed written report of looking at a burgled house together with the residents. The technicians agreed that the effort the patrol had expended on writing would have been much better spent on "brushing," that is, on looking for fingerprints, which really wasn't that hard to do.

This break-in was a thoroughly routine type of case. Domestic burglaries formed a large part of the crime scene division's work, and they were what the crime scene technicians tended to talk about when they spoke of examining crime scenes in general terms. This may have to do with not wanting to be sensationalistic, but it was probably also because burglaries were an everyday crime. But since they affect victims significantly, they are given attention. Suspected murders on the other hand, the staple of crime fiction, are comparably rare occurrences in Sweden.

As this case illustrates, crime scene technicians typically do a number of things simultaneously at crime scenes. By examining the places where the residents' belongings had been for traces and the doors and windows for indications of force, the crime scene technician I accompanied had been looking both for opportunities to find traces of the burglar(s) and for confirmation that a crime had taken place. The latter was one reason he preferred not having residents watch him; if he had doubts about the veracity of a resident's report, their presence would not be helpful.

When working with the shoe print, the carton, and the money, the technician was looking for and trying to recover traces that could be analyzed in the laboratory. A trace is only valuable if it is analyzable, so finding traces is inseparable from recovering them and thus transforming them from a possible trace into a usable trace.

During their interaction, the crime scene technician addressed the residents' distress about someone having rummaged through their home and gave advice about changing the locks and cleaning. He conducted his examination in the least disruptive way possible—for example, by using fingerprint powder over the sink to avoid making too much of a mess and by trying to recover fingerprints from the banknotes without ruining them. He also asked them to help the investigation by providing a description of the missing items and sharing their knowledge of their house—explaining how they had left it before the burglary, that they had recently moved and had not yet changed the locks, and that it was possible that some of the house's keys were missing.

What the crime scene technician took away from the crime scene were photographs, a partial fingerprint, a shoe print, some money, and information. These are not the crime scene itself, nor representative of it, and they are not "easily readable and presentable" (Latour 1990, 39) inscriptions either. Rather, they are abstractions. The crime scene technician has abstracted them from the burglarized house both literally and figuratively, having removed them from the crime scene and used them to summarize the burglary.

How does a crime scene technician make this abstraction? How does he or she decide that a place is indeed a crime scene, and which traces, objects, and bits of information sum up the crime that is supposed to have taken place there?

ABSTRACTING FROM CRIME SCENES

Making abstractions of crime scenes can be described as a specialized practice of seeing. Crime scene technicians, like forensic scientists, rely on professional vision (Goodwin 1994, 1995) when examining crime scenes. Their seeing and feeling of a crime scene builds on shared practices and understandings. It builds on what they have learned during training and on what they learn from each other in their professional practice. It also builds on understandings shared through stories and discussions. In this way, examining crime scenes is not only a matter of individuals' imagination and experience, it is also a collective matter. However, unlike Goodwin, whose emphasis— perhaps due to the situations on which his notion is based—is on how professional vision is explicitly transmitted, crime scene technicians' talk about imagination, experience, and how a crime scene feels suggests a tacit dimension. "You need imagination," said one technician when asked to explain how he examines crime scenes. "It depends on the crime. Break-ins, you have to imagine how [the burglar] got in. Follow those traces. That's what you need to do." Stressing his initial point, he continued: "You need *a lot* of imagination. And then there are different alternatives. With a forced window, there's only one way to get in, where you can hold on and how you can lever yourself up. Crimes of violence are worse, of course, because there, well, you can hit this way or that way and all kinds of things." His hands moved with his words, mimicking heaving himself through an imaginary window frame and swinging an invisible bat. In addition, he emphasized, technicians need experience, which is acquired "over the years." They combine this with their skills and knowledge into the ability to see promising traces.

In practical terms, what crime scene technicians look for is that which "you can see has been moved"—traces of the presumptive crime but not of the place's everyday activity. In the case of the break-in, the residents' testimony that the carton belonged in the back of a cabinet and had not been handled a lot, certainly not since they had moved into the house, was what made the carton interesting. As analyzing forensic evidence, particularly fingerprints, requires quite a lot of "manual" work, lifting all the fingerprints in the house and sorting them out after analysis is not an option, especially considering the number of burglaries. There are not enough resources in the criminal justice system to carry out this kind of investigation for each case. Thus, crime scene technicians do the first sorting—or, in other words, make a first abstraction—at the crime scene, often based on information from the plaintiffs.

To do this, knowing the "normal" state of a crime scene is important:

> If you have the plaintiffs along [. . .] you get to ask, what did it look like to start with? Weeell, maybe it always looks like this, a little like this. Then it's even harder, because then you don't know where to look, if it's a mess and everything's ripped out. Not everyone's all that neat. [. . .] Because it's different if you come to a tidy home, where there's a bit of order. Then you can see that something's been pulled out and thrown on the floor and stuff like that. That has not been done by them, the plaintiffs.

While talking to the plaintiffs may be helpful, they may also be unavailable or forgetful, or they may have an obvious interest in being less than truthful. Since the crime scene technicians have never seen the crime scene in its normal state, their imagination and experience is all the more important.

When telling stories about their work, the crime scene technicians talked about understanding crime scenes in terms of "look" and "feeling." It was a matter of being able to see possible points of entry and promising places to look for traces. They spoke of being able to tell traces of everyday legal activities apart from those of potentially criminal ones. They had also seen so many crime scenes that, even considering that "there are many varieties of burglars [. . .] how all of them think, we don't know," they were able to tell "normal" crime scenes from surprising ones. Thus, they were able to draw conclusions on whether there were indications of a crime and where potential traces might be recovered.

This became particularly clear when the crime scene technicians talked about crime scenes that had felt wrong. One, for example, talked about a home that had allegedly been broken into where she had not been able to find any traces. It was "chemically clean," as she put it—although the residents had been adamant that they had not cleaned before her arrival. In addition, one of the residents had been looking over the technician's shoulder during the whole examination, asking questions. Neither of these things was unusual in itself. According to crime scene technicians, people clean after a burglary for a number of understandable reasons. They may feel their home has been violated and start to clean without thinking; they may be embarrassed to show the police a messy home; they may have walked into a room that they had been told not to touch and want to cover up their noncompliance. People also deny having cleaned, mainly because they are embarrassed about having done something they should not have. Asking questions is not unusual either, especially because popular crime fiction has gotten people interested in forensics, "*CSI*, you know."

However, taken together, the two things made the technician look at the (presumed) crime scene and the potential points of entry with particular care. She wrote in her report that she had been unable to find any traces of a forced entry. Clearly a little uncomfortable with what this implied, she said to me that, after all, she had not accused the residents of attempting to defraud their insurance company.

One of her colleagues talked about finding himself in a very difficult position when dealing with such cases. On the one hand, the crime scene "feels" wrong, but on the other hand, offenders sometimes act in unusual ways, and crime scene technicians certainly do not want to wrongfully accuse the victim of insurance fraud: "You need to have done your homework rather well to be able to say that it's totally impossible [that there could have been a break-in]. [. . .] You have to take a little more care if you get the feeling when you get there that this doesn't look normal. Then you have to put in a little more work if you want to say that this is not how it happened."

When asked whether "not normal" means that a crime scene does not look like such scenes usually do, the technician elaborated by telling me about a case in which he wrote, in his words, "quite harshly":

> It's almost impossible that [there was a burglary]—well, it's not impossible, but it hasn't happened like this. [. . .] Everything, I mean vases and stuff hadn't been knocked over but moved and set aside. There wasn't a broken thing in the whole place. [. . .] It would have been impossible to go through the place without knocking over a vase or something. Oh, some vase had even been laid on its side—if [a burglar] had knocked it over, it would have broken. But it was so nicely and neatly set aside. [. . .] And it's a little knotty with those [types of cases]. You need to really have done your homework. You must be able to stand up in district court and say, this is a sham.

His concern about needing to have done his "homework" arose in part from his own professional pride; he did not want to have to be ashamed about being wrong later on. But he did not want to cause trouble for victims of crime either. If he mistakenly put in his report that the break-in never happened, the victim might not receive any compensation from their insurance, despite having suffered quite a loss.

However, even with professional vision—in the technicians' words, imagination, experience, skills, and knowledge—success cannot be taken for granted. There might simply not be any traces there to find: "Those who are sober, the thieves that is, of course they know what they are doing, they protect themselves the whole time. So there's not a lot we can do, unfortunately. That's why the success rate is so low. But the dopeheads and those who are a little high and a little drunk, they usually botch up." Thus, it is unrealistic to expect results every time, especially as there are "real professionals who make it absolutely impossible. All these airbag thieves and those crews that come and break into houses, it's absolutely hopeless. They don't leave any traces. [. . .] That's difficult, really difficult, but they're professionals, so you have to catch them in the act."

In addition, not all crime scenes retain the traces that may have been left there equally well or for a long time. Interference at the crime scene also affects what can be found. The police patrol who walks through an apartment, the passer-by who throws a cigarette butt through the broken window of a car, the ambulance crew who takes an injured person to the hospital, or the fire brigade who lets a house burn down rather than trying to save it—all of these people can influence a crime scene, either deliberately or unintentionally.

Crime scene examinations contain their own type of uncertainty. Crime scene technicians may miss something or there may be nothing (or nothing else) to find. A surface or object on which a crime scene technician cannot find any traces may be made of a material that does not easily retain traces, may have been exposed to the elements and therefore lost its traces, may never have held any traces in the first place, or may yet yield results if subjected to more scrutiny. These things are impossible to know in all cases.

Accordingly, examining crime scenes also contains an element of luck, as one technician emphasized: "I took a chance yesterday. [. . .] It was at a break-in, and there was a glove lying in the garden. But the guy who lived there said, 'Oh, that should be, or that could be, the builders', but it could just as well be the thief's. So of course we took that in, you have to take a chance sometimes." Taking a chance on traces can pay off in the form of DNA evidence that generates a cold hit and thus moves the investigation forward, but it could also turn out to be a dead end. As one technician put it, "You don't always find out; you just have to realize that. Like those cars[8], how they burned—when there's just a shell left, it's almost impossible to say."

The crime scene technicians' seeing also incorporates and transforms others' accounts. One example of this is the plaintiffs' explanation of the possibly missing keys, which could explain the lack of traces of forced entry in the break-in. The crime scene technicians' work also incorporates what the criminal investigation division has accumulated so far. In regard to a particular fire, a crime scene technician said, "there wasn't anything around it, in the story,[9] that pointed to it being set." What she meant was that, often, "you can rule out a lot of things: there may not be electricity, no one has done any repairs with oils and stuff, so someone must have set the fire." In the case of this fire, however, there had not been anything to indicate arson; no witness had reported seeing someone near the house at the time of the fire, and the residents did not report having been threatened.

Thus, crime scene examinations bring together the "stories" known at the time of their examination, the traces technicians have found and have not found, and the technicians' experience of crime scenes and stock scripts. Their experience and stock scripts include, for example, how houses do or do not catch fire and how a total absence of evidence can in some cases be explained by upset plaintiffs' cleaning. Crime scene technicians transform the messy and material presumptive crime scene into an ordered and understandable contribution to the pretrial investigation's multiple legal stories. In other words, the crime scene technicians make crime scenes meaningful and understandable to others—a transformation that requires mediation between a number of epistemic cultures (Knorr Cetina 1999).

MEDIATING BETWEEN EPISTEMIC CULTURES

The crime scene technicians' experience of police work and their specialization in forensics and crime scene work puts them in a position where they have insight into several epistemic cultures. In addition, the reports they write are directed at police investigators, prosecutors, the court, and the defense—none of them forensics experts.

At a crime scene, crime scene technicians mediate between the controlled, standardized world of the laboratory and the definitely unstandardized crime scenes they encounter. To use one of Latour's terms, crime scene technicians are the "vanguard" of the laboratory (1999, 46). Crime scene technicians turn a messy, ill-defined site into a form that is analyzable in the laboratory.

Being the laboratory's vanguard also means that the crime scene technicians need to know enough about how the laboratory works to be able to recover and transport potential traces in a way that promotes the laboratory's work. Precautions must be taken not to degrade evidence. One can damage evidence—for example, by walking on it, smudging or obliterating fingerprints with a thoughtless or clumsy touch, or by contaminating potential DNA traces, either by leaving DNA of one's own or by cross-contamination between objects or places. Special containers are used for recovered knives to prevent them from cutting through paper or plastic wrappings and rubbing against each other during transport.[10] There are separate rooms for unpacking and examining material, so that clothes from suspects and victims never touch the same surfaces.

During a pretrial investigation, crime scene technicians mediate between the laboratory on the one hand and the prosecution and the police on the other. Some crime scene technicians would say they get caught between these different institutions and their demands.

One aspect of this mediation is reducing pressure on the laboratory. A crime scene technician described it like this: "The investigators want loads of things and the SKL cannot investigate loads. So we're sitting in between. Well, now they've started to call the SKL and hassle them by themselves instead, and that's not that great either. We're supposed to be sort of a filter." If every pretrial investigation leader had the laboratory do every analysis possible on the remote chance that it would turn up something useful, the SKL would be bogged down. Thus, not every trace that is collected should necessarily be analyzed, certainly not at first.

In large cases—usually serious crimes with a lot of material—the crime scene technicians advise the prosecution and police on how to proceed with the material: "You have to do certain things in the right order. [. . .] You have to think before you start on a material, so to speak. But not all investigators understand that. And then, after a while it occurs to them, this is what we should've done. Yes, well, that bird has flown." They also explain, sometimes with the help of a senior forensic scientist from the SKL, what types of answers the police and prosecution can expect from an analysis: "Usually, I let them decide. I give them my arguments, this is how it is, and they get to decide. So they can't come back later and complain. [Laughs] But that's something you learn over the years—it's not something you do with every case. But with large cases, when you have all this material, then you go through it with the investigator and with the SKL, you sit down and establish priorities."

This crime scene technician described the crime scene division's role in the criminal justice system as "kind of like the spider in between them," alluding to the Swedish idiom "the spider in the web," which describes a person who knows everything and everyone there is to know and thus can pull a lot of strings (i.e., the "web"). In this case, the crime scene technicians are spiders moving between different webs, so to speak, because the laboratory is "a completely different world" for many police officers—in STS terms, a different epistemic culture. The crime scene technicians were, for example, concerned about how "clinically" the laboratory's expert statements sometimes were written. They said that even they, who were reasonably familiar with the laboratory and forensic science, occasionally needed to read a statement several times to understand it. Accordingly, they sometimes felt they needed to explain the laboratory's statement and make it more accessible to the prosecutor.

This does not mean, however, that crime scene technicians are the laboratory's advocates. They are certainly also aware of the police's work and concerns—for example, the police's knowledge of "troublemakers" and the time restraints under which they work. The technicians keep track of whether there is a suspect under arrest or in custody and whether, consequently, the laboratory analyses can be given priority. And just like the prosecutor and the police investigators, the crime scene technicians I met were concerned about plaintiffs, worried about troublemakers being at large, and hoped that the laboratory would be able to deliver their results in time for the committal proceedings or trial.

Finally, crime scene technicians mediate between the civilian world and the worlds of the police and the laboratory. They explain to plaintiffs what they can expect from an investigation, and they assess how useful the plaintiffs' accounts of their houses or cars or suspicions are for the crime scene investigation. And even though the crime scene technicians I spoke with did not appear overly optimistic about the chances of domestic break-ins being solved, they seemed to think that they were doing something useful by investigating them, not least demonstrating to the public that the police care about victims of crimes. The crime scene technicians talked about residents' "appreciation" when they "see that the police are at least doing something" more than just writing down names and phone numbers and leaving. Even when their homes were left grubby with fingerprint powder, residents were "happy anyway"—if, the technicians amended, "happy" was a term that could be applied to the situation.

Crime scene technicians also encounter plaintiffs' expectations of crime scene investigations, one of which is the belief that clear fingerprints can be lifted from just about any surface. All the crime scene technicians I talked with had stories about crime victims' disappointment on learning that not all surfaces retain fingerprints and that many of the fingerprints that can be recovered are smudged or incomplete. To the crime scene technicians, crime victims' ideas of how the police work were often quite unrealistic. A plaintiff might, for example, point someone out as the offender and then be disappointed and perhaps insulted when a technician explained that the police cannot make arrests based on an accusation.

In these situations, the crime scene technicians seemed to experience a sort of "*CSI* effect," a term that denotes a cluster of several conceivable effects of the fictional on perceptions of nonfictional forensic science (see, for example, Cole 2015; Cole and Dioso-Villa 2007; Ghoshray 2007; Stephens 2007; Tyler 2006). One of the most prominently discussed effects is juries acquitting defendants because television shows like *CSI* (*Crime Scene Investigation*) have led them to expect more forensic evidence. Another is the almost blind faith in forensic scientists as expert witnesses because *CSI* depicts them so positively (for a comprehensive discussion of the *CSI* effect, see Cole and Dioso-Villa 2007).

Thus, an important part of the crime scene technicians' work is that of mediating the cooperation between the criminal justice system's different epistemic cultures, helping the flow of forensic evidence-to-be through these epistemic cultures, and contributing to the translation of forensic evidence-to-be between them, a translation that the following chapter will examine more closely by tracing how the SKL's expert statements travel through the criminal justice system.

CHAPTER SIX

Colluding and Colliding Worlds

MOVING FORENSIC EVIDENCE

For forensic evidence to complete its social life it must be moved through the criminal justice system. But in some cases the differences between the justice system's epistemic cultures will lead to friction. What is clear to one actor might not be clear to another. What is meaningful to one actor might not be meaningful to another. For example, as discussed in chapter 3, an investigator and a prosecutor clashed because, although the investigator *knew* that a suspect was guilty of car theft, based on previous knowledge and interrogations, the prosecutor needed to *prove* the guilt using legally acceptable evidence. Similarly, as this chapter will discuss, the forensic scientists sought a careful distribution of responsibility in their written expert statements, leaving it to the court to make the final conclusions about the forensic evidence, while the prosecution and defense might try to push the scientists to say more than they feel they have a mandate to.

These perhaps inescapable frictions must be dealt with so the evidence-to-be can be moved through the system with its meanings intact. In the Swedish criminal justice system, the frictions are addressed through what can be called "translation work," in which the intended meanings that are read into both written and verbal expert statements are aligned with their intended meanings.

To illustrate these frictions and discuss the criminal justice system's translation work, this chapter focuses on one way (of several) of moving forensic evidence-to-be through the criminal justice system, namely on how the expert statements produced by the Swedish National Laboratory of Forensic Science (SKL) were transported from the laboratory to the court. I will look at the concerns and the focal points of the different actors involved in the transport and discuss what is required to transport laboratory results and their value from the epistemic culture of forensic science to those of the judges, prosecutors, and defense lawyers.

To be clear, friction did not occur around every expert statement. Quite the contrary, most expert statements seemed to be transferred quite smoothly to the police, the prosecution, the defense, and the court. Focusing on frictions thus means focusing on the exceptional. The exceptional, however, will be able to shed light on the usual, as it makes the transfer visible and explicit.

MOVING KNOWLEDGE BETWEEN EPISTEMIC CULTURES

As shown in the previous chapters, the criminal justice system's epistemic cultures (Knorr Cetina 1999) have different understandings of what valid knowledge is and how it should be produced. Such diverging perspectives should make the exchange of knowledge difficult. Karin Knorr Cetina does not address the question of how knowledge might travel between epistemic cultures. Her focus is on the inner workings of epistemic cultures, "the machineries of knowledge construction" (1999, 3). But others have pointed out that cooperation across professions can be difficult. Andrew Abbott (1988), for example, has coined the term "jurisdictions" to describe how professions define their specific core activities and competencies and defend them against others' intrusions. This "boundary work," as Thomas Gieryn (1983) would put it, of maintaining jurisdictions makes for internal cohesion and cooperation, but it also impedes interprofessional cooperation. Moving evidence-to-be with its meanings intact and distributing decisions and responsibilities between the epistemic cultures (or professions) of the criminal justice system is an example of such cooperation.

Science and Technology Studies (STS) scholarship points—albeit implicitly—to a tension in the exchange or transport of knowledge, namely the tension between stability and plasticity of understanding. Stability is central in Bruno Latour's notion of "immutable mobiles," objects that by virtue of being inscriptions can easily be transported from one place to another without losing their message. In his words, they are "objects which have the properties of being *mobile* but also *immutable, presentable, readable* and *combinable* with one another" (1990, 26; italics in original). As immutable mobiles can travel unchanged and be reproduced, combined, and superimposed on one another, they are, according to Latour, prime instruments of domination—and of transporting knowledge.

Plasticity, on the other hand, is a characteristic of Susan Leigh Star and James Griesemer's (1989) "boundary object." Boundary objects are explicitly akin to immutable mobiles, but they draw attention to the heterogeneous ways people understand the "same" object even if they have common goals: "In conducting collective work, people coming together from different social worlds frequently have the experience of addressing an object that has a different meaning for each of them. Each social world has partial jurisdiction over the resources represented by that object, and mismatches caused by the overlap become problems for negotiation" (Star and Griesemer 1989, 412). Boundary objects "form a common boundary between worlds by inhabiting them both simultaneously" (Star and Griesemer 1989, 412), and Star and Griesemer emphasize that these common objects do not imply consensus but rather contain "the traces of multiple viewpoints, translations and incomplete battles" (1989, 413). The boundary object's plasticity enables it to participate in different contexts or epistemic cultures.

Star and Griesemer focus on common goals and collective work. Their inhabitants of "different social worlds" (1989, 412) are willing and thus tolerant collaborators. Latour's scientists, however, are not. Latour's understanding of producing facts and artifacts in science and technology is one of convincing, enrolling, and manipulating others—in short, one of competition and combativeness. Consequently, his view of transporting knowledge is a rather aggressive one of cornering "the dissenter" and of making dissent costly and impractical (1990, 41f.), with immutable mobiles constituting the main tools or, perhaps, weapons. Latour's scientists do not want to be enrolled in others' fact-making; they want others to ally themselves with them, and therefore they are not tolerant of plasticity and expend quite a lot of effort to make diverging understandings untenable.

What about the SKL's expert statements, then? On the one hand, members of the criminal justice system often emphasize their common goal of solving crimes—or, more precisely, making sure that the right person is convicted of the right crime in a legally secure way. As with Star and Griesemer's boundary objects, the different parts of the criminal justice system bring different understandings to that common goal and make different contributions to it.

On the other hand, this common goal does not allow for plasticity in forensic evidence. If there is to be legal security, neither the verdict nor the evidence it is based on can be tainted by instability or alteration. For forensic evidence, that means that, in order to be acceptable, it must be stable—from the crime scene through the crime scene division, the laboratory, the criminal investigation division, the prosecution's office, and the court. Like an immutable mobile, it must move through the criminal justice system's epistemic cultures with their differences in expertise and professional vision without changing meaning.

That tension between stability and plasticity in forensic evidence manifests in frictions between different epistemic cultures.

FRICTIONS

Two types of friction around expert statements illustrate how difficult it is for them to move through the criminal justice system without losing meaning. One is centered on the distribution of responsibility and the other on how to understand uncertainty.

As discussed in chapter 4, the SKL's Bayesian approach to evaluating laboratory results implies a distribution of responsibility in such a way that leaves the uncertainty inherent in evaluating forensic evidence to be resolved by the court, not by the laboratory. In this way, the forensic scientists take responsibility for the result and its evaluation, but not for "how it is." The forensic scientists I interviewed emphasized that even a result that very strongly supported one proposition over the other could not eliminate any and all uncertainty and that there might be circumstances affecting the result that they did not know about. The court, they emphasized, knows these circumstances—or at least those that the investigation has been able to turn up—and thus the decision on the propositions is left to the court.

However, this division of responsibility is not necessarily a focus of interest in court. The court's interest is focused on the whole of the evidence and whether it proves the defendant's guilt. Consider this district court judge's (fairly typical) description of a hypothetical situation: "The fact that your DNA has been recovered from a particular place, [. . .] ordinarily, you accept the fact that the point has been proven, so there won't be any discussion there."

The judge collapsed the nontrivial issue (for the forensic scientists) of what a DNA match means into "your [the defendant's] DNA has been recovered." Then he immediately moved on to the (for the judge) more interesting issue of whether the presence of the defendant's DNA at the crime scene means that the defendant has been there or whether the DNA might have gotten there without the defendant's presence. That is, the laboratory result was—implicitly—taken as establishing that the DNA originated from the defendant.

This judge's stance was echoed by other judges as well as by prosecutors and defense lawyers. For them, as discussed in chapter 1, the central question was how to interpret forensic evidence in terms of the defendant's actions and culpability. They focused predominantly on what forensic scientists call the "offense level" and what Lynch et al. call the "field of possibilities" (2008, 345).

When forensic scientists were summoned to court as expert witnesses, the prosecutors' and defense lawyers' implicit closure of the forensic evidence seemed on occasion to cause friction. A forensic scientist described testifying as an expert witness like this: "Both the court and the prosecutor would very much like to get us to say that we think that this very strongly shows that it happened like this, but we try to guard against that, [. . .] and I guess there's a risk that they don't see a huge difference there. Often, they ask how likely is it, roughly, that it should have happened like this, [. . .] [but] that's not for us to say." In her view, the court and prosecutor were asking forensic scientists to overstep their authority and responsibility in these instances. The prosecutor and the court want to know what could be concluded to have happened, but the forensic scientists consider that that is for the court to decide.

The forensic scientist described defense lawyers' questions in corresponding terms: "Similarly, the lawyers try to devalue [our evaluation] in the opposite direction. The prosecutor wants [. . .] us to talk about how likely we estimate this to be or how strongly we think it has happened like this [i.e., to make a statement about the propositions instead of the results of the analysis]. But the lawyers [. . .] usually say, 'But it could look like this even if it happened that way, couldn't it?' But you can't answer a question like that straight-out." A direct answer would compromise the distribution of responsibility, albeit in a different way from giving in to the court and the prosecutor's wish for unambiguity. The lawyers' suggestions might very well have been included in the forensic scientists' evaluation. But conceding that "it could look like this even if it happened that way" would undermine the expert statement because such an answer does not communicate value or weight.

Another forensic scientist's account suggests that judges, prosecutors, and defense lawyers might not recognize the careful distribution of responsibility in the written expert statements in the first place: "Well, it happens that when an experienced lawyer asks his question, and you've suddenly said yes to something he's said, and you realize, no, wait, now he's saying something I haven't written at all. [...] They can distort what you've written when they ask questions. They believe they're reading from the statement [but they] inflate what it says."

By being scrupulous about how they answered questions and worded their written statements, the forensic scientists actively and continuously maintained the distribution of responsibility. That is, they did not express an opinion on what "really" happened and subsequently were not responsible for the consequences if the court followed that opinion.

This distribution of responsibility echoes the handing off of responsibility for the risks associated with the uncertainties of technologies to users that Brian Rappert (2001) discusses based on the use of pepper spray by the British police. In the case of forensic evidence, the friction could be interpreted as the forensic scientists trying to shift responsibility to the judges, prosecutors, and defense lawyers and vice versa. The forensic scientists wanted the court to make a potentially consequential decision, and the court, prosecutors, and defense lawyers attempted, through their questions, to escape that responsibility.

However, I think there is more to the friction than the desire to evade responsibility, especially if one considers the second type of friction that arose around expert statements, namely friction about the sources of uncertainty.

When forensic scientists were summoned to court as expert witnesses, they were typically asked to explain how the analysis in question had been performed and how they had arrived at a particular grade. Both in the hearings I attended and in my interviews with forensic scientists, questions in such situations revolved around what was wrong with a comparably "weak" result:

[The prosecutors and lawyers] often don't understand the cause of the uncertainty. [...] If it's a grade +2 or +3 they think it's a bad result, you know? Something's gone wrong with the machine or something, that's why it turned out a bit second-rate. But it's not like the result is wrong or something. [...] It can be a terrific and neat result all the same. [...] When it comes to DNA, for example, they think there's something wrong, they think there's a deviation in the profile [i.e., a partial mismatch], that's why it's only a +2. So there they want to pressure us: [...] "What's wrong, where's the deviation, why is it only a +2?"

While the forensic scientists talked and wrote about how strongly the results supported one proposition over the other (i.e., their weight), the judges, prosecutors, and defense lawyers seemed to believe that grades referred to the results themselves (i.e., their accuracy)—for example, their belief was that a low grade meant there had been an imperfect match.

Using Latour's term, one might say that the forensic scientists did not close the "black box" of forensic evidence for transport out of the laboratory, no matter how closed it might appear at first glance in court. In a black box, "uncertainty, people at work, decisions, competition, [and] controversies" are closed or at least hidden away (Latour 1987, 4) so that the users will not need (or be able) to concern themselves with them. But the forensic expert statements consciously and deliberately left uncertainty visible and decisions open. However, they did not leave *all* the intricacies of forensic science visible; questions of contamination, mix-ups, or accuracy, for example, were closed in the laboratory.

Forensic evidence is not the only "box" that is neither fully open nor fully closed. Michael Lynch and Kathleen Jordan (1992, 107) use the term "translucent box" for processes and technologies whose "outlines [...] are not clearly resolved" and whose "inner workings remain clouded by uncertainty and dispute." However, unlike the molecular biology technique Lynch and Jordan discuss, a forensic expert statement is a stable and standardized artifact. Thus, to avoid confusion, I want to call the forensic evidence produced at the SKL "a semitransparent box"—one that is neither fully opaque nor fully transparent, which leaves some issues to be closed by the court.

Even if forensic evidence is intended to be a semitransparent box, however, it seems that the intention is not enough for the recipients of expert statements to see all of the unresolved decisions and uncertainties they are meant to see. In order to actually look through forensic evidence's semitransparent walls, judges, prosecutors, and defense lawyers require help from forensic scientists. This help bears similarities to the "articulation work" that Anselm Strauss et al. (1985) describe as being a part of medical work. Medical work, Strauss and his colleagues argue, might consist of standard procedures, but these standard procedures require (the often invisible) coordination of resources and people (Strauss et al. 1985, chapter 7). As Susan Leigh Star elaborates: "Articulation work is work that gets things 'back on track' in the face of the unexpected, and modifies action to accommodate unanticipated contingencies. *The important thing about articulation work is that it is invisible to rationalized models of work.* Those representations of work and production that consider a smooth, unproblematic sequence of events as an adequate representation cannot, and will not, admit of local, unique, unexpected solutions to problems" (1991, 275; italics in original).

Articulation work smooths out inevitable difficulties and makes standard procedures standard and unproblematic. Similarly, the standard procedure of using written expert statements seems to require that their readings be brought back on track. When the forensic scientist quoted above talked about when lawyers "believe they're reading from [a] statement," he drew attention to a defense lawyer interpreting the statement in a way that the forensic scientist had not meant it to be understood—in other words, he was pointing out that there were communication difficulties. Therefore, I argue that forensic evidence requires *translation work.*

TRANSLATION WORK

Translation does not necessarily need to be performed between literal languages. Peter Galison uses language as a metaphor to understand cooperation across epistemic cultures. Inspired by anthropological studies of trade between cultural groups, Galison uses the image of "trading zones" (1997, 783) to describe how the "subcultures" of physics (1997, 46ff.), despite their different "languages," manage exchanges (1997, particularly chapter 9). In his words: "Two groups can agree on rules of exchange even if they ascribe utterly different significance to the objects being exchanged; they may even disagree on the meaning of the exchange process itself" (Galison 1997, 783).[1] But what works for objects does not necessarily work for knowledge, which may be difficult to exchange on such "most minimal understandings." Galison goes on: "Nonetheless, the trading partners can hammer out a *local* coordination despite vast *global* differences" (1997, 783; italics in original).

Prolonged exchange, he continues, might lead to the development of common trading languages, from instrumental "pidgins" to hybrid and nuanced "creoles." However, he underlines, this does not mean that differences are obliterated—rather, the partners make it possible to trade *despite* their differences (Galison 1997, 783f.). To bring together several notions, one might say that immutable mobiles are expected to transcend language (and, perhaps not surprisingly, Latour's rhetoric of immutable mobiles and inscriptions is about *vision* rather than *words*), whereas one could call boundary objects a good-enough approximation of communication, one that leaves the partners satisfied that a conversation is taking place.

Language as a metaphor, however, makes it possible to think about stability and plasticity in a different way. Words can (and must) be translated between different languages, but languages do not map onto each other seamlessly, and thus stability and plasticity become entangled with each other. How can one change from one language to another while keeping both content and connotations?

Translation studies distinguish between formal and dynamic equivalence in translations, that is, between aiming "to reveal as much as possible of the form and content of the original message" and focusing on "the receptor response" (Nida 2000, 157). A translator must, of course, keep both concerns in mind, but a translation that leans more toward formal equivalence may, for example, translate an idiomatic expression literally, perhaps providing additional information about its connotations in a footnote, whereas a translator leaning toward dynamic equivalence may instead choose an expression that exists in the target language. In terms of forensic evidence, the scale the forensic scientists always attach to their expert statements would correspond to the footnote in formal equivalence. The crime scene technicians' explanations of the statements mentioned in chapter 5, on the other hand, correspond to dynamic equivalence.

Similarly, Paula Rubel and Abraham Rosman discuss anthropological translation from one culture (and often language) to another: "How does one preserve the cultural values of the source language in the translation into the target language, which is usually the aim of the translation. The values of the local culture are a central aspect of most of the cultural phenomena which anthropologists try to describe, and these may differ from and be in conflict with the values of the target culture. How to make that difference comprehensible to audiences is the major question at issue" (2003, 6). They emphasize the importance of providing "supplementary information," since "incompatibilities will always be present which must be dealt with by additional discussion and contextualization" (Rubel and Rosman 2003, 10). In order for a translation to transport the original's meanings, its (implicit) context must be (explicitly) included.[2]

These points are a far cry from both Latour's immutable mobiles and Star and Griesemer's boundary objects. In both of them, contexts are not part of the traveling object—immutable mobiles transcend context, and boundary objects "work" despite differing contexts. But context is important in the criminal justice system and its epistemic cultures, as illustrated by the frictions around the laboratory's expert statements. Both recipients and producers *expect* the statements to be stable. Judges, prosecutors, and defense lawyers expect expert statements to fit smoothly into the epistemic culture of the court, and forensic scientists expect them to transport knowledge unchanged. By understanding expert statements within the context of their own epistemic cultures, however, recipients and producers *treat* them as if they were plastic.

What prevents expert statements from becoming so plastic that they are unable to transport meaning is the work that makes them comprehensible and moves them back toward stability. What these statements require is the coordination of writing and reading, that is, not articulation but *translation* work.

When Translation Work Is Performed . . .

Translation work is what moves meaning from one epistemic culture to others. Forensic scientists did this in court as expert witnesses, in writing their expert statements, and in informal discussions.

As the discussion of the friction hints at, translation work in court around expert statements was predominantly done in cases of comparably weak evidence. This may have to do with judges not encountering weak evidence very often, certainly less often than the SKL's forensic scientists encounter it. One reason for this is that prosecutors do not always include weak or ambiguous evidence in their cases (it is always included in pretrial investigation reports, but not everything in these reports is referred to in court). Thus, judges are more likely to encounter evidence that strongly supports one of the propositions than to encounter rather weak evidence.

The need for translation in court regarding the cause of a low grade was illustrated by a judge speaking about a recent case, in which he appreciated having a forensic scientist as an expert witness: "Yes, I felt it was a good thing that they came and [witnessed]. Because [. . .] it would probably have been harder to understand from just the written material. [With an expert witness] you get the scale a little more, and what I felt wasn't clear if we'd only had the written material was that he said, 'We only found positive indications.'"

This judge clearly did not feel that the cause of the low grade (and thus the uncertainty) of the forensic evidence was decipherable from the expert statement alone. He needed the forensic scientist's explanation about "positive indications" in order to understand that, in this case, the low grade for a comparison of two photographs had to do with the low quality of one of the photographs, not with any discrepancies between the two. The expert statement and the prosecutor's presentation of it were not by themselves enough to convey that.

Unfamiliar methods also made translation work necessary in order to understand whether and how a particular forensic analysis was "reputable work" and thus produced valid knowledge. A judge talked about a case in which the SKL had done a type of handwriting analysis:

> One does think that's a little dodgy, [. . .] [but] when [the forensic scientist] also talked about what they do—how they do a handwriting analysis, that is, how one can determine whether it's the same person who has written these two documents—[I thought,] oh, great. Because that can also strengthen credibility—when one sees it's reputable work. [. . .] There can be different things that one can point to and say yes, I didn't think about that, but it seems that they seriously . . . in a scientifically acceptable way—arrived at their conclusion.

In this case, the evidence was not only weak (there was very little written material to compare, apparently) but was also of an unusual type. The translation work necessary to make this piece of forensic evidence understandable to the judge was thus in part about its grade, but the analysis itself was just as important to him.

In the writing of expert statements, translation work was also a part of everyday, routine practices. The forensic scientists were quite concerned about how the police and the prosecutors would read and understand their statements, and so they expended quite a lot of effort both on developing standards and templates for their statements and on formulating individual statements.[3] They wanted to write correctly, clearly, and understandably to ensure that the distribution of responsibility was maintained and the results' value was conveyed accurately and intelligibly.

The use of the laboratory's scale to report results is intended as a tool to reduce the risk of misunderstandings. This is illustrated by a forensic scientist contrasting the Bayesian approach with the statistical frequency of a DNA profile, something the SKL has apparently done in the past:

> We stopped doing that because [. . .] it's easy to get it wrong in court—[the prosecutor, the defense lawyer, and the court] get carried away. If they, for

example, learn that this DNA profile occurs at a frequency of one in 10 billion—no, let me exaggerate even more—10 quintillion—there aren't even that many people on earth—then they'll think there can't be anyone else [with the same profile]. But there can. The frequency is not the same thing as [saying that] there can't be anyone else. We don't know whether there's anyone else—what we know is, if this person has a[n identical] twin, there is another one with the same [profile], regardless of the low frequency. This is easily misunderstood.

In this forensic scientist's eyes, what makes the laboratory's current approach superior is that it is not as easy to misunderstand as the previous method. To the forensic scientist, the Bayesian approach conveys uncertainty in such a way so that judges, prosecutors, and defense lawyers do not get "carried away" as easily in court.

The forensic scientists also described the scale as a more user-friendly and accessible way of conveying a result's value than raw likelihood ratios. They thought the likelihood ratios might be more difficult to understand for people who were not forensic scientists. Moreover, in January 2011, after a survey on how members of the criminal justice system understood different phrasings, the SKL changed the wording that corresponds with the verbal scale for grade +4 from "The results of the examination support with certainty" to "The results of the examination extremely strongly support." This change, the forensic scientists said, had been long overdue. The old wording really had not expressed what they wanted to convey. As one forensic scientist put it, "we're not talking about certainty, which you might be deceived into believing."

There had been discussion of introducing a higher grade to be able to express stronger support, but the forensic scientist quoted above regarded this as quite problematic, saying:

> Today the line [...] between +3 and +4 [...] is a million;[4] if it's more than a million, it's a +4. But for DNA, you often get much higher figures, so the question is, should we introduce another grade, a grade +5, or should we raise the threshold for grade +4? But we decided not to [introduce a grade of +5], because a million is already so strong, you already reached the wall, and if we would raise it, you'd just hit the wall a little harder, but it doesn't have any practical significance for whoever uses these results. [...] We see a danger in introducing another grade, because then [the recipients of the expert statements] would automatically think that the other ones are less valuable.

A new grade might have been meaningful within the laboratory, where the likelihood ratios behind the grades are visible, but the forensic scientists decided that it was not of practical significance. To the forensic scientist quoted above, it appeared that the police and the prosecutors treated the scale as relative rather than absolute, and thus a higher grade might weaken the other grades, thereby causing more harm than benefit.

Translation work was not only carried out in such formal contexts. There were also informal telephone calls, through which mainly prosecutors and defense lawyers initiated translation work[5] (such informal avenues are not open to judges or lay assessors). For example, prosecutors concerned with understanding the cause of the uncertainty in a piece of low-graded evidence might ask for an explanation. They would often wonder why the evidence had not received a higher grade. One of the prosecutors I interviewed talked about being puzzled by the low grade of a particular piece of DNA evidence. So she called the forensic scientist, who explained to her that the bodily fluid found at the crime scene had been badly degraded (and the reasons for that degradation) and that the laboratory had thus only been able to attain a partial DNA profile. The loci of the partial profile matched the suspect in the case—who had been produced by the investigation, not through a cold hit— but, the forensic scientist had pointed out, it was impossible to know whether the missing loci would have matched the suspect's loci or differed from them, hence the low grade. The prosecutor said that this conversation had been really helpful. It was good to know that a partial profile was to be expected in that kind of situation and that the low grade did not speak against the suspect's involvement. She added that she had asked the forensic scientist to put the explanation into writing, but the scientist had refused.

Occasionally, forensic scientists also performed similar informal translation work before doing an analysis. They might, for example, talk to a "customer"—a prosecutor, investigator, or crime scene technician—about the analysis they had commissioned to explain why that particular analysis did not appear meaningful to them, considering the result it could be expected to yield. For example, one forensic scientist told me, "We're very restrictive with analyzing cigarette butts. [. . .] Before you do the analysis, [. . .] you often have to call up and talk to the, oh, it's usually the [crime scene] technicians, but sometimes it's the pretrial investigation leader, because the pretrial investigation leader might be persistent and really want this analyzed, and then it can, at the end of the day, be easier if I [. . .] talk to them directly and explain why it's not meaningful that we should do all these analyses."

Here, the forensic scientist describes the translation work of explaining exactly how the result of the analysis is going to fit into the investigation. In this case, producing DNA evidence from a (highly mobile) cigarette end would most likely not be able to contribute significantly to the investigation, even though it probably would result in a high grade. This type of translation work is done together with crime scene technicians, who, as was explained in the previous chapter, mediate (i.e., translate) between the laboratory and the police and prosecution.

The forensic scientists also talked about having to point out to the police or prosecution "that a DNA match is not the one and only salvation." A cold hit, they explained, does not mean that the person in question is guilty: "That depends of course on what kind of trace it is and how it can conceivably have gotten there." They saw a need to emphasize that "everything shouldn't turn on our results;" instead, "you need to investigate more, you need to collect more things, before you can, so to speak, convict a person."

In these conversations, the forensic scientists strove for what Nida calls dynamic equivalence (2000, 157) in their translations. One forensic scientist said, "The prosecutor perhaps thinks that this is important, this is central, but we think that, based on what we know, there is no chance that our result will be able to illuminate the question you're after, although the prosecutor thinks it will. Or the prosecutor will claim it will—and then we feel even more perhaps that, if we produce a result, it will perhaps be used incorrectly. That can be an additional reason to actually not produce, because [. . .] if you procure that, they'll claim that it's like this." This forensic scientist thus not only translated the analysis and its possible result into the terms of the pre-trial investigation, he also anticipated a reaction to the result and translated that back into action of his own. Conversely, forensic scientists may some-times argue that a certain analysis is more important than a pretrial investiga-tion leader may think it is, an argument that requires the same type of trans-lation between the laboratory and the investigation.

Similarly, when the forensic scientists maintained the difference between what they had written in their statement and what the recipients wanted the statement to say, they adapted their responses to the effect they anticipated: "When we tell [the police and the prosecutors] that for glass cases, for exam-ple, we seldom get a higher grade than +2, they say, 'Well, then we'd like you to put that into your statement, say that it doesn't get any higher than +2.' 'All right,' we say, [. . .] 'why should we write that? Won't you take that as [. . .] the same as certainty?' 'Yes,' they admit. That's how they'll interpret it in any case: 'this is as good as it gets, so it's certain.' And that's not what we're saying. +2 is only +2."

That forensic scientist did not content herself with accommodating the police and prosecution's desire for more information—which, in this case, entailed writing into the statement that mass-produced glass does not often support very strong conclusions. Instead, she looked for the reason for that desire, anticipating—a bit exasperatedly—from past experience that the police and the prosecutors might treat the scale as relative. She did not simply provide context or supplementary information (Rubel and Rosman 2003) about the origin of the laboratory result but also tried to anchor her answer in the context in which it would be received and to achieve the effect she wanted. In other words, she strove for dynamic instead of formal equivalence. While it would be formally "correct" to add the requested information to the expert statement, the effect, at least as predicted by the forensic scientist, would be "incorrect." In this case, a formal equivalent translation would look quite different from a dynamic equivalent one.

Like the crime scene technician in the previous chapter, the forensic scientists seemed to perceive such situations in terms of different worlds meeting. One of them, for example, underlined the importance of the SKL arranging courses for prosecutors and training for crime scene technicians so that the inhabitants of these worlds could learn more about each other: "We have seen the necessity to, well, convey [more about our work conditions] to their worlds [...] at the same time as we need to learn about their conditions."

Thus, in the Swedish criminal justice system, translating—although its members would not describe it in these terms—seems to be a question of learning about the "worlds" of others in order to be able to, firstly, provide salient supplementary information and, secondly, to put this information into the context of these other worlds.[6] But such translation work is not done for every piece of forensic evidence.

. . . And When It Is Not

Sometimes, translation work is not performed because it is not perceived as necessary or desirable, and in some cases, because it is difficult to initiate.

Strong, routine forensic evidence was perceived as not requiring any explanation. In court in particular, this may have to do with the fact that the Swedish criminal justice system does not use juries. Judges and, to a lesser extent, lay assessors have more experience of forensic evidence than a lay jury might have. They are exposed to more routine types of forensic evidence on a regular basis, thus there seems to be the expectation that they do not need explanations of those technologies. This came out, for example, in the comment of one of the prosecutors quoted in chapter 2, who said that the court should trust expert statements and that summoning a forensic scientist to court should therefore not be necessary.

The judges' descriptions of their work suggest that they share this attitude. For example, one judge told me that when dealing with everyday DNA samples, "often [the forensic scientists] say that [. . .] this DNA comes from this person, and that's certain[7]—if you disregard the possibility that it comes from a close relative." So in these cases, he continued, "you wouldn't need to hear anyone [from the SKL as a witness]." In his eyes, strong, routine forensic evidence did not require any supplementary information.

In other parts of the criminal justice system, the nuances of expert statements were not always important enough to their recipients to make translation work necessary. At the criminal investigation division, for example, I did not often hear grades or uncertainty come up in conversation, nor did the investigators talk about forensic evidence in terms that might be understood as translation work. This may well be because I was at the wrong place at the wrong time or because I did not listen properly, but it may also have to do with how the investigators use forensic evidence in their work. When investigators ask a suspect for an "explanation" of why a bloodstain at a crime scene matches their DNA profile or why the force marks on a window frame match the crowbar that was found in their possession, the details of the laboratory result are secondary. This is not necessarily because of a temptation to oversell forensic evidence but because the forensic evidence has not been resolved yet. The interrogations can contribute vital elements to that resolution.

Translation work was not necessarily desired in all contexts. Forensic scientists did not want, for example, to teach potential criminals how to avoid leaving usable traces. This can happen because pretrial investigation reports, including expert statements, become public documents when charges are pressed, which can make formal, routine, and public translation work problematic for the forensic scientists. Anyone can request public documents, and thus also expert statements (although parts of some statements are occasionally classified, usually to protect a plaintiff's privacy in a sensitive issue), and, according to the forensic scientists, this is sometimes done with the intention of learning how to better commit crimes. "Troublemakers learn," one forensic scientist said, citing that expert statements had been found at offenders' houses (presumably during house searches carried out in connection with investigations). Thus, the forensic scientists were very careful not to put too much supplementary information in their expert statements. However, this of course also makes the statements less transparent for their intended recipients.

An interview with one defense lawyer suggests that there may be impediments to initiating translation work. Like the prosecutors or the police, defense lawyers can initiate translation work by making informal telephone calls to the SKL and asking the forensic scientists to explain or elaborate on an expert statement. They can also summon forensic scientists to court as expert witnesses. In addition, their questions and objections during trial are very much a part of the translation work around forensic evidence.

However, at second glance, there are difficulties inherent in this process. The lawyer passionately described what he perceived to be an imbalance in expertise between the defense on the one hand and the police and prosecution on the other:

> Of course it's a problem of education. [. .] If you're a judge, prosecutor, and police officer, well then you have a lot of resources in terms of education. [. .] Here, we have lots of law firms that are very small and that do this kind of work [i.e., criminal defense]. Some are self-employed, and of course it's really difficult for them—for one, to find the time to acquire this knowledge [. . .] but also perhaps to understand. And that puts you at disadvantage as a lawyer. [. . .] But the most important thing is of course to see to it that the courts get this knowledge. It's they who decide.

This lack of knowledge makes it difficult for defense lawyers to look into the semitransparent box of forensic evidence, and the result of this is that they very rarely question forensic laboratory results. However, having such knowledge is essential for one to be able to, as he put it, "question the results that are being presented and not just stand there, cap in hand, and say, all right, okay." Instead of questioning results, though, defense lawyers appear to focus principally on their explanation or interpretation.

The lawyer's conclusion was: "We lawyers could be much better at this—we must get much better at this." He then went on to describe the practical difficulties of obtaining knowledge about forensic technologies and the evidence they produce. Members of the forensic science community publish their research in international forensics journals, which are not "something we [lawyers] normally read," he said. It was hard, he added, to find the time to keep up with forensic science as well as with jurisprudence, especially as keeping up does not generate income, at least not immediately. In consequence, "the imbalance in trial increases," as the police and the prosecution have many more resources at their disposal. And, if defense lawyers "fall behind" in competence, it affects defendants and might lead to an increased risk for miscarriages of justice. "That's not something you want under the rule of law, is it?"

In the perception of the lawyer I spoke to, there are questions and objections that defense lawyers cannot pose:

> You rely on the results that the lab delivers to be correct, and [...] I don't think that the SKL deliberately delivers incorrect results in order to favor the police or the prosecutor, I really don't believe that, but of course there can be errors even at the SKL. [...] I don't know of any enterprise where there aren't any mistakes, and I find it hard to believe that the SKL should be the only authority, the only actor, that never makes mistakes. Then again, of course, there are occasional objections that there has been a mix-up or something like that, and in 99.9 percent of these cases there certainly hasn't, but it could have happened, and it's very difficult to know.

While the lawyer was careful not to question the SKL's work or its impartiality, part of his acceptance was rather involuntary and had to do with the practical obstacles to checking the results' correctness.

Obtaining a second opinion or counter-expert opinion to supplement the lawyer's understanding has its practical difficulties. Defense lawyers can—just like any member of the public—commission analyses from the SKL at their own cost. But such private analyses are not given a high priority,[8] since, in the words of the SKL's administration, "you shouldn't be able to buy your way past the queue." Thus, by the time the forensic scientists get to a privately commissioned analysis, the trial it was to be used in might be over.

The defense can have traces analyzed with higher priority by going through the pretrial investigation leader or the court, but then the results will automatically become part of the pretrial investigation. As the results might make the client's situation worse, lawyers can be reluctant to take this route. It is technically possible to commission a second opinion from a forensic science laboratory abroad, but the lawyer I spoke to described that as so impractical it was almost impossible, primarily because of tight time frames. In addition, language barriers might be difficult to cross even with highly qualified interpreters. So, as another lawyer put it, "unfortunately there's no tradition in Sweden to obtain [a second opinion]." Johanne Yttri Dahl (2009) describes a similar situation in Norway at the time of her study, and she discusses

Norwegian defense lawyers' perspectives on DNA evidence. The lawyers she interviewed expressed similar views to those of the lawyers I met. Most of them felt that it was very difficult to call DNA evidence into question.

However, the defense lawyers I talked to did seem to be able to obtain second opinions on, and subsequently question, other types of evidence, such as medical evidence. Yet the first lawyer's example of trying to find a medical examiner for a second opinion sounded at first very much like the situation with forensic evidence being produced by the SKL, that the small size of the professional community makes it difficult to obtain second opinions: "There are quite few medical examiners in Sweden. All know each other and exchange experiences with each other. It's very difficult to find someone who will criticize a colleague's conclusions. And that also means that on those occasions [when you can't get an examiner to give a second opinion], you'll have to go abroad to find that expertise. And that makes it more difficult and expensive and it takes longer." But he continued, saying, "a colleague here at the firm [. . .] had a case a couple of years ago where a little boy had died, [. . .] and the medical examiner who, at the prosecutor's request, had looked at this, said the father had killed the boy. On purpose. But then [the colleague] found a retired professor of forensic medicine who concluded it wasn't certain at all that that was how it had happened. And the man was acquitted, but had [the colleague] not been able to get hold of the retired professor, well, there would have been a very high risk that the man would have been convicted for that." In the interviewee's perception, the retired professor's second opinion was thus instrumental in calling the medical examiner's evidence into question; involving another expert in the translation work might have made an opaque box more transparent.

Such transparency was also achieved in the high-profile 2012 trial of a man who was suspected of carrying out a series of shootings in the city of Malmö, in the south of Sweden.[9] The defense took the extremely exceptional measure of bringing in an expert from the United States in order to question the SKL's bullet analysis. The verdict contained several pages that detailed exactly how the SKL had examined the bullets and the guns and what, in the eyes of the court, made their results reliable and credible. When ruling on the defense's reimbursement, the court deemed the counter-expert's appearance in court to be unnecessary (although it approved of her advising the defense) and thus only granted part of the sum requested. But the court's unusually extensive reasoning about the bullet analysis was clearly carried out at least in part in response to the defense's objections.

I only managed to interview two lawyers during my fieldwork, and just one of them spoke at length—spontaneously—about the difficulties of questioning forensic evidence. A single lawyer's opinion is, of course, not representative, and I do not have any ethnographic data on defense lawyers' work to complement the interview. In addition, the opinion of the lawyer I interviewed could be dismissed as a predictable complaint; after all, defense lawyers are obliged to be on their clients' side. However, when one considers the translation of forensic evidence between epistemic cultures, the lawyer's concerns can illuminate an important aspect of translation work: successfully initiating translation work might require a measure of expertise. Just as the semitransparent box could be quite opaque to prosecutors and judges (and, presumably, also defense lawyers) when it came to sources of uncertainty, lack of expertise can make it difficult for a defense lawyer to ask the questions that make it possible to discuss the insides of the box. As a consequence, meanings might be lost or changed, affecting not only the individual piece of evidence but also the case as a whole and the people involved in it.

There can be different (and opposite) reasons for why translation work was not routinely performed around expert statements. The "worlds" of the criminal justice system might—through contact, through training, through the crime scene technicians' mediations—have come close enough to each other for most expert statements to be quite stable. In other words, members of the criminal justice system might have acquired enough fluency in each other's cultures to be able to make their own translations. In this case, frictions would be the exception, not because gaps and dissimilarities go undetected but because it is only under exceptional circumstances that they cannot be bridged without translation work that involves members of several epistemic cultures. But at least on occasion, translation work might not be performed because members of the criminal justice system are not aware of the dissimilarities and gaps between their epistemic cultures. That is, expert statements might sometimes effectually be boundary objects, holding different meanings for different epistemic cultures.

LANGUAGES, FRICTIONS, AND TRANSLATIONS

Even though the forensic scientists took care to make their expert statements semitransparent boxes rather than black boxes, the effect of this semitransparency was not necessarily what they expected it to be. While with "strong" evidence, recipients did not seem to see any need to look into the box (with the possible exception of defense lawyers), in looking at "weak" evidence, they did not always see what the forensic scientists expected them to see. Some of the frictions that occurred around the expert statements might have had to do not only with different epistemic languages but also with differences in focus and aims. Forensic scientists often focus on individual pieces of evidence, while police investigators typically focus on the people involved in the case, and judges, prosecutors, and defense lawyers, in their focus on legal storytelling, have to maintain a double focus on both the pieces and the whole of the evidence. Although the recipients of the expert statements do not necessarily refuse or neglect to look into the box, trust, practical hurdles, or differences in focus or expertise can render it opaque.

In the laboratory, different specialties—different epistemic subcultures— share their worlds with each other through the shared practices and ensuing organic objectivity discussed in chapter 4. In terms of Galison's language metaphor (1997), these practices have contributed to a shared creole used throughout the laboratory, a language that can be employed to talk about a result's value or weight.

Forensic scientists on the one hand and judges, prosecutors, and defense lawyers on the other, however, do not have many points of contact where they could develop shared understandings and languages. There are the (relatively rare) occasions when an expert witness appears in court and the informal conversations that prosecutors or defense lawyers occasionally have with forensic scientists about particular expert statements. Such sporadic contact might make it difficult to extend organic objectivity beyond the laboratory. Furthermore, translation work seems to be prompted predominantly by frictions. The forensic scientists took contact with prosecutors or police investigators when they disagreed with commissions, and prosecutors and defense lawyers instigated translation work only when they had additional questions or anticipated contention. As the role of judges and lay assessors is to listen to the evidence presented in court, not to conduct inquiries, they are even more passive in this respect.

For the forensic evidence, the criminal justice system's translation work suggests that expert statements are neither immutable mobiles that transport unchangeable meanings and thus transcend the need for translations, nor boundary objects that allow for enough flexibility or multiplicity of meanings to gloss over the incomplete translations or incompatibilities of language that arise around that transport. Instead, the stability of forensic evidence is not an inherent quality but one that is achieved through translation work, that is, through members of the criminal justice system actively—and at times informally and invisibly—supplementing information and aligning writing and reading. To use Galison's trade metaphor (1997, 783), global alignment in the criminal justice system might depend on local coordination continuously being worked out through translation work. Instead of developing a shared language, be it a creole or a pidgin, the criminal justice system maintains translation practices.

CHAPTER SEVEN

In Court, Reprise

LEGAL TRUTH

Having traced the pretrial biography of forensic evidence from the court to the crime scene, I want to return to the end of the legal chain. Despite what crime fiction suggests, crimes are solved in court, not through the conviction of a police investigator, a crime scene technician, or even a prosecutor. A verdict in court holds a particular person responsible for a particular crime.

At the end of the legal chain, the evidence in the case is complete—not complete in an absolute sense, but in the sense that the investigation is concluded and the collection of evidence is finished. The evidence has been collected and put together by a sequence of experts, each with a specific expertise and focus within their different epistemic cultures. Thus, what reaches the court is a conglomeration of different kinds of knowledge, forensic and other evidence, woven together, intertwined with legal stories, and translated from epistemic culture to epistemic culture.

In coming to a verdict, the district court is not trying to find an absolute truth, rather, it evaluates the evidence to make a decision about what has been proven and will be held as the (legal) truth. Legal storytelling is used to determine whether the prosecution has proved the defendant's culpability beyond a reasonable doubt. The court evaluates whether the evidence makes the connections that it is claimed to make beyond a reasonable doubt. At the same time, the court determines the meaning of each piece of forensic evidence, settling their multiple possible interpretations into a single interpretation. Through the verdict, the court provides closure to what each trace means for the defendant's culpability at the same time as it provides closure to what the laboratory results and the other information in the case mean for each trace's origin. Thus, the verdict is the conclusion of the forensic evidence's biography and, simultaneously, the end of its social life.

In looking in more detail at how verdicts are reached, this chapter will focus on professional judges. Their votes do not weigh heavier than those of the lay assessors, but they are responsible for the trial being conducted in accordance with the law, and, more importantly for this chapter, they have much more experience of making judgments.

MAKING VERDICTS

In making its verdict, the court depends on the pretrial investigation. It cannot investigate additional possibilities—and it is extremely rare for the court to have the prosecution supplement the pretrial investigation. It can only evaluate the evidence put before it. Thus, the quality of the pretrial investigation plays a crucial role in a court coming to a verdict. One of the judges I interviewed commented that an incomplete pretrial investigation might produce a strong suggestion of culpability but not the certainty beyond a reasonable doubt required for a conviction. He spoke of his frustration: "Sometimes you get a little ... annoyed at this, when you see that there actually is a lot that suggests that this person is guilty of this crime, but you don't have a complete investigation for some reason. And you think, [...] it should have been possible to do this better or more completely. That's not fun." There can be a number of reasons why an investigation is not complete, he conceded, but it is frustrating regardless.

All of the judges I talked with—as well as the prosecutors and defense lawyers—emphasized that a trial is not about the truth but about the evidence and whether it allows sufficient certainty for a conviction. Similarly, the Swedish National Courts Administration emphasizes the centrality of evidence in an information leaflet (2010), quoting a judge, "It is not the district court's task to decide what is true or false." Instead, "the court's task is to make a decision on the evidence there is." And many of my interlocutors pointed out that only the offender—perhaps—knew "what really happened." In other words, there is uncertainty even in court.

From the time an investigation starts up to the point when the prosecutor decides whether to press charges, reducing uncertainty is the main concern. Throughout an investigation, there is a substantial, albeit decreasing, measure of uncertainty. By the time the prosecutor presses charges, the investigation has reduced uncertainty enough that he or she deems a conviction to be a more likely outcome than an acquittal.

For the court to convict a defendant, even less uncertainty is allowed. But there *is* room for uncertainty. As in many other criminal justice systems, the Swedish standard of evidence is "beyond a reasonable doubt," which is an acknowledgment of there being, as one of the judges put it, "no such thing as absolute knowledge about anything in this world."

The "beyond a reasonable doubt" standard is a pragmatic acknowledgment of uncertainty because a standard of absolute certainty would make it virtually impossible to convict anyone and would thus paralyze the criminal justice system. The risk of paralysis has to be balanced against avoiding arbitrariness or miscarriages of justice, which would affect individuals' lives and undermine trust in the criminal justice system and, by association, in the state. But the expression "beyond a reasonable doubt" is also a little obscure. In the words of a judge, "You don't need absolute knowledge, you need to be convinced it is a certain way. It's [...] not 100 percent certainty—it's 97, 98, 99, somewhere. It's a delicate issue. Judges always put up a fight, don't like to set a percentage. Well, but it's difficult to set a number, actually."

This judge was not the only one to find the concept of "certainty beyond a reasonable doubt" difficult to pin down. Another judge talked about it in a similar manner, giving his level of acceptable certainty as 95 percent. None of the judges seemed to intend the number to be a precise measurement; rather, they appeared to use it to convey a scope of sufficient certainty and acceptable uncertainty.

How the court arrives (or does not arrive) at the hard-to-pin-down level of certainty that makes a conviction seemed difficult for judges to explain. A district court judge said, "Someone once said it's supposed to be easy to convict in criminal cases. If it's not easy to convict, you shouldn't [convict]." With a laugh, he went on to explain that the remark was not a comment on the lightheartedness of judges, but rather that it pointed out that, unless the court was fully convinced that the defendant had done the things outlined by the prosecution, it should acquit.

On the surface, his words are about the presumption of innocence and reasonable doubt. But he was also, less obviously, talking about *how* he as a judge makes the decision on whether a defendant's guilt has been proven beyond a reasonable doubt: he is supposed to be so convinced that the decision is easy.

When asked about how they reached a decision, the judges' answers tended to be rather sweeping. It was "a feeling, of course," was how one of them put it. Only one of them, one with a little less experience than his colleagues, explicitly talked about having difficulties in putting the evaluation into words. It was a "gut feeling," he said; with time, he continued, one learned to feel whether the evidence held up for a conviction.

This "feeling" does not seem to be uncomplicated. One of the judges, for example, said, "of course you can have a feeling [. . .] that someone is guilty but [still] feel that you have to acquit this one, that the evidence doesn't hold up." Another expressed a similar caution: "You can [. . .] be of the opinion that it happened differently, but . . . you have to rid yourself of that and only look at the evidence, the body of evidence." In other words, there are different kinds of feelings: personal feelings about what happened or whether someone is guilty and professional feelings about the evidence.

The judges' descriptions of coming to a decision can be compared to how the professors interviewed by Michèle Lamont talked about evaluating grant proposals. They were not always able to give a definition of academic excellence but would often simply say, "I know it when I see it" (Lamont 2009, 107). To be sure, judging in court is different from assessing academic grant proposals. The professors in Lamont's study served on interdisciplinary panels on a voluntary basis, not as a core function of their occupation, and they reviewed their peers' proposals. These were all certainly factors that shaped both interactions and evaluations. But there are similarities.

Firstly, neither the professors nor the judges are individually responsible for the final decision. The academic panels make collective decisions based on their members' advance ratings of proposals and their discussions of these ratings and the proposals. Similarly, the court's decisions are collective. A tie between the four people—one judge and three lay assessors—on the committee in district court equals an acquittal; at least three of the court's members must be convinced of the defendant's guilt for a conviction to be possible. The fact that each member of the court has an equal vote also means that the lay assessors can overrule the judge. Thus, while the members of the court hold individual opinions—and, on rare occasion, express them as a diverging opinion in the written verdict—none of them can sway the decision on their own.

Secondly, both academics and judges are free to decide how to evaluate, but their evaluation is expected to be professional, not personal, and to be anchored in a professional community. Lamont's professors draw on notions of academic excellence that, while not necessarily identical, are shared (Lamont 2009, 159ff.). The judges orient themselves and their "feeling" for the evidence against the court community:

I've had that struggle with myself: whether I've set the bar high enough. [. . .] You do get at least some kind of response in the way that [cases] often go to the court of appeal, who then changes [the verdict] in one direction or the other. Although I think that it lately has happened more often that they've convicted where I've acquitted and the other way around. [. . .] It's not very enjoyable when that happens. Sometimes they have other facts to consider than I had—so, of course, you don't break down because of that, but you do think about it. I guess it's important to constantly kind of think about whether you've set the bar high enough.

The sports metaphor of evidence standards as a bar, such as in high jumping or pole vaulting, is a rather common way to speak about setting or meeting standards also in other parts of society. Similar to the prosecutors who assessed their safety margins (and thus also their standards of evidence) on how frequently and on what grounds their cases were dismissed, the judge measured his "bar" and practice against the higher court. He set and reset them in relation to how his verdicts fared.

Another factor in setting the bar is the seriousness of the case. One judge called the assessment of evidence "kind of a risk evaluation as well," explaining that, "of course, it's considered more [. . .] serious if someone, on a confession that is false, should be given a life sentence for murder than someone who is fined for shoplifting on a false confession." Society, he explained, "can accept a fine being imposed based on a false confession," but it cannot accept that someone would be given a long prison sentence for a crime they did not commit. Thus, the more severe the crime for which a defendant is being tried, the higher the standards on the investigation. When someone falsely confesses to shoplifting and is fined, it is of minor consequence to them and a small risk to society. But a confession in a murder case cannot be taken at face value, as miscarriages of justice in murder cases have much more severe repercussions, for the person wrongly convicted, for possible additional victims and their families and friends, and for society as a whole.

Lamont not only describes the evaluations the panelists made as rooted in a professional community and its shared notions of excellence but also provides further insights on how judgments are made in her analysis of the panelists' descriptions and discussions. Academic excellence in the context of a grant proposal, she demonstrates, is, among other things, a question of craftsmanship, of the cultural capital of affiliation and recommendations, of appropriate self-display, and of anticipated trajectories (Lamont 2009, chapter 5). In other words, even though the panelists could not describe in detail how they arrived at their decisions, Lamont's analysis makes it possible to see the practices (and criteria) they use when judging proposals.

The same applies to the judges in district court. While I was not able to observe the court's deliberations after a trial, I did talk with the judges about how they evaluated evidence and the grounds the courts gave for their decisions. Even though members of the court may find it difficult to describe their evaluation as a whole, they do talk about evaluating pieces of evidence. The evaluation made by the court is, of course, not about excellence but about evidentiary value.

EVALUATING EVIDENCE

In terms of legal storytelling, evaluating evidence is about determining how the evidence contributes to understanding the central action in the legal stories told in court (Bennett and Feldman 1981, 41). The judges all emphasized that their verdicts were based on an evaluation of "a combination of all the circumstances" (i.e., considering *all* the evidence presented in court). "Of course it depends on which type of evidence you've got," a judge told me. "If you have [...] only accounts from witnesses and perhaps the plaintiff, [...] you have to take them as your point of departure and see how credible they are. [...] Hopefully the witnesses are a little more careful with what they say, perhaps, than the defendant and of course also the plaintiff. [...] Witnesses are supposed to be impartial. Then you have to look at how credible these accounts are, that is, weigh them together." This same judge said that the evaluation itself "can be difficult."

One support for making evaluations can be found in Swedish legal doctrine, which has developed several detailed models for evidentiary evaluation (see, for example, Björkman et al. 1997; Diesen 1994; Schelin 2007; see also Axberger et al. 2006, chapter 3). These models are rather theoretical, making it possible to think about credibility and reliability as separate notions, to differentiate between several types of evidence and auxiliary evidence, and to consider weighing chains of evidence together in a mathematically probabilistic way.

However, doctrine and praxis live rather separate lives. Hans-Gunnar Axberger and his colleagues ascribe these separate lives to doctrine being quite theoretical and abstract and cases being, by necessity, concrete and particular. This makes the theory of evidentiary evaluation difficult to apply to actual evaluations (Axberger et al. 2006, 63ff., 471), and the judges I interviewed certainly did not refer to doctrine when they tried to explain how they assessed evidence.[1]

All of the judges I spoke to seemed to find the process through which they arrived at their convictions—in both senses of the term—difficult to describe, especially in general terms, and they seemed more comfortable with talking about particulars. The difficulty with generalization can be perceived in one judge's comments. He talked about how forensic evidence is considered in weighing the evidence and how forensic evidence is assigned a supportive role in relation to verbal accounts, which serve as the main evidence, but he did not make the assessment process much clearer. "But of course, if you then have . . . support from other forensic evidence—for example, that what one person says also can be verified in another way, with forensic evidence, [. . .] for example, that you can find . . . DNA, fingerprints, footprints, what have you, then it of course strengthens that narrative. [. . .] That's how you have to weigh and look at the different factors. [. . .] That's how we do it." When talking about concrete—albeit hypothetical—cases, judges seemed to find it much easier to discuss the weighing of evidence. Here, the judge describes a hypothetical case in which the evidence is easy to evaluate:

> When it comes to sex crimes, for example, [the question is,] has there been intercourse? Well, how do you then determine whether it was consensual or not? I usually say that the best [i.e., the most straightforward] rape cases are those where [the plaintiff and the defendant do not know each other and where the offender] attacks someone out of the bushes, because [if the plaintiff and defendant had] some form of contact—a relationship—beforehand, that makes it more difficult. If they haven't, and it can be shown that there has been intercourse, well, that makes it easier, of course. If the woman is attacked out there in the park, for example, which is the usual way, [. . .] of course it strengthens her credibility if she can point out the man and if you then find DNA. [. . .] [Then it becomes] difficult for him to explain.

Unlike in cases in which the plaintiff and defendant have had a prior relationship, there are very few possible interpretations of the evidence in such an attack, and thus there is less uncertainty.

Sometimes, the evidence available is not enough to dispel uncertainty, as the judge illustrated in similarly concrete terms: "It usually is not enough that [. . .] a window has been smashed and then you find a blood stain from a particular person there. That can't possibly be enough to say he's the one who took something that's missing from the house, that's not enough at this point. [...] I don't think you'd get a conviction. Even if it's a well-known petty burglar." In this case, while there may be evidence that the hypothetical defendant has been at or even in the burgled house, there is no evidence that he has appropriated the missing property.

Even though the cases quoted here are generic, they appear to be a condensation of the judge's experience with rape and burglary cases. In both examples, the conclusion was easily arrived at and made explicit. Due to the circumstances of the rape case, the DNA evidence was "difficult for [the defendant] to explain," meaning that he would most likely be convicted. In the other case, the judge didn't think there was enough evidence to get a conviction—unless, of course, the loot could be found in the suspect's possession. In which case, "they're in trouble."

This difference in talking about evaluating evidence is not one of personal style; all three descriptions come from the same judge. What is more, the other judges I interviewed spoke about the process in a similar way, giving very vague descriptions when describing the evaluation of evidence in general terms and quickly moving on to clear-cut, concrete cases as examples with which to illustrate the evaluation.

To put it in terms of legal storytelling, the court evaluates how each story element—each piece of evidence—is connected to each other element, forming the interpretive context of the story's central action, the allegedly criminal act (Bennett and Feldman 1981, 41). In the rape example, the relationship (or rather the lack thereof) between the plaintiff and defendant is well defined—they do not know each other at all—and there is a course of events that evokes not only a stock script but also a stereotype of rapists lurking in the bushes. The other case also arranged well-known stock scripts into a typical legal story: a previously convicted offender who presumably has broken a window to burglarize a house. The only disruptive element in that case was the lack of evidence for the theft itself. The (hypothetical) evidence, both forensic and verbal, is connected through the story framework and thus processed into judgments (cf. Bennett 1978, 1979).

MAKING REASONABLE CONNECTIONS

Evaluating evidence is not only about determining how different pieces of evidence fit together into a whole. It is also about assessing the pieces of evidence and making (or, sometimes, implying and inferring) connections between the story elements and deciding which conclusions can be reasonably drawn from people's behavior. In the case of a witness account, a judge named several aspects that could be factored into the evaluation, among them how the witness related to the defendant: "What it was like then, how long has it been since it happened, and have they [the witness] told it in the same way during the entire investigation and also today in district court and so on. [. . .] What kind of relationship do they have to the defendant?"

On one level, taking this relationship into account may seem unproblematic: of course a friend will both perceive and try to display a friend in a favorable light, and of course enemies will do the opposite. To take such things into consideration when evaluating the evidence seems only sensible. Relationships are even formally taken into consideration in the criminal justice system. Family members are not obliged to testify against one another, and if a close relative does testify in court, they are not put under oath and thus not placed in a position where they could commit perjury.

However, the consideration of personal relationships is also part of the larger pattern of making connections between story elements based on expectations of how people in a certain relationship, position, or situation would act, or, conversely, of inferring from people's actions how they perceive a situation or relationship. Consider the defendant in chapter 1 who had been observed going into a mailbox that did not belong to him. The witness reported that he left the mailbox when, as the witness thought, he realized he was being observed. This was implicitly taken as an indication of being aware of breaking the law. Consequently, the defendant's account that he was performing work in good faith was dismissed by the prosecution as a falsehood, and an act of unlawful disposal was proposed as the only viable conclusion. The underlying assumption was that someone pursuing a lawful errand would not be expected to react in such a way to being noticed, and thus the defendant's reaction could be understood as awareness of being in the wrong.

Max Gluckman discusses such reasoning in relation to his idea of the "reasonable man" (1963, chapter 7) and how such a person would act. From his fieldwork in what was then Northern Rhodesia and his familiarity with British law, Gluckman argues that, during trial, "the truth is arrived at mainly by contrasting the behavior of the parties, as witnesses report it and as the parties themselves describe it, against the standards of how a reasonable man would behave" (1963, 184). These standards of reasonableness are different for different kinds of people. For example, a reasonable father behaves differently toward his daughter than a reasonable daughter does toward her father. Likewise, what is considered to be reasonable fatherhood may differ between cultures. However, the concept of reasonable behavior itself, Gluckman argues, can be found in all legal practice (1963, 189ff.). This universality has been questioned (Moore 2001, 99ff.), but Gluckman's concept does makes it easier to see how notions of how people can be expected to "work" in general are part of creating meaning out of disparate accounts and pieces of evidence in trial. A reasonable person who knows that they are pursuing lawful employment does not stop their work, much less stop it in a furtive manner, when they find themselves observed. Someone knowingly breaking the law, however, would reasonably want to avoid being observed.

Similar reasoning can be found in verdicts. In the fraud case examined in chapter 1, for example, where the defendants maintained that the frauds had been committed by a relative, the court concluded that "there is reason to doubt [the relative's] existence."[2] The main reason for this doubt was that the relative had been impossible to trace, but the court also commented that it was "a remarkable circumstance that [one of the defendants], when he was asked to describe [the relative] during the hearing, was not able to give a closer description of him." Thus, the apparent assumption in this situation is that a person should reasonably be able to describe their relatives; it is considered "remarkable" if they cannot.

In the verdict of the car crash case, also discussed in chapter 1, the court appears to have based its decision on what the defendant could reasonably have been expected to know and how he could reasonably have been expected to feel. It reasoned about the crime like this:

> The circumstances are such that [the defendant] must, as the driver of the large car, have been aware enough of the forces his actions developed on the smaller car to in the moment of the deed have had insight into the considerable risk that [the plaintiff] could be killed. A possible realization of this effect cannot be considered to have in this moment provided a relevant reason for [the defendant] to refrain from the deed. This assessment must, among other things, be based on what has been come to hand about [the defendant] harboring anger against and being deeply stirred by his perception of [the plaintiff's] having been disrespectful and ungrateful, as well as [the defendant's] interest in escaping the difficult relationship with him. Thus, it is proven that [the defendant] in the way that has been specified in the indictment through so-called indifferent intent[3] has committed attempted manslaughter.

The defendant was convicted of attempted manslaughter and given a four-year sentence. The court argued that, as an experienced driver, the defendant must have known that he was driving a larger and consequently heavier car and that his car was able to inflict serious damage on the smaller car and its driver. In addition, he was "harboring anger" toward the plaintiff and thus could be concluded to have had an "interest in avoiding the difficult relationship" to the plaintiff. Both factors together, then, made it possible for the court to consider it proven that the defendant had attempted manslaughter.

Motive is sometimes a factor in assessing the different legal stories, as it was in the above case, but as judges and others frequently emphasized, a motive is not required for a conviction,[4] and often, motives are never revealed. However, if someone kills or tries to kill a person they do not know, for example, that is not regarded as reasonable behavior, and thus a motive should (preferably) be explained for the legal story to make sense (cf. Bennett and Feldman 1981, 10). As one of the judges remarked about a trial being conducted in the north of Sweden at the time of the interview, "I guess that's what they're wrestling with up there in Gällivare . . . where [the suspect has] been tied to [the case] in a different way. But I think the motive's a bit weird—what kind of motive would he have actually to kill this person he doesn't know?" Other crimes may need less explanation, as the motive is implicitly understood as quite reasonable. For example, there was no question as to why the defendants in the fraud case should want to defraud people they did not know.

In their verdict on the case of serial shootings in Malmö (mentioned in chapter 6), the local district court drew on ideas of how people typically and reasonably behave in order to make sense of the defendant's uncooperative silence during the pretrial investigation and the trial. It was the defendant's right, the court stated, to remain silent, and the silence could, of course, never "automatically be equaled with a confession." Additionally, the court stressed, the burden of proof is on the prosecution, no matter how cooperative or uncooperative the defendant is, and it is the court's duty to assess the defendant's silence as part of the case. However, the court's assessment suggested that the defendant's silence had been evaluated in terms of reasonable behavior when he was asked about his whereabouts and activities at the times of the alleged crimes: "The answers have consistently been that he does not remember, moreover often with the addition that he, having been fully occupied with other things in custody, has not even tried to remember what he did, either. This behavior appears extremely odd for an innocent person who has wrongfully been accused."[5]

The court went on to comment on the oddness of the defendant's decision to tell the police that he had made "agreements of significance to the case" with two acquaintances but refused to describe the contents of these agreements. These "vague statements about agreements with other people cannot reasonably be interpreted in any other way than that a report of the agreements' contents would be beneficial to him in the case. That he still withholds the content appears, in the light of the very serious transgression he is indicted for, to be wholly unexplainable if there really were agreements. [. . .] In the district court's opinion, the significance that must be attached to [the defendant's] silence is that it appears unlikely that a completely innocent person would choose to behave in the way [the defendant] has done." The court ended its argument about the defendant's silence by noting that its significance was "virtually negligible." Still (perhaps prompted by an extensive argument during the hearing), they apparently found the issue important enough that they devoted almost two pages to explaining it.

These three verdicts illustrate different types of reasonableness used to make connections between story elements. One can reasonably expect an adult to give a detailed description of a relative; one can reasonably assume that an experienced driver knows that his or her car will inflict serious damage and one can infer his or her feelings from witness accounts of family relationships; and one can expect an accused person to behave in a way that is most beneficial to him or her.

In this way, everyday skills are a factor in differentiating between legal stories. While it may take legal expertise to assess which prerequisites are fulfilled and which crime the defendant should (or should not) be convicted of, it does not take legal education and experience to make the connection between, for example, a young couple's troubled relationship, the involvement of the young woman's family, and her father's presumed feelings toward the plaintiff upon spotting him in his car. These everyday understandings are not only emphasized as being important to legal storytelling (Bennett and Feldman 1981) but are also acknowledged in legal doctrine: "The knowledge relevant to the assessment of evidence is [. . .] based foremost on experience of life and on general education" (Björkman et al. 1997, 23; my translation). This does not mean that judges should base their assessments on intuition or prejudice (Axberger et al. 2006, 40) but rather that the evaluation of evidence in court is based on a combination of legal and everyday knowledge and experience, not only in practice but also in intention.

This everyday knowledge and experience of how people "work" and of which conclusions can be reasonably drawn from their behavior and their accounts bridges the gap between not knowing "what's happening inside another person's head," as one of the judges put it, and attaining (or not attaining) sufficient certainty for a conviction. What happens inside other people's heads is salient not only when it comes to assessing what people say in court—together with supportive evidence—but also when it comes to such prerequisites as intent, which can mean the difference between different crimes and sentences.

If the criminal justice system is to be able to convict, it must be able to distinguish between different legal stories—that is to say, different explanations of evidence. In both the car crash case and the fraud case, the defenses' legal stories—that the crash was an accident and that the elusive relative was responsible for the frauds, respectively—were discounted as not being equipotent to the prosecution's, in part because of the forensic and other evidence but also because of everyday knowledge.

But relying on everyday understandings and skills is not always unproblematic. Firstly, as Mariana Valverde (2003) points out, everyday or common knowledge is a somewhat knotty concept. Secondly, the court is required to be impartial in its evaluation of the evidence and, more than that, to err on the side of acquittal. But impartiality can be a difficult position to achieve, especially when it is expected to be based on "common" understandings. Donna Haraway argues that although a position may be understood to be universal (and impartial), it is as local and incomplete as other views from other positions. To ascribe a position a view from nowhere, she writes, is to perform the "god trick" (Haraway 1988, 581), that is, to pretend that one's vision is infinite and free from earthly concerns. Similarly, while the members of the court are expected to be detached and impartial, they still draw on understandings and experience from their specific gendered, classed, and ethnified positions—both personal and professional—which may unconsciously bias them toward or against the people whose accounts they assess (see Rosen 2006, 177ff.; Bennett and Feldman 1981, 170ff.).[6]

Even though they might not necessarily put it in these terms, judges seem to be aware of this issue. Judges interviewed by legal scholar Olof Ställvik on the role of the judge in Sweden emphasized not only the need for integrity and knowledge of the law but also "a broad-minded and tolerant outlook on people" (2009, 213; my translation). They also emphasized the need for empathy, flexibility, and knowledge of human nature—qualities that, at least in the descriptions Ställvik quotes, take into account different realities of life. The judges I interviewed emphasized that there was no "standard template" for how people work and for what constitutes a credible narrative.

However, as Haraway and others point out (Haraway 1988; Harding 2004), a completely detached view is impossible. Perspective is always a part of perception. That both tellers and listeners draw on everyday knowledge and communicative skills in legal storytelling requires, of course, shared knowledge and understandings. Consequently, it entails certain biases (Bennett and Feldman 1981, 6, 170ff.).

One aspect of bias is connected to the repertoire of language and communication styles available (Bennett and Feldman 1981, 170ff.). A defense lawyer, for example, talked about helping clients to convey their perspectives, saying that not everyone was "all that good at expressing themselves" and that some people's "extremely meager language," due perhaps to having grown up in an "intellectually poor environment," made it very difficult for them to communicate. A legal story conveyed by means of such "meager" language, which perhaps does not conform to conventional story structure or is not perfectly clear, may appear less convincing and reasonable than one told in a more eloquent way. In the same vein, a judge talked about how, in cases where interpreters were used, it was difficult for him to assess the interpreter's skill and thus to determine whether an "unreasonable" narrative was just unreasonable or only translated badly.

Another aspect of bias is the repertoire of notions of what constitutes reasonable behavior. Standards of reasonableness may vary between cultures, but they can also differ with gender, class, and ethnicity (see Bennett and Feldman 1981, 170ff.). The life experience of a judge may be considerably different from that of a defendant, witness, or plaintiff, and this may affect their evaluation of evidence.[7] As the defense lawyer put it when talking about the evaluation of injuries in rape cases, "should a sixty-year-old judge's sexual preferences be . . . the norm for what's normal? I guess that's also tricky." He pointed out that some consensual sexual practices may cause injuries, and thus, even though this may seem improbable to the hypothetical judge—with his implied old-fashionedness and thus lack of imagination and adventurousness—injuries do not automatically prove the absence of consent. While certainly disquieting in concrete cases, his objection also poses a relevant question: what is "the norm for what's normal" and reasonable?

This is an issue that a judge also touched upon in an interview when talking about filling in spaces around verbal evidence. "I sometimes think," he said, "that [the parties] ask the court to fill in the gaps in the evidence with their own knowledge." He went on to enumerate cases involving children, mentally disturbed people, and immigrant women as instances in which the court, in his opinion, sometimes was "expected to realize that they live under different circumstances" and thus may express themselves differently than other people. "There it's not easy for us to say, oh, he says 'a' but means 'b.'" Clearly uncomfortable, he pointed out that the court cannot be expected to understand if and when a statement means something else:

> Well, we can't [fill in] with knowledge of our own. Perhaps [the parties] could bring in an expert, a psychologist or something who can come and [make an expert statement]. It's a bit dangerous if the court is to sit there and fill in with their own knowledge. [. . .] The prosecutor is the one to put forward the evidence, and it has to be complete evidence. We're not supposed to sort of sit there and, with knowledge of our own, to sort of say, well, now the prosecutor has produced 90 percent, so we'll add the last 5 percent by ourselves.

What makes such gaps between what is said and what is understood visible seems to be the perceived otherness of the defendant, witness, or plaintiff; perhaps one of the parties even points out that the usual notions of reasonableness do not apply to a certain account. Sometimes, the gaps are so obvious that the judge would like the parties to provide an expert to make the person in front of him—presumably other to him through differences in culture, experience, education, horizon, mental maturity, or mental health—understandable.

But in other cases, gaps may go unnoticed, and thus the verdicts risk being biased. These discrepancies may not become as visible and noticeable when the background against which a witness, defendant, or plaintiff makes their statements is less obviously different than the notions against which the court assesses these statements.

Of course, not interpreting the evidence at all because of the possibility of bias is not an option; the evidence must be made legally meaningful for the legal system to function. But what is problematic about evaluating evidence, and evidence already intertwined with legal stories at that, also illustrates another inseparability. Evidence not only requires interpretation—through legal storytelling—it also requires ways of discriminating between interpretations, and these ways are as rooted in sociocultural understandings and experiences as is the legal storytelling.

PROVIDING CLOSURE ON FORENSIC EVIDENCE

The verdict the court makes on a case is an interpretation of the available evidence. This also means that the court is less of a fact finder and more of a fact *maker,* or, as Latour would put it, a fact builder (1987). In Latour's examination of how technoscience is made, nature or reality is the outcome of settling controversies, not the cause of the settlement (1987, 99). While scientists and engineers may refer to reality as the reason their knowledge claims hold, this reality is made through technoscience. Thus, facts are not convincing by virtue of being inherently true, but they become true by being convincing. A similar thing can be said about the outcomes of trials and, by extension, of criminal investigations. Defendants are not convicted because they are offenders, but they become offenders through being convicted. The court does not discover the truth; rather, it makes the truth.

Since it is impossible to know whether the outcome of a trial is in alignment with "what really happened," the court does not concern itself with "what really happened." This does not mean that judges and lay assessors— and the other members of the criminal justice system for that matter—do not care about accuracy or justice, but rather their exclusive focus on the evidence before them is an acknowledgment of the criminal justice system's limitations. To put it differently, since the court cannot access or uncover an absolute truth, it does the next best thing, namely, it makes legal truth out of what *can* be accessed: the evidence.

Thus, a verdict is not synonymous with a convicted offender "actually" having committed the crime he or she has been convicted of; it means that the evidence has been presented to the court and the case has been considered to establish certainty of their culpability beyond a reasonable doubt. Likewise, an acquittal means that the evidence has not been found adequate to establish such certainty. With the verdict, what has been proven becomes fact: the defendant is either acquitted and remains innocent or is convicted and thus becomes an offender. Through a conviction, a specific action is defined as a particular crime; plaintiffs become recognized victims and are awarded damages, and defendants become convicted offenders and have to serve sentences and pay damages. Once the verdict has gained legal effect,[8] none of the uncertainty that pervaded the pretrial investigation is left. The defendant is either unequivocally culpable, if convicted, or unequivocally innocent, if acquitted. Thus, reality is the outcome of the trial.

The legal truth that is made in court is not only the truth about a crime and who is involved in what way, but also the truth about the forensic evidence. As discussed in chapters 4 and 6, forensic scientists consciously choose to not make a statement about the propositions of their evaluation; they only comment on how strongly their results support (or do not support) one of the propositions over the other. The decision about what that support means for the propositions, let alone for the case, is left for the court to make. The court may make this decision implicitly, like the judge who talked about "the fact that your DNA has been recovered from a particular place" and thus evidently took the DNA match to mean identity; or they may make this decision consciously, as in the case of the serial shooting, where the court dismissed the defense's objections to the forensic evidence and thus actively engaged with the forensic evidence, the laboratory's evaluation, and the defense's counter-expertise.

Conclusion

THE SOCIAL LIFE OF FORENSIC EVIDENCE

Examining the social life (Appadurai 1986) of forensic evidence makes it possible to see the wide range of expertise that goes into concluding the biography of a piece of forensic evidence. That in turn makes it possible to use forensic evidence to think about how knowledge can be produced in the cooperation of an array of epistemic cultures and how that knowledge can be transported between contexts. More specifically, I want to suggest that acknowledging the biography of forensic evidence makes it possible to simultaneously and fruitfully think about stability and change in producing and moving knowledge.

The expertise going into the production of forensic evidence is constantly being combined and intertwined during the forensic evidence's social life as it is moved through the different epistemic cultures of the criminal justice system. Some of this expertise is professional: the crime scene technicians' imagination in finding traces and their skill in recovering them; the forensic scientists' laboratory and evaluation skills; the police investigators' knowledge of people; the prosecutors', defense lawyers', and judges' knowledge of the law; and not least the varied expertise needed to be able to perform translation work. Other expertise is rooted in everyday understandings of the world as well as in everyday communicative skills, such as the telling and receiving of legal stories. In its assessment of what the prosecution has or has not proven about the defendant's culpability, the court brings together all this expertise into a final decision. This makes the court dependent not only on the evidence being assembled during the pretrial investigation but also on it being transported to the court in an understandable manner (i.e., on it being successfully translated).

The biography of forensic evidence is both lived and written: at the same time as the forensic evidence lives its social life, that life is being documented.

However, that does not mean to say that the lived life and the written biography are identical. Just as crime scene technicians make abstractions (Latour 1999) from crime scenes to produce their crime scene reports, so the other biographers of forensic evidence make abstractions, recording that which is deemed relevant and appropriate. Police investigators, for example, do not put everything an interrogee says into their reports, but only what to them appears to have a bearing on the case, and forensic scientists are careful not to give the kind of details in their expert statements that may be helpful to criminals. Thus, the written biography of forensic evidence is an abstraction of the lived biography—a documentation of what is judged salient by the members of the epistemic cultures through which the forensic evidence travels.[1]

This perspective has allowed me to make the argument that forensic evidence is collaboratively produced by a chain of epistemic cultures that "create and warrant knowledge" (Knorr Cetina 1999, 1). Crime scene technicians use their professional vision (Goodwin 1994, 1995) and experience of crime scenes to transform a crime scene into traces and an accessible report. Forensic scientists analyze and evaluate single traces against the background of their professional vision and experience and their (inherently limited) knowledge about the material in question. Police investigators use relationships with and personal knowledge of suspects, plaintiffs, and witnesses to produce evidence. Prosecutors transform a case's evidence into legally meaningful stories while at the same time overseeing the assembling of this evidence. Judges and lay assessors simultaneously provide closure to cases and evidence by combining knowledge of the law with everyday experience to come up with verdicts.

As the previous chapters have shown, the epistemic cultures of the criminal justice system differ in terms of expertise, in terms of which kind of knowledge they contribute to the forensic evidence, and in terms of how they produce that knowledge. Many of these epistemic cultures rely on professional vision—for example, in order to "see" sameness and difference in the laboratory, to "see" promising places to look for traces at a crime scene, or to "see" what is needed for a case to be proven. This professional vision is sometimes consciously and deliberately standardized within one epistemic culture but more or less foreign to the others.

But the epistemic cultures also are mutually dependent. Without the work of the police investigators, the forensic scientists, and the crime scene technicians, prosecutors would have no evidence to transform into stories. In the police investigators' work, forensic evidence, which is produced by the forensic scientists and crime scene technicians and interpreted in collaboration with the prosecutor (or the investigator) who leads the pretrial investigation, is an important tool. The forensic scientists depend on the crime scene technicians to examine crime scenes and abstract traces, on the investigators to produce suspects and comparison samples, and on the prosecutors to develop propositions. The crime scene technicians use "the story" around a case to examine the crime scene, and the abstractions they produce would not be useful to the investigation without the subsequent work of the forensic scientists, the investigators, and the prosecutors. And the meanings assigned to the evidence during trial depend on the pretrial investigation. There is certainly scope for the legal stories of the defense and the court alongside those of the prosecution, but how a bit of evidence can be credibly interpreted and which stock scripts can be drawn on in court is affected by, among other things, the other evidence available and how that evidence was assembled in the pretrial investigation.

With this dependence comes a distribution of responsibility. The prosecutors pointed out that it was not they who decided whether a suspect (and, subsequently, defendant) was guilty, but the court. The investigators underscored that it was not them but the prosecutor who decided whether to go to court to have a suspect arraigned or to press charges. And the forensic scientists emphasized that it was not for them to develop the propositions in their evaluations (that is what the leader of the pretrial investigation did) or to settle for one of them (that was the court's province). This distribution has to do with checks and balances, but it is also in alignment with competences and perspectives. The court, which has to make the final decision, sees the whole of the (assembled) evidence, whereas the other links of the legal chain have narrower perspectives. The forensic scientists see only the forensic part of the evidence, the prosecution sees (multiple and perhaps equivalent) avenues of investigation and legal stories, the police investigators see a perhaps distressed plaintiff and cocky suspect (or vice versa), and the crime scene technicians see a place that may (through the investigation and perhaps trial) turn out to have been the scene of a crime.

My argument is based on fieldwork carried out in particular sites at a particular time. Crimes vary between regions. For example, poaching is described by members of the criminal justice system as committed predominantly in the north of the country, probably due to the sparse population and a partiality for hunting in the region. The practices for solving crimes may also differ. Prosecutors, crime scene technicians, or police investigators other than those whose work I followed may work differently or may emphasize other aspects of their work as important. Thus, I do not claim that my description of forensic evidence practices is representative for the whole of the Swedish criminal justice system or for forensic evidence in general. I do think, however, that it makes it possible to raise interesting issues about how to think about the production of forensic evidence and, more generally, of knowledge, issues that may be also relevant for other contexts.

THE MULTIPLE LIFE OF FORENSIC EVIDENCE

Having visited the different parts of the criminal justice system and observed their distinct epistemic cultures, it is possible not only to see how these epistemic cultures differ but also to understand the frictions that sometimes arise between them. Chapter 6 discusses friction around the meaning of forensic evidence that arises around expert statements and is managed through translation work, but there were other kinds of friction.

One example was friction about time. Many of the calls to the forensic scientists were from pretrial investigation leaders who were pressed for time, with the trial or the arraignment hearing approaching fast, and were anxious to receive their analysis results before it was too late. After such a call, forensic scientists might remark that while they obviously tried to deliver results in time for court, sometimes there was simply too much to do. And besides, the forensic scientists frequently emphasized, "it's more important that [the statement] is right than that it comes out fast, isn't it?"

There was also occasional friction between the parts of the criminal justice system about how other parts performed their work. Crime scene technicians complained about police patrols walking all over crime scenes, forensic scientists complained about how order forms were filled out, and judges complained about incomplete investigations. Even though crime scene technicians, forensic scientists, and judges conceded that there were sometimes reasons for shortcomings, the friction was still there, since the work is collaborative. A crime scene that has been walked on makes the crime scene technicians' work more difficult and might destroy traces that could become evidence, incomplete orders are at best a waste of time and at worst a source for misunderstandings, and incomplete investigations can fall short of the bar in court.

Seeing the whole of the criminal justice system makes it possible to understand both sides in those frictions. For example, a patrol police officer I interviewed talked about having to take care of upset or even frightened residents who have found their house broken into and who may be very difficult to reassure if the patrol does not look through the house for intruders. She also mentioned that on busy days, patrols are often dealing with the time pressure of being sent to a number of places in quick succession, meaning that they may not be able to leisurely brush for fingerprints or give lengthy explanations. In consequence, a relatively simple crime scene may be passed on to the crime scene division because it comes on an exceptionally busy day. In addition, the patrol police are less specialized in and familiar with crime scenes,[2] so a crime scene that appears complicated or difficult to a police patrol might be passed on to the crime scene division, who in turn may judge it to be exasperatingly simple and therefore feel that the patrol should have dealt with it. Similarly, crime scene technicians may shake their heads at the exact demands the Swedish National Laboratory of Forensic Science (SKL) places on traces and orders, explaining that the forensic scientists, while very good at their laboratory work, did not always understand what it meant to work at a crime scene and within an investigation. Police investigators and prosecutors could likewise be frustrated at the judges when cases they thought would hold up in court were dismissed.

Looking at the passage of forensic evidence through the criminal justice system also makes it possible to reflect on the different meanings and functions of forensic evidence in different phases of its social life in the different parts of the criminal justice system. Rape cases and the evidence produced in them, for example, look different in the different epistemic cultures. Police investigators meet the plaintiffs. The investigators may be aware that many cases will not be solved (i.e., lead to a conviction), and they may be aware that people sometimes report other people to the police for reasons other than the reported crime having taken place. But they still meet a plaintiff who is often obviously upset, and so they investigate not only because of their professional responsibility but also out of (professional) compassion. They hope that it will be possible to recover traces that can be turned into forensic evidence, which can then be used to assess the plaintiff's statements and to produce a suspect, especially in the cases where the plaintiff cannot name a suspect. Such evidence can then be used to interrogate that suspect and, eventually, perhaps even to achieve a conviction.

Crime scene technicians, on the other hand, do not meet the plaintiff, and therefore, their involvement is impersonal. Their experience with rape cases is that it is often impossible to find traces at the alleged crime scene or on the plaintiff's or suspect's clothes, especially if the crime has not been reported for several days or weeks. Thus, they can have rather low expectations of success in solving the case. But that does not mean that they refuse to participate in the investigation or that they drag their feet.

Forensic scientists at the SKL, however, have higher expectations for rape cases. They only see cases in which the crime scene division has already examined the crime scene or a set of clothes and found traces, and thus, in their view, it is quite common for forensic evidence to be found in rape cases. In addition, the cases that they become involved in are precisely the kinds of cases in which forensic evidence would make a difference. These are typically cases where the point of contention is whether there has been sexual contact, not whether it has been consensual. Thus, the forensic scientists' understanding of rape cases is strongly influenced by a particular subset of cases. For them, rape cases are typically an issue of bodily fluids on clothes or bedclothes and of meticulous work that could yield a DNA profile that will be of central importance as evidence.

Prosecutors see a variety of rape cases, not only the subset that hinges on forensic evidence. For them, rapes are cases that, as violent crimes, are assigned high priority but are notoriously difficult to prove. In their experience, rapes are typically committed in seclusion, and thus it is often one person's word against another's. Forensic evidence is not necessarily helpful, as it may not be able to clarify the contested issues.

Judges see yet another different subset of rape cases, namely those cases in which there is enough evidence for a prosecutor to expect a conviction. Still, one of the judges I interviewed talked about the most straightforward rape cases being those with clear-cut circumstances and where forensic evidence can and does contribute clarity.

In all these different perspectives of the "same" crime, forensic evidence has different meanings, which illustrates how forensic evidence has different value in different contexts during its life cycle. In some contexts, the presence or absence of forensic evidence indicates whether there is a case. In others, it cannot solve the legally pertinent question and is thus marginal at best. At the SKL, forensic evidence is of central importance, but judges may de-emphasize it, saying that "in the majority of cases, you don't get forensic evidence, and you don't need forensic evidence, either." Perhaps the judges perform identity work (Snow and Anderson 1987) by emphasizing that a judge's skill does not become obsolete with the arrival of forensic evidence. But the de-emphasis of forensic evidence may also have to do with precisely the different meanings and functions given to forensic evidence in the criminal justice system's different epistemic cultures. In some cases, forensic evidence is of crucial importance early on in the investigation—for example, in eliciting a statement that then becomes a case's central piece of evidence. Of course, in such cases, these statements are prompted by forensic evidence, but the forensic evidence's importance in court is then indirect, as it serves to support a statement rather than carrying story elements on its own. From a judge's perspective, then, the forensic evidence does not seem as important as the statement, especially considering that the court emphasizes verbal evidence. A piece of forensic evidence may therefore never make it into the courtroom or may be assigned a very minor role there, but it can still be very valuable.

As the previous chapters have shown, forensic evidence can also be important because it can change a pretrial investigation's course or cause a pretrial investigation to come to an end. For example, forensic evidence can strongly indicate a different course of events than that given by a plaintiff or witness, or it can indicate a suspect's lack of involvement in a crime. The value of forensic evidence can also change in other ways over time. Early on in an investigation, it can help in the assessment of whether a crime has been committed—for example, if tool marks are found where a window has been forced open. Later on, forensic evidence can contribute to producing not only suspicion, but also a suspect—for example, if a bloodstain yields a cold hit in a database. It can also be used to solidify or dispel suspicion and to narrow down multiple legal stories to an indictment. Finally, it can become part of the assessment of whether the prosecution has proved their version of events beyond a reasonable doubt.

These different values, together with the different functions that forensic evidence has in the different parts of the criminal justice system (e.g., potential trace, analysis result, tool, story element), make it difficult to talk about forensic evidence in the singular, as a homogeneous object. Indeed, these different forensic evidences may even suggest that talking about a biography or a social life of forensic evidence is a narrative affectation that creates an illusion of coherence and stable singularity where there is only disjunct multiplicity.

I want to argue, however, that it is possible to think about forensic evidence in terms of (flexible, plastic) multiplicity and (stable) singularity simultaneously. Forensic evidence depends on stability *and* change; both are needed if forensic evidence is to fulfill its role in the criminal justice system.

What is more, these issues tie not only into thinking about forensic evidence in the criminal justice system but also in thinking about the production of knowledge in more general terms.

MULTIPLICITY AND STABILITY

One way of understanding multiplicity is by looking at how Annemarie Mol (2002) has traced atherosclerosis, or rather atheroscleroses, in a Dutch hospital. Atherosclerosis, Mol shows, is "done" in different ways in different parts of the hospital. To vascular surgeons, atherosclerosis is pulsations in the arteries of the feet, clammy skin, and patients complaining about pain in their legs when they walk. To pathologists, atherosclerosis is a cross section of an artery under a microscope that exhibits a thickened innermost layer. To medical technicians, atherosclerosis is a difference between the patient's blood pressure in the ankles and that in the arms. To patients, it is a hindrance, making it difficult to, for example, go grocery shopping or visit friends and family. And there are more atheroscleroses, which are enacted, as Mol puts it, in different ways. These different—multiple—atheroscleroses may or may not correspond to each other, and, as Mol argues, the contradictions make it clear that there are, indeed, *several* atheroscleroses, not different ways of enacting "the same" atherosclerosis. "The difference between them," Mol writes, "may not attract attention as long as the objects they enact coincide, but as soon as they contradict another it becomes apparent that the clinic is two places. The interview. And the physical examination" (2002, 51).

A doctor interviewing a patient about his or her experience and a doctor physically examining a patient's legs are not the only sites where atherosclerosis is enacted in the clinic. "Blow up a few details of any site and immediately it turns into many" (Mol 2002, 51). There is an innumerable multiplicity of atheroscleroses being enacted, and Mol shows how different practices enact this multiplicity in parallel to each other, the outcomes sometimes coinciding and sometimes not.

This multiplicity is similar to that of forensic evidence. To a crime scene technician, forensic evidence is something that can be produced from traces he or she may, with the help of experience and imagination and professional vision, be able to recover from a crime scene. To a police investigator, forensic evidence is something that may be able to help him or her to assess a person's narrative. To a forensic scientist, forensic evidence is a trace that is to be analyzed and evaluated against a background of what forensic science knows about the world. To a prosecutor, forensic evidence is something that will help him or her to convince the court of a defendant's culpability. And to a judge, forensic evidence is something reliable, an anchoring point in their assessment of a case. One might say that each epistemic culture—and perhaps every workplace within it—enacts a specific forensic evidence through its specific practices. These forensic evidences may also be specific to particular cases or types of cases. For serious crimes, "you might really turn every stone," as a prosecutor in chapter 2 put it, whereas the investigation of a burglary or a vandalized bus shelter does not produce as much evidence, both because there typically are fewer traces to begin with and because fewer resources are spent on these cases.

Mol's concept of multiplicity can draw attention to the differentness of forensic evidence in the various epistemic cultures of the criminal justice system in a way that the notion of a biography cannot. It makes it possible to think about how forensic evidence is made—enacted—in a specific context, within a specific epistemic culture, and through specific practices. Granted, in their discussions of the social lives or biographies of objects, neither Appadurai (1986) nor Kopytoff (1986) focus on stability; their focus is the (ex)change that forms a commodity's trajectory. As Appadurai points out, commodities as objects may travel without their meanings; all an exchange requires is agreement about the exchange itself, not about the object (Appadurai 1986, 15). But still, both the idea of the circulation of objects and the notion of objects' biographies presuppose that there *is* an object to circulate and to accumulate a biography. The enactment of multiple forensic evidences presupposes no such thing.

The criminal justice system strives for stable, singular forensic evidence. Similarly, the multiplicity in the hospital that Mol studied was not appreciated by the doctors. They "don't like it" (Mol 2002, 51) when atheroscleroses do not coincide because this reveals that their diverse practices do not produce a single, coherent object. When discussing how the doctors achieve (a measure of) coherence, Mol does not talk about stability but about coordination. "The different forms of knowledge," she argues, "aren't divided into paradigms that are closed off from one another" (Mol 2002, 55). In other words, while there are multiple and different atheroscleroses in the hospital she studied, the atheroscleroses are connected. More than that, they are *being* connected. They are being connected when diagnoses and treatments are decided on, when different tests are done on the same patient, when the results are added, and when social and emotional reality are brought into diagnosis and treatment. Connecting them also implies that one atherosclerosis is given precedence or at least an advantage over others. While connecting them does not necessarily bring about a single reality—there might still be incoherence and incompatibilities during and after, for example, a treatment is decided on—it brings about (or to use Mol's term, enacts) sufficient coherence to settle on a course of treatment.

When it comes to forensic evidence, the translation work discussed in chapter 6 could be understood as a form of coordination that connects the different forensic evidences in the criminal justice system's different epistemic cultures. The translation work in court, for example, when forensic scientists answer questions on how they performed a particular analysis and the subsequent evaluation, could be described in terms of coordination making the court's decision on the evidence possible, and so could the meetings that the crime scene technician in chapter 5 talked about, during which crime scene technicians advised prosecution and police on how to proceed most fruitfully with the material collected in a case. The final act of coordination, then, is the verdict, which provides closure to the forensic evidence and determines its meaning for the case.

Regarding these activities as coordination also emphasizes their temporality and fragility. Multiplicities do not stay coordinated; their coherence must be enacted continuously. Forensic evidence may require particularly tight coordination—because the Swedish criminal justice system is not tolerant of incoherencies and incompatibilities and, as the frictions discussed in chapter 6 suggest, because forensic evidence is not always stable or coherent by itself. As chapter 6 shows and Mol discusses, stability and coherence may require work.

Understanding forensic evidence as being multiple, like atherosclerosis, could also cast a different light on the frictions between epistemic cultures. With multiple forensic evidences, the question of how to move the same object through the criminal justice system without it losing its stability is irrelevant, since it is not the same forensic evidence that is being moved but rather a new forensic evidence that is being enacted. That coherence between these enactments requires new coordination should not be surprising, nor should it be surprising that different "machineries of knowledge construction" (Knorr Cetina 1999, 3) enact different forensic evidences.

Thus, there are points in favor of seeing forensic evidence as multiple. An analytic concept of multiple forensic evidences makes it much less of a struggle to look at the criminal justice system's different epistemic cultures and the different forensic evidences they deal with. Most of all, it makes it much less of a struggle to reconcile these forensic evidences—recognizing their multiplicity means that they do not need to be analytically reconciled into a single, coherent forensic evidence.

BIOGRAPHICAL SEQUENTIALITY

Thinking about forensic evidence only in terms of multiplicities makes it difficult, however, to see its accumulative character. Mol's multiplicity allows for a certain accumulation; her notion of coordination includes running several tests on a patient and combining the different atheroscleroses they enact. Mol's atheroscleroses are—through coordination—connected: "It is one of the great miracles of hospital life: there are different atheroscleroses in the hospital but despite the differences between them they are connected. Atherosclerosis enacted is more than one—but less than many. *The body multiple* is not fragmented. Even if it is multiple, it also hangs together" (Mol 2002, 55; italics in original). The same could be said about forensic evidence: even if it is multiple, it also hangs together.

However, if forensic evidence were multiple in the same way as atherosclerosis, it would not matter much in which order the different forensic evidences were enacted. But the different forensic evidences are not parallel, as Mol's atheroscleroses are. Their accumulation is, of necessity, sequential. The prosecutor's forensic evidence is not enacted simultaneously with the forensic scientist's, but after. The crime scene technician's forensic evidence is not only enacted through different practices and in a different place than the forensic scientist's, but also before it. The court does not provide closure to a new enactment in the multiplicity of forensic evidences being enacted by different epistemic cultures but to forensic evidence that has been produced by these epistemic cultures together and additively.

More precisely, forensic evidence's sequentiality is fixed. Traces cannot be analyzed before they have been recovered, and the SKL must produce its results before they can be used to narrow down the legal stories being told during the pretrial investigation. What is more, the past of a piece of forensic evidence affects its present and future. How a trace has been recovered affects how it can be analyzed, and how it has been documented affects its place in a legal story. In addition, there may not always be a possibility of going back, so to speak, and changing the past. Once a crime scene has been released, it is more difficult, if not impossible, to find traces that have been overlooked. A trace that has been recovered cannot be re-recovered using a different method. The undocumented origin of a trace is lost forever. A suspect who has been confronted with forensic evidence cannot be asked for their pre-confrontation statement. Once the blood from a bloody fingerprint has been submitted to DNA analysis, it is impossible to examine the fingerprint instead. If a laboratory analysis uses up a trace—for example, a very small bloodstain— while carrying out an analysis, the analysis cannot be redone if it should go wrong. Only in rare cases is "going back" possible. For example, there may be enough of a trace to redo an analysis, or it may be possible to re-examine a seized piece of clothing if it has been correctly stored. But even these exceptions entail only a partial going back, and even they are dependent on how the trace has been recovered or the garment has been stored.

The notion of forensic evidence having a biography makes it easy to conceptualize this strictly sequential multiplicity. Just as a person's past has bearing on their present and future, so does the forensic evidence's. How a crime scene is examined and documented, a trace is handled in the laboratory, or an interrogation is conducted affects how forensic evidence can and cannot be treated later on in its biography. Like the huts Kopytoff describes—which typically go from living quarters, to guest huts, to kitchens, to goat or chicken houses, and, finally, to ruins (1986, 67)—forensic evidence has an expected biography as it moves (or is moved) from crime scene to laboratory, to the police and prosecution, to the defense, and, finally, to court.

To be sure, the life cycle of forensic evidence, unlike that of the huts, is not typically one of gradual deterioration and loss of status, but, as with the commodities Kopytoff discusses, there are "biographical expectations" (1986, 67). "To us," he explains, "a biography of a painting by Renoir that ends up in an incinerator is as tragic, in its way, as the biography of a person who ends up murdered" (Kopytoff 1986, 67). To police investigators and crime scene technicians, an investigation that is closed by the prosecutor because he or she deems that the evidence is not sufficient for an indictment is frustrating. To forensic scientists and prosecutors, forensic evidence that ends up being useless in court, for example, because there is too little documentation on where at the crime scene it was recovered, is at the least annoying, if not infuriating. And, as one of the judges put it, it is "not fun" when a defendant must be acquitted because the pretrial investigation is incomplete. These biographical expectations and the practices that fulfill (or fail to fulfill) them would be rather difficult to talk about with a notion of forensic evidence that focuses on parallelism instead of sequentiality.

Even though stability is not a focus for Appadurai or Kopytoff, it is the Renoir painting's stability that would make its incineration a tragedy—the expectations rely on it retaining its connection to the artist, that is, that the painting is conceptualized as "the same" ever since the artist created it. But at the same time as remaining "the same," it *does* change. A Renoir painting, for example, will have a string of successive owners, and its paint will crack over time. Furthermore, it has become completely irreplaceable (and much more valuable), since Renoir is dead and cannot paint more pictures.

Using the metaphor of a biography thus makes it possible to understand stability and change as occurring simultaneously. Forensic evidence is—and must be—"the same" throughout the criminal justice system. As chapter 6 shows, translation work contributes to this stability. On the other hand, forensic evidence changes constantly as it travels from the crime scene to the courtroom. It transforms from the material to the symbolic, from being an analysis result to giving support to a proposition, and from being a singular piece of evidence to being part of a legal story. Without these changes, forensic evidence would be as useless for the criminal justice system's purposes as it would be without stability. For example, a crime scene itself cannot be looked at during a trial that is taking place weeks or months after the alleged crime, and a court cannot determine the source of blood on a bloody shirt just by looking at it.

Thus, the differences between the criminal justice system's epistemic cultures are not merely a source of friction; they are also an integral component of the criminal justice system's collaboration. The police investigators' personal relationships and knowledge are just as important a part of the biography and social life of forensic evidence as are the prosecutors' exclusive focus on evidence and its legal meanings, the forensic scientists' analyses and evaluations, and the court's holistic evaluation of cases. It is not only the "*how we know what we know*" (Knorr Cetina 1999, 1; italics in original) that differs between the criminal justice system's epistemic cultures but also "what we know," that is, the knowledge that will be part of establishing, at the end of the biography of a piece of forensic evidence, what it means.

Each piece of forensic evidence is a combination of the different epistemologies of which it has been a part during its social life. In its evaluation, the court is not restricted to the legal stories or, in emic terminology, "explanations," of the evidence provided by the opposing legal parties. But by the time the court makes its evaluation of a case, it becomes quite difficult to separate out the forensic evidence from the other evidence in the case and from the legal stories with which it is intertwined. The forensic evidence supports, weakens, and shapes the legal stories, and the legal stories give the forensic evidence its meaning.

Thus, I argue that forensic evidence may be best understood neither as singular nor multiple, but as both. Certainly, the notions of multiplicity and the biographies and social lives of things are based on very different epistemologies. However, they can still be, if not combined, at least brought together in thinking about forensic evidence. There are different forensic evidences in the different epistemic cultures of the criminal justice system, but these different forensic evidences are also part of each other, part of a more or less stable forensic evidence being sequentially assembled as it is moved through the criminal justice system. If the criminal justice system were not made up of such disparate epistemic cultures, the forensic evidence would have a much less rounded personality (to appropriate another term usually applied to people), as it would have a much less diverse biography. This arrangement requires translation work in order to bridge differences and overcome (perhaps inevitable) frictions, but it also makes a diverse biography based on a combination and collaboration of different epistemic cultures possible. The differences in expertise in the criminal justice system's epistemic cultures are needed in order to produce and transport forensic evidence from crime scene to the court; the forensic evidence's different stages of life require different expertise if there is to be forensic evidence in court.

This simultaneity of forensic evidence—which is both singular and multiple at the same time—recalls Anni Dugdale's (1999) analysis of the negotiations around a consumer leaflet on a particular intrauterine contraceptive device (IUD). These negotiations, she shows, perform "a kind of oscillation, an oscillation between the (presupposition) that there is a single object on the one hand and the performance of different objects on the other" (Dugdale1999, 125). Moreover, she argues, "Indeed, more strongly, I want to say that the conversation and the agreement [. . .] is only possible at all because of this oscillation. For it is something like this: at least in this conversation, the enactment of a single IUD demands or depends on the mobilization of several different IUDs. If we all had to agree on the nature of the IUD, then the conversation would come to an abrupt halt" (Dugdale 1999, 125). Just as in the negotiations she discusses, where different IUDs are enacted in different parts of the conversation, it seems that the singular forensic evidence depends on the multiple ones. But, as chapter 6 has discussed, in the criminal justice system, the conversation—or its equivalent, the cooperation—comes to a halt or becomes at least very difficult and fraught with friction when it becomes impossible to agree on a single forensic evidence.

This does not mean that the translation work that contributes to that agreement is always successful or sufficient. The complaints about members of a different epistemic culture committing blunders because of their lack of familiarity with others' work are an example of imperfect translation work. A similar indication of concern about the efficacy of translation work is when forensic scientists wondered aloud how often pretrial investigations were closed solely because the prosecutor did not understand the forensic evidence and thus mistakenly thought it was worthless.

I was not able to give the forensic scientists an answer when I heard these concerns during my fieldwork, and I have no answer now. I have seen some friction in the criminal justice system, I have heard stories about other instances of friction, and I have heard hesitation about forensic evidence as well as seen the glossing over of issues that were important in other parts of the criminal justice system. But I have also seen (and heard) translation work that resulted in agreement and coordination and thus stability and singularity. In addition, forensic evidence is being made part of verdicts on a routine basis, so there must be at least the illusion of the different parts of the criminal justice system understanding each other.

I do think, however, that the frictions between the epistemic cultures are constructive; they seem to make possible the coordination that Mol (2002), Galison (1997), and Dugdale (1999) emphasize, not the least by drawing attention to coordination and translation being necessary in the first place. Friction can lead to translation work, and thus, paradoxically, it promotes stability. Without noticeable friction, there would be a risk of multiplicity without the stability for which the criminal justice system strives.

So, if forensic evidence in the criminal justice system is rather messy—being hard to pin down and both multiple and singular, depending on where one is looking—what can we learn from studying it?

LESSONS FROM FORENSIC EVIDENCE

I have, throughout this book, treated forensic evidence as a form of knowledge—not general knowledge but knowledge about particular cases that is gradually and collaboratively assembled by the criminal justice system.[3] Through evidence—forensic and other—the case's initial uncertainty is transformed into certainty beyond a reasonable doubt, at least in the cases in which the crime can be solved and the result is a conviction. So, what can understanding forensic evidence in the Swedish criminal justice system contribute to understandings of knowledge in society?

Forensic evidence is social and cultural not only through being (made) a participant in different social situations through the course of its biography but also through its production. Most tangibly, forensic evidence is an illustration of knowledge being inseparably material and social. As the previous chapters have hinted, forensic evidence is not only made by differing epistemic cultures, it is also made within a particular society.

"Death is [. . .] a social event," Stefan Timmermans (2006, 1) asserts, and his analysis of how medical examiners determine causes of death shows just *how* social it is. Death requires a medical act to become official. The investigation of a suspicious death requires legitimacy, authority, and a legal mandate. Death relies on medical as well as social practices—for example, to determine whether a suspected suicide was indeed a suicide. The outcome of the process of death and its cause has consequences—for example, for insurance claims.

Crime is just as social as death, as I have shown; it is established, and thus made, through collecting and organizing evidence, both forensic and other. Through this process, forensic evidence is both assembled and made meaningful, simultaneously being produced and being assigned roles in criminal justice. To borrow a term and a phrase from Karen Barad, forensic evidence is a "phenomenon," a "place where matter and meaning meet" (1996, 185); it is inseparably matter and meaning, inseparably material and cultural.

The making of forensic evidence requires organization—a laboratory, trained forensic scientists and crime scene technicians, police investigators, courts, laws, paths of communication—and this organization is sociocultural. There is no universally predetermined way to organize criminal justice; indeed, criminal justice itself is a cultural concept. That the SKL is a state-run laboratory, for example, can be seen in connection with the Swedish welfare state and its tendency, although weakened in past years, to keep the functions important to its citizens publicly run.

The practicalities of making forensic evidence are intertwined with and dependent on sociocultural factors. The shoe print at the crime scene of the burglary I described in chapter 5, for example, was interesting to the crime scene technician in part because people in Sweden generally do not wear shoes in a home. Similarly, individuals can be connected to clothes because clothes are not typically shared between individuals and thus usually carry only single DNA profiles (cf. Lynch et al. 2008, 284ff.).

The legal stories through which forensic evidence is assembled, interpreted, and evaluated draw on (culture-specific) stock scripts and assumptions of reasonableness. As forensic evidence is inseparably intertwined and entangled with the legal stories that produce and assess it (and that are produced and assessed through it), it is also inseparably cultural and therefore includes cultural biases.

There is also the issue of legitimacy, of what counts as knowledge and how different types of knowledge are put in relation to each other. Placing emphasis on knowledge associated with science is a historically and locally developed practice, and so is defining the delimitation of what is relevant and admissible to a case and what is not (e.g., Rosen 2006, particularly chapter 2). Such emphases are just as cultural as the role of the Azande oracles, which were brought to anthropological fame by E. E. Evans-Pritchard (1937).

This means that forensic evidence is produced not only by the whole of the legal system but also by wider society. Thus, in order to understand forensic evidence, it is not enough to only look at the courtroom, the forensic laboratory, or the crime scene, or to look at structural bias in forensic laboratory analyses (e.g., Lynch et al. 2008, 166; Meintjes-Van der Walt 2003) or the use of forensic databases (e.g., Duster 2006; Hindmarsh and Prainsack 2010; McCartney 2006). It is necessary to widen the perspective on forensic evidence to take into consideration the practices and circumstances that produce it.

A similar widening may be interesting when studying other forms of knowledge. The atheroscleroses studied by Mol (2002), for example, seem not only to be made in the hospital but also to be entangled with patients' personal lives and their expectations of their bodies. Regarding the production of general rather than particular knowledge, Emily Martin (1991), among others, has pointed out how cultural understandings are an integral part of (supposedly acultural) scientific knowledge, and this study of forensic evidence underlines the importance of taking that issue seriously.

Studying forensic evidence can contribute more than a new illustration to a well-known notion. As forensic evidence in the Swedish criminal justice system is produced in collaboration between a number of disparate epistemic cultures, it can help to think about the multiplicity and stability of knowledge at the same time. In other words, it can help thinking about not only how pieces of knowledge (or facts) are sequentially and collaboratively made, but also how they can be moved between disparate epistemic cultures in the course of their cooperation.

Moving artifacts (de Laet and Mol 2000), skills (Collins 1985, chapter 3), or concepts (Galison 1997, chapter 9) between contexts has been described as fraught with complexity and difficulty, with the central issue being the question of how to achieve stability and retain flexibility without giving in to plasticity. How much stability is required and how much plasticity is allowed (or necessary) varies, both between contexts and between agents. The Swedish criminal justice system, and in particular its forensic scientists, strive against plasticity and toward stability, whereas the museum studied by Star and Griesemer (1989) accepted quite a high degree of plasticity.

Typically, artifacts or facts are black-boxed in preparation for moving them from producer to user. For example, the user of a computer or cell phone is neither expected nor required to know much about its inner workings; the consumer of a drug is neither expected nor required to understand how it affects her body on a molecular level, nor to concern herself with how it has been tested; and the student learning about DNA is not necessarily expected or required to delve into the controversies that preceded the currently accepted DNA model. All these (arti)facts are just as usable when black-boxed and much less unwieldy. When (arti)facts are not black-boxed, the reason might be that a controversy—or a Science and Technology Studies scholar—has reopened them (Latour 1987), or that they are so new as to still harbor some uncertainty or controversy and thus require looking into (e.g., Lynch and Jordan 1992).

Forensic evidence is not so strictly black-boxed, although it is produced with tried and tested analyses and evaluation methods and interpreted within the long-developed framework of legal practice. That it is produced within a context of contestation, even though this contestation affects mainly the interpretation part of its production, might of course contribute to keeping forensic evidence from being completely black-boxed (although cf. Jasanoff 1998, 716). But I want to argue that it is primarily the collaboration of disparate epistemic cultures and the ensuing translation work that prevents black-boxing. Translation work brings stability across epistemic cultures to multiple forensic evidences, and such translation work, as chapter 6 shows, requires that supplementary information, details, and contexts, which would in other contexts be black-boxed out of sight, remain—or even be made—visible.

In addition, there is the distribution of responsibility to consider. If the court is to make the final decision on the forensic evidence in a case, the black box cannot be fully closed. What also makes the Swedish criminal justice system different from many other collaborations across professions is its common goal of solving crimes, which sets the tone for the collaboration and makes the members of the various epistemic cultures inclined to share information and to work together. This positive attitude toward collaboration differs from the boundary work (Gieryn 1983) that other professions in other collaborations use to establish and defend their jurisdictions (Abbott 1988) against others. To be sure, collaboration may still be difficult due to the differences between epistemic cultures, but it does not need to overcome distrust. Exceptions to this are that forensic scientists want to avoid teaching criminals to commit better crimes and that they feel occasional apprehension toward defense lawyers when they are perceived to deliberately be trying to distort expert statements.

Forensic evidence thus straddles Latour's (1987) distinction between ready-made science and science in action in more than one way. It is not black-boxed and thus made ready-to-use, but its recipients are expected to look into a semitransparent box and to be able to keep its contents stable. It is not produced in one part of the criminal justice system—say, the laboratory—and consumed by the other parts, but rather its production is an ongoing process that finishes at the end of the legal chain with a verdict. And after its production is finished, so is its use.

The example of forensic evidence suggests that black-boxing is not necessarily the only solution to making knowledge movable. As long as translation work is performed, the semitransparent box enables more stability than either boundary objects (Star and Griesemer 1989), which, employing Galison's (1997) language metaphor, rely on a good-enough approximation of communication, or immutable mobiles (Latour 1990), which are expected to transcend language. Translation work does not necessarily make the different languages mutually intelligible, but it achieves coordinated communication about specific pieces of forensic evidence.

For people dealing with knowledge—and this applies not only to those working with forensic evidence—this implies that moving knowledge between epistemic cultures and keeping it stable during the transition might be made easier by sharing general knowledge specific to these epistemic cultures. Shaping a common trading language (Galison 1997) may not be sufficient to assure stability; shared understandings and the means and the ability to put oneself in the other side's shoes may also be required. Thus, for cooperation across professions, especially in large-scale knowledge production organizations, practitioners may want to create points of contact that make it possible for epistemic cultures to exchange understandings and form a shared knowledge base.

For scholars studying practices of knowledge, a semitransparent box and the translation work it requires may be an interesting alternative perspective to Latour's black box. It also allows for a less manipulative view of the transport of knowledge than Latour's perspective of silencing and overpowering dissenters offers. However, as it builds on mutual trust—the participants in the translation work rely on each other to provide translations in good faith—and the willingness to engage, this mode of moving knowledge between epistemic cultures may not, of course, be possible in all contexts.

NOTES

INTRODUCTION

1. The Swedish term for plaintiff is *målsäganden,* literally, "the owner of the case." In many cases, this is the person who contacts the police to report having been harmed or wronged. I will use the term "plaintiff" instead of the more customary "victim," not only because this is the word my interlocutors have used, but also because, strictly speaking, it is not legally certain before the verdict whether the plaintiff is actually a victim of crime. However, this choice is not intended to minimize their possible distress; a plaintiff may, of course, be quite clearly suffering physically, emotionally, or financially.

2. In January 2015, after my fieldwork was complete, the Swedish police was reorganized, and the twenty-one regional police authorities were consolidated into a single authority. In the course of the reorganization, the Swedish National Laboratory of Forensic Science became a part of the police (before, it had been a separate authority under the National Police Board) and was renamed the National Forensics Centre. As my interlocutors called the laboratory by its old name and referred to the old structure, I will use the now-obsolete name throughout the book.

3. For a concise and very readable overview of the field of STS and its sensibilities, see Thompson (2005, chapter 1).

4. Mol's point is that "atherosclerosis" does not exist from the outset but rather that it (and presumably other conditions as well) comes into being as a result of various practices, some of them medical. Moreover, different practices enact different atheroscleroses. In other words, the practices don't "give" patients a disease in terms of infecting them with it, but they do "give" patients a disease in terms of combining the patients' experiences with medical practices to come up with a diagnosis of and a treatment for atherosclerosis—which looks different and is treated differently in different parts of the hospital.

5. The SKL is state-owned and part of the criminal justice system, and thus forensic analyses, while subject to allotting and prioritizing resources, are not paid for directly. In criminal justice systems where they are, forensic evidence

may very well be perceived in terms of economic value (see Lawless and Williams 2010).

6. For an introduction to ethnographic work, see Agar (1980), Marcus (1998), Peacock (1986), and Spradley (1979, 1980).

7. The interviews (and the other parts of my fieldwork) quoted in the book were conducted in Swedish. I have translated them from my transcriptions (or field notes).

8. *Kriminalteknik* [Forensics] is available at http://nfc.polisen.se/trycksaker /tidningen-kriminalteknik/.

9. These terms are police slang. In Swedish they are *en buse, en allmänhet,* and *göra husis,* respectively—a petty criminal, a member of the public (literally, "one public"), and doing a house search (see also Granér 2004).

1. IN COURT

1. For a concise overview of the Swedish criminal justice system, see Svensson (1995).

2. Unlike in other criminal justice systems, the plaintiff in the Swedish legal system is part of a criminal trial both as a witness and as an injured party, since he or she is seen as having been wronged by the offender. Thus, criminal trials are about both society and individuals having been wronged; accordingly, the verdict addresses both the sentence and damages.

3. Throughout the book, I've used ellipses in square brackets to indicate omissions and suspension points to indicate a pause or a speaker's hesitation.

4. What made the issue a bit less clear-cut than it might seem was that the relative was not a citizen or a registered resident in Sweden and that there was some difficulty and uncertainty involved in dealing with the foreign bureaucracy in question.

5. Chapter 6 will discuss the (non)questioning of forensic evidence in more detail.

6. When the members of the criminal justice system I interviewed discussed rape cases in general, they typically spoke about female plaintiffs and victims and male suspects and offenders.

2. THE PUBLIC PROSECUTION'S OFFICE

1. Giving a case an obviously unreasonable classification (in order to use more resources or certain coercive measures and thus perhaps obtain more evidence) does not mean that the evidence recovered will become inadmissible. It may, however, lead to the prosecutor being charged with professional misconduct.

2. For a more extensive discussion of the pretrial legal storytelling in this particular case, see Kruse (2012).

3. At the time of our conversation, the examinations and analyses were not complete yet, so the prosecutor did not know what their results would be.

4. A possible such case—a person convicted of multiple murders—was being discussed in the media at the time of my fieldwork because an in-depth television documentary claimed that the convictions had been based on (at best) sloppy investigations and an unbalanced person's false confessions. Since then, the verdicts have been recanted as miscarriages of justice, and the person in question has been released from forensic psychiatric care.

5. An (albeit nonrepresentative) overview of DNA evidence in trial made by a regional public prosecution office in 2008, however, suggests that it is rather common that defendants deny participation in a crime or, more often, state that they cannot remember what happened and thus can neither confess or deny involvement (Regional Public Prosecution Office Gothenburg 2008). Merckelbach and Christianson (2007) and van Oorsouw and Cima (2007) suggest that these claims of amnesia may be strategic, at least in connection with violent crimes, as they allow defendants to appear cooperative while being selective with information, to escape having to talk about unpleasant events, or to gain access to psychiatric evaluations. For a thorough and insightful analysis of convicted offenders' attitudes to forensic evidence, see Machado and Prainsack (2012), who have interviewed prisoners in Portugal and Austria.

6. Spohn et al. (2001) describe US prosecutors using similar reasoning when they decide whether to file charges in a case.

7. The most famous still-open investigation in Sweden is that of the 1986 murder of Prime Minister Olof Palme.

8. Like many other workplaces that are funded by the government, prosecutors' offices are expected to use taxpayers' money efficiently. For prosecutors, efficiency is measured in indictments and convictions; in absolute numbers, but also in relation to the number of pretrial investigations carried out.

9. Prosecutors and defense lawyers occasionally clash on what should and should not be included in these reports. The prosecution and police say that, in order to keep the reports at a manageable length, they must leave out clutter, such as unsuccessful door-to-door questioning, whereas defense attorneys claim that that amounts to suppressing evidence.

3. THE CRIMINAL INVESTIGATION DIVISION

1. Almost all Swedish employees are paid on the twenty-fifth of the month.

2. Swabbing—taking buccal swabs from known persons in order to obtain a comparison DNA profile—is in the hands of the police in Sweden.

3. Because of the family's distress, I experienced this case only from the relative distance of the investigators' discussions among themselves. It was the investigators' decision to keep me out of direct contact with the family, as they were, the investigators felt, too upset to have to deal with my presence on top of everything else.

4. The Swedish word for a "troublemaker" is *buse* (plural *busar*). It is a colloquial term, used especially in police jargon, for a criminal, typically an unspecialized petty criminal. Someone who makes their living from petty crime might be called a "professional troublemaker." See also Ekman (1999) and Granér (2004) for discussions of police categorizations and jargon.

5. On the other hand, violent crimes, such as murders, were understood as typically being committed either within "addict circles" or, more rarely, in exceptional situations by someone who is quite law-abiding both before and after.

6. This does not mean that there is always agreement on *how* a case is police solved. For example, some of the investigators I met spoke, unprompted, about the murder of Prime Minister Olof Palme in 1986 as having been police solved. In that case, a suspect was first convicted but then won an appeal. However, in other contexts, other members of the police favor other possible culprits or talk about the murderer still being unknown.

7. In Sweden, carrying a knife in a public place—including keeping one in one's car in a public place—can be a criminal offense, so the question of who had placed the knife in the car was relevant.

8. Prosecutors and investigators do not *necessarily* clash, though. For example, I once heard a prosecutor who had decided that there was not enough evidence to keep a suspect in custody apologize to the police investigator in charge of the case, who, having dealt with the suspect on and off for years, was not convinced of their innocence.

9. Innes (2002) describes similar police humor as a distancing strategy that police officers use to deal with potentially disturbing situations and to manage their emotions.

10. The official investigation of how the cases had been handled pointed out other problematic factors, as well, such as noncompliance with protocols and unsatisfactory treatment of tip-offs from the public (National Police Board and the Public Prosecution Service 2010).

11. Lars Holmberg's (2003) study of police work in Glostrup, Denmark, shows that suspicion—and thus the making of suspects—could, in addition to personal knowledge, also be based on general categories of behavior and appearance. The investigators whose work I studied typically only talked about known troublemakers, but the police on the street, who delivered these suspects, may very well have used similar categories in their work.

12. See chapter 4.

13. With a law that took effect on January 1, 2006, the police's power to take DNA samples was extended. Before this law was passed, police were allowed to take DNA samples from persons suspected of a crime whose range of punishment included imprisonment, but only if such a measure was deemed necessary for the investigation. The new law allows them to take buccal swabs for registration purposes from persons suspected of a crime whose range of punishment includes imprisonment, even if swabbing is not considered to be necessary for the current investigation. This made it possible to swab many "professional troublemakers" and register their

DNA profiles. They also are allowed to take buccal swabs from non-suspects (who must be at least fifteen years of age) in order to facilitate identification in investigating crimes whose range of punishment includes imprisonment, but only if there is an extremely strong justification for the swabbing's significance for the investigation.

14. Their work becomes visible primarily through annual efficiency statistics. See Manning (1997 [1977], 122ff.) for a discussion of these statistics and how police are affected by them and affect them.

4. IN THE LABORATORY

1. In January 2015, the laboratory changed its name to the National Forensics Centre (Nationellt forensiskt centrum).

2. The police's crime scene divisions do have smaller laboratories in which they perform analyses that require less equipment and specialization. In addition, the National Fingerprint Department (Nationella Fingeravtrycksavdelningen) in Stockholm—which is part of the national police—identifies some of the fingerprints recovered at crime scenes. (The SKL typically recovers and identifies fingerprints from objects sent to them.)

3. Since January 2015, the laboratory has been part of the police service.

4. In this context, a "case" is not necessarily a court case or an investigation; in the laboratory, a case can be a single trace, a single material, or a conglomeration of objects and the traces recovered from them. The differences between how police investigators and forensic scientists use the term can, however, be quite fluid.

5. Drug analyses were the exception. In those cases, the forensic scientists identified substances instead of doing comparisons.

6. Recently, a fourth database was added, namely an elimination database that contains the DNA profiles of SKL staff and other relevant persons and is used to screen out false traces.

7. For discussions of the social consequences of forensic databases, see, for example, Hindmarsh and Prainsack (2010) or McCartney (2004, 2006).

8. A locus is a place on the genome. These specific ten loci are located in areas of the genome that are considered without function, so-called junk DNA, where mutations can accumulate without affecting function and where, therefore, variation between individuals is great. This variation consists of a varying number of repetitions of short sequences of DNA. As there are two copies (or alleles) of each gene on the human genome, one from each parent, the analysis of each locus results in two numbers.

9. Every resident in Sweden has such a number, called a *personnummer*. The number is used as a unique identification in contact with the authorities—not only with the criminal justice system but also with the medical, education, and tax systems—as well as with companies.

10. A +4 is the highest possible result for a match. The next sections of the chapter will discuss this in detail.

11. I use the term "Bayesian approach" to describe the conceptual framework as a whole, including the courts' role; the SKL would call their part a "likelihood ratio approach." In either case, a Bayesian approach is not a synonym for Bayes' theorem (see, for example, Evett et al. 2011) but rather a way of reasoning about probabilities.

12. The random match probability denotes the probability that a given DNA profile matches a person selected at random.

13. This is not one of the three forensic DNA databases, nor is it connected to them.

14. Linköping is the city where the SKL is located.

15. The analysis the interviewee talks about involves the activity level (i.e., whether the items have been in contact with each other). While the reasoning is the same as for the source level, drawing conclusions on the activity level requires more information about a case and its circumstances.

16. Alternatively, a grade of +3 could be reached if fibers from three separate items worn together are found on a chair made of a fabric that does not release fibers.

17. This applies to fiber analyses. When dealing with other types of analyses, forensic scientists do not require as much information and may prefer to remain ignorant about the details of a case.

18. STR is short for "short tandem repeat" and refers to a DNA technology that measures the number of repetitions of short (and, it is believed, "meaningless") sequences of DNA in particular loci on the genome.

19. The suggestion of addressing the question of guilt in court mathematically (see, for example, Fienberg and Kadane 1983) could also be seen as striving for impartial objectivity.

20. The SKL adopted the Bayesian approach in 2008.

21. In the cases where the defense keeps the defendant's version of events, or parts of it, a secret until the court hearing, the defendant's version can of course not be considered for the propositions.

22. This standardization and transparency encompasses, of course, only the SKL. The forensic scientists also participate in regular accreditation practices and in international expert groups, which calibrated them against national and international standards of their respective forensic specializations.

23. See chapter 6 for more on communicating results and their value.

5. THE CRIME SCENE DIVISION

1. In Sweden, many suburbs consist of large apartment buildings with cheap housing, not idyllic single-family homes with gardens.

2. I am aware that the usual term is "trace evidence." However, as one of the points I want to argue for in this book is that the process of producing forensic evidence is not finished until the court makes its verdict, I will go for consistency with my argument and use the unusual term "trace."

3. Crime scene technicians have received training from the SKL since 1998. Before that, the police academy trained technicians.

4. For severe crimes, the prosecutor and the police investigators sometimes visit the crime scene during the investigation to get an idea of the place's layout; a trial may include a similar visit.

5. For a thorough discussion of science and forensic science, see Cole (2010, 2013).

6. In most Swedish homes, people take off their shoes at the door and walk around barefoot or in socks, so one does not expect shoe prints in living rooms.

7. For safety reasons, doors leading into apartments and houses can be unlocked from the inside without a key.

8. The technician is referring to the burned-out cars discussed at the beginning of the chapter.

9. In the original Swedish, the crime scene technician used the word *berättelse,* which does not connote fictionality in the same way that the everyday use of the English term "story" does.

10. This also prevents the forensic scientists who receive the knives from getting cut and thus exposed to biohazards when opening the packages.

6. COLLUDING AND COLLIDING WORLDS

1. Incidentally, Galison's description of exchange is quite close to Appadurai's, who talks about it in the following terms: "the commodity context, as a social matter, may bring together actors from quite different cultural systems who share only the most minimal understandings (from the conceptual point of view) about the objects in question and agree only about the terms of trade" (1986, 15).

2. What is more, as Lawrence Venuti (1995) points out, a translation that obliterates visible difference may promote (post)colonial domination and subjugation.

3. This did not necessarily preclude the need for more translation work, for example, by the crime scene technicians who translated "clinically" written expert statements for the prosecution, as mentioned in chapter 5.

4. The forensic scientist is talking about the difference in the likelihood ratios behind the grades on the scale. If the likelihood ratio arrived at through the evaluation of the laboratory result (see chapter 4 for details) is a million or higher, that corresponds to a +4. In other words, a likelihood ratio of a million is the line between a +3 and a +4.

5. One forensic scientist mentioned receiving a telephone call from a suspect who had wanted her to spend more time on a particular analysis. He was innocent, he had insisted, and was sure that if she extended the examination she would find proof of it. She had answered that if she were to do that, she would "just become more certain" about what she had written in her statement, but he kept on calling, which "was a little disconcerting," although he had not actually said anything out of the ordinary. In the end, she gave him a few addresses abroad for a second opinion.

6. In this attitude, the Swedish criminal justice system seems to differ from that of the United States. Sheila Jasanoff, for example, points out that the "dynamics of litigation" that affect criminal trials in the United States serve as a strong incentive for parties to keep forensic evidence black-boxed (1998, 716).

7. This interview was conducted before the SKL changed the wording on their verbal scale. Still, the judge's choice of the word "certain" does not echo the expert statements' phrasing of a grade +4 result. (The following phrase about disregarding close relatives does, however, match.)

8. Cases that are assigned high priority are those with juvenile suspects and with suspects in custody, in which time frames are tight.

9. Malmö district court 2012, case B 10425–10.

7. IN COURT, REPRISE

1. When the judge quoted above talked about the credibility of accounts, he did not make a distinction between credibility and reliability. In fact, only one of the judges I interviewed—the youngest of them—acknowledged a difference between them. Even the Supreme Court subsumes both as credibility.

2. The verdicts quoted in this chapter are in Swedish; I have translated the quotes.

3. "Indifferent intent" means that the defendant did not actively intend the plaintiff to die from the crash but was indifferent to the possibility that he might.

4. Motive can be important, however, in the investigation phase of some cases, especially in those of so-called investigation murders (*spaningsmord*), which are suspected murders that lack a suspect at the outset.

5. Malmö district court 2012, case B 10425–10.

6. Also see Lacey (1998), for a discussion of how the British criminal justice system shapes as well as relates to different gendered subject positions.

7. The lay assessors are meant to contribute a layperson's perspective, and thus the people's influence, to the judges' legal expertise, but they do not necessarily contribute diversity in all respects.

8. A district court verdict has a three-week period of appeal, after which, if not appealed, it gains legal effect. For a verdict from a court of appeal, the period is four weeks.

8. CONCLUSION

1. What is not documented may still be conserved, at least for a time. Forensic scientists may talk about why a particular case was interesting or difficult to analyze or evaluate, and police investigators may talk about how respectable a witness appeared at the time of an interview.

2. One of the features of a patrol officer's work is doing tasks that someone else in the police force is more specialized to handle—for example, interrogations and crime scene examinations—so they are quite used to specialists having opinions on their work.

3. For a discussion of scientific and forensic knowledge production, see Cole (2010, 2013).

REFERENCES

Abbott, Andrew

1988 *The System of Professions: An Essay on the Division of Expert Labor.* Chicago: University of Chicago Press.

Agar, Michael H.

1980 *The Professional Stranger: An Informal Introduction to Ethnography.* San Diego: Academic Press.

Amsterdam, Anthony G., and Jerome Bruner

2000 *Minding the Law.* Cambridge, MA: Harvard University Press.

Appadurai, Arjun

1986 "Introduction: Commodities and the Politics of Value." In *The Social Life of Things: Commodities in Cultural Perspective,* edited by Arjun Appadurai, 3–63. Cambridge: Cambridge University Press.

Axberger, Hans-Gunnar, Feryal Mentes, Karin Palmgren Goodhe, and Jens Västberg

2006 *Felaktigt dömda: Rapport från JK:s rättssäkerhetsprojekt* [Wrongly convicted: Report from the legal security project at the Office of the Chancellor of Justice]. Visby: JK:s rättssäkerhetsprojekt.

Bal, Roland

2005 "How to Kill with a Ballpoint: Credibility in Dutch Forensic Science." *Science, Technology, & Human Values* 30 (1): 52–75.

Barad, Karen

1996 "Meeting the Universe Halfway: Realism and Social Constructivism without Contradiction." In *Feminism, Science and the Philosophy of Science,* edited by L. H. Nelson and J. Nelson, 161–194. London: Kluwer Academical Publishers.

1998 "Getting Real: Technoscientific Practices and the Materialization of Reality." *Differences: A Journal of Feminist Cultural Studies* 10 (2): 87–128.

2003 "Posthumanist Performativity: Toward an Understanding of How Matter Comes to Matter." *Signs: Journal of Women in Culture and Society* 28 (3): 801–831.

2007   *Meeting the Universe Halfway: Quantum Physics and the Entanglement of Matter and Meaning.* Durham: Duke University Press.

Bennett, W. Lance

1978   "Storytelling in Criminal Trials: A Model of Social Judgment." *Quarterly Journal of Speech* 64: 1–22.

1979   "Rhetorical Transformation of Evidence in Criminal Trials: Creating Grounds for Legal Judgment." *Quarterly Journal of Speech* 65: 311–323.

Bennett, W. Lance, and Martha S. Feldman

1981   *Reconstructing Reality in the Courtroom: Justice and Judgment in American Culture.* New Brunswick: Rutgers University Press.

Björkman, J., C. Diesen, F. Forssman, and P. Jonsson

1997   *Bevis: Värdering av erkännande, konfrontationer, DNA och andra enstaka bevis* [Evidence: Evaluation of confessions, confrontations, DNA, and other singular pieces of evidence]. Stockholm: Norsteds Juridik.

Bruner, Jerome

2002   *Making Stories: Law, Literature, Life.* Cambridge, MA: Harvard University Press.

Callon, Michel

1986   "Some Elements of a Sociology of Translation: Domestication of the Scallops and the Fishermen of St Brieuc Bay." In *Power, Action, and Belief: A New Sociology of Knowledge?*, edited by John Law, 196–233. London: Routledge and Kegan Paul.

Caudill, David S.

2002   "Ethnography and the Idealized Accounts of Science in the Law." *San Diego Law Review* 39: 269–305.

Caudill, David S., and Lewis H. LaRue

2006   *No Magic Wand: The Idealization of Science in Law.* Lanham: Rowman and Littlefield Publishers.

Cole, Simon

2001   *Suspect Identities: A History of Fingerprinting and Criminal Identification.* Cambridge, MA: Harvard University Press.

2009   "Forensics without Uniqueness, Conclusions without Individualization: The New Epistemology of Forensic Identification." *Law, Probability and Risk* 8 (3): 233–255.

2010   "Acculturating Forensic Science: What Is 'Scientific Culture', and How Can Forensic Science Adopt it?" *Fordham Urban Law Journal* 38 (2): 435–472.

2013   "Forensic Culture as Epistemic Culture: The Sociology of Forensic Science." *Studies in History and Philosophy of Biological and Biomedical Sciences* 44: 36–46.

2015   "A Surfeit of Science: The 'CSI Effect' and the Media Appropriation of the Public Understanding of Science." *Public Understanding of Science* 24 (2): 130–146.

Cole, Simon, and Rachel Dioso-Villa

2007 "*CSI* and Its Effects: Media, Juries, and the Burden of Proof." *New England Law Review* 41 (3): 435–469.

Collins, Harry M.

1985 *Changing Order: Replication and Induction in Scientific Practice.* Chicago: University of Chicago Press.

Cook, R., I. W. Evett, G. Jackson, P. J. Jones, and J. A. Lambert

1998a "A Model for Case Assessment and Interpretation." *Science and Justice* 38 (3): 151–156.

1998b "A Hierarchy of Propositions: Deciding Which Level to Address in Casework." *Science and Justice* 38 (4): 231–239.

Daemmrich, Arthur

1998 "The Evidence Does Not Speak for Itself: Expert Witnesses and the Organization of DNA-Typing Companies." *Social Studies of Science* 28 (5–6): 741–772.

Dahl, Johanne Yttri

2009 "Another Side of the Story: Defence Lawyers' Views on DNA Evidence." In *Technologies of Security: The Surveillance of Everyday Life,* edited by Katja Franco Aas, Helene Oppen Gundhus, and Heidi Mork Lomell, 219–237. Abingdon: Routledge.

Dahl, Johanne Yttri, and Ann Rudinow Sætnan

2009 "'It All Happened So Slowly': On Controlling Function Creep in Forensic DNA Databases." *International Journal of Law, Crime and Justice* 37: 83–103.

Daston, Lorraine

1992 "Objectivity and the Escape from Perspective." *Social Studies of Science* 22 (4): 597–618.

1995 "The Moral Economy of Science." *Osiris* 10: 2–24.

Daston, Lorraine, and Peter Galison

1992 "The Image of Objectivity." "Seeing Science," special issue, *Representations* (40): 81–128.

2007 *Objectivity.* New York: Zone Books.

de Laet, Marianne, and Annemarie Mol

2000 "The Zimbabwe Bush Pump: Mechanics of a Fluid Technology." *Social Studies of Science* 30 (2): 225–263.

Derksen, Linda

2000 "Towards a Sociology of Measurement: The Meaning of Measurement Error in the Case of DNA Profiling." *Social Studies of Science* 30 (6): 803–845.

2003 "Agency and Structure in the History of DNA Profiling: The Stabilization and Standardization of a New Technology." PhD thesis, University of California, San Diego.

Diesen, Christian

1994 *Bevisprövning i brottmål* [Evidence assessment in criminal cases]. Stockholm: Norstedts Juridik.

Dugdale, Anni

1999 "Materiality: Juggling Sameness and Difference." In *Actor Network Theory and After,* edited by John Law and John Hassard, 113–135. Oxford: Blackwell Publishing.

Durkheim, Émile

1984 [1893] *The Division of Labour in Society.* Basingstoke: Macmillan Education.

Duster, Troy

2006 "Explaining Differential Trust of DNA Forensic Technology: Grounded Assessment or Inexplicable Paranoia?" *Journal of Law, Medicine, and Ethics* 34 (2): 293–300.

Ekman, Gunnar

1999 *Från text till batong: Om poliser, busar och svennar* [From text to nightstick: On police, troublemakers, and citizens]. Stockholm: Ekonomiska forskningsinstitutet.

Ericson, Richard V.

1981 *Making Crime: A Study of Detective Work.* Toronto: University of Toronto Press.

Evans-Pritchard, E. E.

1937 *Witchcraft, Magic and Oracles among the Azande.* Oxford: Clarendon Press.

Evett, I. W., et al

2011 "Expressing Evaluative Opinions: A Position Statement." *Science and Justice* 51 (1): 1–2.

Fienberg, Stephen E., and Joseph B. Kadane

1983 "The Presentation of Bayesian Statistical Analyses in Legal Proceedings." *Journal of the Royal Statistical Society,* series D (*The Statistician*), 32 (1/2), Proceedings of the 1982 I.O.S. Annual Conference on Practical Bayesian Statistics: 88–98.

Galison, Peter

1997 *Image and Logic: A Material Culture of Microphysics.* Chicago: University of Chicago Press.

Ghoshray, Saby

2007 "Untangling the *CSI* Effect in Criminal Jurisprudence: Circumstantial Evidence, Reasonable Doubt, and Jury Manipulation." *New England Law Review* 41 (3): 532–562.

Gieryn, Thomas F.

1983 "Boundary-Work and the Demarcation of Science from Non-Science: Strains and Interests in Professional Ideologies of Scientists." *American Sociological Review* 48 (6): 781–795.

Gluckman, Max

1963 *Order and Rebellion in Tribal Africa: Collected Essays with an Autobiographical Introduction.* London: Cohen and West.

Goodwin, Charles

1994 "Professional Vision." *American Anthropologist* 96 (3): 606–633.

1995   "Seeing in Depth." *Social Studies of Science* 25: 237–274.
Granér, Rolf
2004.   *Patrullerande polisers yrkeskultur* [Police patrols' occupational culture]. PhD thesis, Lund University.
Haack, Susan
2003   "Trials & Tribulations: Science in the Courts." *Daedalus* 132 (4): 54–63.
Hald, Camilla
2011   *Web without a Weaver—On the Becoming of Knowledge: A Study of Criminal Investigation in the Danish Police.* Boca Raton: Dissertation.com.
Halfon, Saul
1998   "Collecting, Testing and Convincing: Forensic DNA Experts in the Courts." *Social Studies of Science* 28 (5–6): 801–821.
Haraway, Donna
1988   "Situated Knowledges: The Science Question in Feminism and the Privilege of Partial Perspective." *Feminist Studies* 14 (3): 575–599.
Harding, Sandra, ed.
2004   *The Feminist Standpoint Theory Reader: Intellectual and Political Controversies.* New York: Routledge.
Hindmarsh, Richard, and Barbara Prainsack, eds.
2010   *Genetic Suspects: Global Governance of Forensic DNA Profiling and Databasing.* Cambridge: Cambridge University Press.
Holmberg, Lars
2003   *Policing Stereotypes: A Qualitative Study of Police Work in Denmark.* Berlin: Galda and Wilch Verlag.
Huntley, Jill E., and Mark Costanzo
2003   "Sexual Harassment Stories: Testing a Story-Mediated Model of Juror Decision-Making in Civil Litigation." "Psychology in Civil Litigation," special issue, *Law and Human Behavior* 27 (1): 29–51.
Innes, Martin
2002   "Organizational Communication and the Symbolic Construction of Police Murder Investigations." *British Journal of Sociology* 53 (1): 67–87.
2003   *Investigating Murder: Detective Work and the Police Response to Criminal Homicide.* Oxford: Oxford University Press.
Jackson, Graham
2009   "Understanding Forensic Science Opinions." In *Handbook of Forensic Science,* edited by Jim Fraser and Robin Williams, 419–444. Uffculme: Willan Publishing.
Jasanoff, Sheila
1998   "The Eye of Everyman: Witnessing DNA in the Simpson Trial." *Social Studies of Science* 28 (5–6): 713–740.
2001   "Judicial Fictions: The Supreme Court's Quest for Good Science." *Society* 38 (4):27–36.
2006   "Just Evidence: The Limits of Science in the Legal Process." *Journal of Law, Medicine & Ethics* 34 (2): 328–341.

Johnson, Jim (Bruno Latour)

  1988   "Mixing Humans and Nonhumans Together: The Sociology of a Door-Closer." *Social Problems* 35 (3): 298–310.

Knorr Cetina, Karin D.

  1999   *Epistemic Cultures: How the Sciences Make Knowledge.* Cambridge, MA: Harvard University Press.

Knorr-Cetina, Karin D., K. Amann, S. Hirschauer, and K.-H. Schmidt

  1988   *"Das naturwissenschaftliche Labor als Ort der 'Verdichtung' von Gesellschaft"* [The Sciences laboratory as a location of social 'condensation']. *Zeitschrift für Soziologie* 17 (2): 85–101.

Koehler, Jonathan J.

  1996   "On Conveying the Probative Value of DNA Evidence: Frequencies, Likelihood Ratios, and Error Rates." *University of Colorado Law Review* 67: 859–886.

Kopytoff, Igor

  1986   "The Cultural Biography of Things: Commoditization as a Process." In *The Social Life of Things: Commodities in Cultural Perspective,* edited by Arjun Appadurai, 64–91. Cambridge: Cambridge University Press.

Kruse, Corinna

  2010   "Producing Absolute Truth: *CSI* Science as Wishful Thinking." *American Anthropologist* 112 (1): 79–91.

  2012   "Legal Storytelling in Pre-Trial Investigation: Arguing for a Wider Perspective on Forensic Evidence." *New Genetics and Society* 31 (3): 299–309.

Lacey, Nicola

  1998   *Unspeakable Subjects: Feminist Essays in Legal and Social Theory.* Oxford: Hart Publishing.

Lamont, Michèle

  2009   *How Professors Think: Inside the Curious World of Academic Judgment.* Cambridge, MA: Harvard University Press.

Latour, Bruno

  1987   *Science in Action: How to Follow Scientists and Engineers through Society.* Cambridge, MA: Harvard University Press.

  1990   "Drawing Things Together." In *Representation in Scientific Practice,* edited by Michael Lynch and Steve Woolgar, 19–68. Cambridge, MA: MIT Press.

  1999   *Pandora's Hope: Essays on the Reality of Science Studies.* Cambridge, MA: Harvard University Press.

  2005   *Reassembling the Social: An Introduction to Actor-Network-Theory.* Oxford: Oxford University Press.

Latour, Bruno, and Steve Woolgar

  1986   [1979] *Laboratory Life: The Construction of Scientific Facts.* Princeton, NJ: Princeton University Press.

Law, John

  1999   "After ANT: Complexity, Naming and Topology." In *Actor Network Theory and After,* edited by John Law and John Hassard, 1–14. Oxford: Blackwell Publishing.

Lawless, Christopher J., and Robin Williams

2010 "Helping with Inquiries or Helping with Profits?: The Trials and Tribulations of a Technology of Forensic Reasoning." *Social Studies of Science* 40 (5): 731–755.

Lindsey, Samuel, Ralph Hertwig, and Gerd Gigerenzer

2003 "Communicating Statistical DNA Evidence." *Jurimetrics* 43: 147–163.

Lynch, Michael

1985a "Discipline and the Material Form of Images: An Analysis of Scientific Visibility." *Social Studies of Science* 15 (1): 37–66.

1985b *Art and Artifact in Laboratory Science: A Study of Shop Work and Shop Talk in a Research Laboratory.* London: Routledge and Kegan Paul.

1998 "The Discursive Production of Uncertainty: The OJ Simpson 'Dream Team' and the Sociology of Knowledge Machine." *Social Studies of Science* 28 (5–6): 829–868.

Lynch, Michael, Simon A. Cole, Ruth McNally, and Kathleen Jordan

2008 *Truth Machine: The Contentious History of DNA Fingerprinting.* Chicago: University of Chicago Press.

Lynch, Michael, and Kathleen Jordan

1992 "The Sociology of a Genetic Engineering Technique: Ritual and Rationality in the Performance of the 'Plasmid Prep.'" In *The Right Tools for the Job—At Work in Twentieth-Century Life Sciences,* edited by Adele E. Clarke and Joan H. Fujimura, 77–114. Princeton, NJ: Princeton University Press.

M'charek, Amade

2000 "Technologies of Population: Forensic DNA Testing Practices and the Making of Differences and Similarities." *Configurations* 8: 121–158.

2008 "Silent Witness, Articulate Collective: DNA Evidence and the Inference of Visible Traits." *Bioethics* 22 (9): 519–528.

Machado, Helena, and Barbara Prainsack

2012 *Tracing Technologies: Prisoners' Views in the Era of CSI.* Farnham: Ashgate.

Manning, Peter K.

1997 [1977] *Police Work: The Social Organization of Policing.* Prospect Heights, IL: Waveland Press.

Marcus, George E.

1998 *Ethnography through Thick and Thin.* Princeton, NJ: Princeton University Press.

Martin, Aryn, and Michael Lynch

2009 "Counting Things and People: The Practices and Politics of Counting." *Social Problems* 56 (2): 243–266.

Martin, Emily

1991 "The Egg and the Sperm: How Science Has Constructed a Romance Based on Stereotypical Male-Female Roles." *Signs* 16 (3): 485–501.

McCartney, Carole

2004 "Forensic DNA Sampling and the England and Wales National DNA Database: A Sceptical Approach." *Critical Criminology* 12: 157–178.

2006 *Forensic Identification and Criminal Justice: Forensic Science, Justice and Risk.* Portland: Willan Publishing.

Meintjes-Van der Walt, Lirieka
2003 "The Proof of the Pudding: The Presentation and Proof of Expert Evidence in South Africa." *Journal of African Law* 47 (1): 88–106.

Merckelbach, Harald, and Sven Å. Christianson
2007 "Amnesia for Homicide as a Form of Malingering." In *Offenders' Memories of Violent Crimes,* edited by Sven Å. Christianson, 165–190. Chichester: John Wiley and Sons.

Mol, Annemarie
2002 *The Body Multiple: Ontology in Medical Practice.* Durham: Duke University Press.

Moore, Sally Falk
2001 "Certainties Undone: Fifty Turbulent Years of Legal Anthropology, 1949–1999." *Journal of the Royal Anthropological Institute* 7 (1): 95–116.

Nida, Eugene
2000 "Principles of Correspondence." In *The Translation Studies Reader,* 2nd ed., edited by Lawrence Venuti, 153–167. New York: Routledge.

Nordgaard, Anders, Ricky Ansell, Weine Drotz, and Lars Jaeger
2012 "Scale of Conclusions for the Value of Evidence." *Law, Probability and Risk* 11 (1): 1–24.

National Police Board and the Public Prosecution Service
2010 *Granskning av polisens och åklagarmyndighetens åtgärder i samband med utredningen av mordet på Pernilla Hellgren* [Examination of the police's and prosecution's measures in the investigation of Pernilla Hellgren's murder]. Accessed April 24, 2015. https://polisen.se/Aktuellt /Rapporter-och-publikationer/Rapporter/Publicerat---Nationellt/Ovriga-rapporterutredningar/Inspektion/2010/Granskning-av-utredningen-av-mordet-pa-Pernilla-Hellgren/.

Orr, Julian E.
1996 *Talking about Machines: An Ethnography of a Modern Job.* Ithaca, NY: Cornell University Press.

Peacock, James L.
1986 *The Anthropological Lens: Harsh Light, Soft Focus.* Cambridge: Cambridge University Press.

Pennington, Nancy, and Reid Hastie
1986 "Evidence Evaluation in Complex Decision Making." *Journal of Personality and Social Psychology* 51 (2): 242–258.
1992 "Explaining the Evidence: Test of the Story Model for Juror Decision Making." *Journal of Personality and Social Psychology* 62 (2): 189–206.

Popper, Karl R.
1972 [1959] *The Logic of Scientific Discovery.* London: Hutchinson and Co.

Porter, Theodore M.

1992a "Objectivity as Standardization: The Rhetoric of Impersonality in Measurement, Statistics, and Cost-Benefit Analysis." *Annals of Scholarship* 9: 19–59.

1992b "Quantification and the Accounting Ideal." *Social Studies of Science* 22 (4): 633–651.

1995 *Trust in Numbers: The Pursuit of Objectivity in Science and Public Life.* Princeton, NJ: Princeton University Press.

Prainsack, Barbara, and Martin Kitzberger

2009 "DNA Behind Bars: 'Other' Ways of Knowing Forensic DNA Technologies." *Social Studies of Science* 39 (1): 51–79.

Prainsack, Barbara, and Victor Toom

2010 "The Prüm Regime: Situated Dis/Empowerment in Transnational DNA Profile Exchange." *The British Journal of Criminology* 50 (6): 1117–1135.

Public Prosecution Service

n.d. *Prosecutor: A Part of the Legal System.* Accessed July 10, 2015. www .aklagare.se/Dokumentsamling/Informationsmaterial-och-nyhetsbrev /Prosecutor---a-part-of-the-legal-systempdf/.

Rappert, Brian

2001 "The Distribution and Resolution of the Ambiguities of Technology, or Why Bobby Can't Spray." *Social Studies of Science* 31 (4): 557–591.

Regional Public Prosecution Office of Gothenburg

2008 *DNA som bevis: En sammanställning av domar* [DNA as evidence: A compilation of verdicts]. Accessed July 10, 2015. www.aklagare.se /Dokumentsamling/RattsPM1/2008–05-DNA-som-bevispdf/.

Robertson, Bernard, and G. A. Vignaux

1995 *Interpreting Evidence: Evaluating Forensic Science in the Courtroom.* Chichester: John Wiley and Sons.

Rosen, Lawrence

2006 *Law as Culture: An Invitation.* Princeton, NJ: Princeton University Press.

Rubel, Paula G., and Abraham Rosman

2003 "Introduction: Translation and Anthropology." In *Translating Cultures: Perspectives on Translation and Anthropology,* edited by Paula G. Rubel and Abraham Rosman, 1–22. Oxford: Berg Publishers.

Sarat, Austin

1993 "Speaking of Death: Narratives of Violence in Capital Trials." *Law & Society Review* 27 (1): 19–58.

Schelin, Lena

2007 *Bevisvärdering av utsagor i brottmål* [Evidentiary evaluation of statements in criminal cases]. Stockholm: Norsteds Juridik.

Schklar, Jason, and Shari Seidman Diamond

1999 "Juror Reactions to DNA Evidence: Errors and Expectancies." *Law and Human Behavior* 23 (2): 159–184.

Simoncelli, Tania

    2006   "Dangerous Excursions: The Case Against Expanding Forensic DNA Databases to Innocent Persons." *Journal of Law, Medicine, and Ethics* 34 (2): 390–397.

Snow, David A., and Leon Anderson

    1987   "Identity Work among the Homeless: The Verbal Construction and Avowal of Personal Identities." *American Journal of Sociology* 92 (6): 1336–1371.

Spohn, Cassia, Dawn Beichner, and Erika Davis-Frenzel

    2001   "Prosecutorial Justifications for Sexual Assault Case Rejection: Guarding the 'Gateway to Justice.'" *Social Problems* 48 (2): 206–235.

Spradley, James P.

    1979   *The Ethnographic Interview.* New York: Holt, Rinehart and Winston.

    1980   *Participant Observation.* New York: Holt, Rinehart and Winston.

Ställvik, Olof

    2009   *Domarrollen: Rättsregler, yrkeskultur och ideal.* [The role of judges: Legal rules, professional culture, and ideals]. Stockholm: Jure förlag.

Star, Susan Leigh

    1991   "The Sociology of the Invisible: The Primacy of Work in the Writing of Anselm Strauss." In *Social Organization and Social Process: Essays in Honor of Anselm Strauss,* edited by David R. Maines, 265–283. New York: Aldine De Gruyter.

Star, Susan Leigh, and James R. Griesemer

    1989   "Institutional Ecology, 'Translations' and Boundary Objects: Amateurs and Professionals in Berkeley's Museum of Vertebrate Zoology, 1907–39." *Social Studies of Science* 19 (3): 387–420.

Stephens, Sheila L.

    2007   "The '*CSI* Effect' on Real Crime Laboratories." *New England Law Review* 41 (3): 591–607.

Strauss, Anselm, Shizuko Fagerhaugh, Barbara Suczek, and Carolyn Wiener

    1985   *Social Organization of Medical Work.* Chicago: University of Chicago Press.

Sudnow, David

    1965   "Normal Crimes: Sociological Features of the Penal Code in a Public Defender Office." *Social Problems* 12 (3): 255–276.

Svensson, Bo

    1995   *Criminal Justice Systems in Sweden.* Stockholm: National Council for Crime Prevention Sweden.

Swedish National Courts Administration

    2008   *More Modern Court Proceedings: Video Recording and Playback of Examinations in Court.* Accessed July 10, 2015. http://domstol.se/Ladda-ner--bestall/Informationsmaterial/More-modern-court-proceedings---Video-recording-and-playback-of-examinations-in-court/.

    2010   *Tingsrätten* [The District Court]. Accessed March 21, 2013. http://np.netpublicator.com/netpublication/n04443896.

2015 *Court Statistics 2014.* Accessed July 10, 2015. http://domstol.se
/Ladda-ner--bestall/Statistik/.

Swedish National Laboratory of Forensic Science

2014 *Årsberättelse 2013* [Yearly report 2013.] Accessed July 21, 2015. https://
polisen.se/Global/www%20och%20Intrapolis/Arsredovisningar/01%20
Polisen%20nationellt/Polisen_Arsredovisning_2013.pdf.

Thompson, Charis

2005 *Making Parents: The Ontological Choreography of Reproductive Technologies.* Cambridge, MA: MIT Press.

Timmermans, Stefan

2006 *Postmortem: How Medical Examiners Explain Suspicious Deaths.* Chicago:
University of Chicago Press.

Tyler, Tom R.

2006 "Viewing *CSI* and the Threshold of Guilt: Managing Truth and Justice in
Reality and Fiction." *Yale Law Journal* 115: 1050–1084.

Valverde, Mariana

2003 *Law's Dream of a Common Knowledge.* Princeton, NJ: Princeton University Press.

van Oorsouw, Kim, and Maaike Cima

2007 "The Role of Malingering and Expectations in Claims of Crime-related
Amnesia." In *Offenders' Memories of Violent Crimes,* edited by Sven Å.
Christianson, 191–213. Chichester: John Wiley and Sons.

Venuti, Lawrence

1995 *The Translator's Invisibility: A History of Translation.* London: Routledge.

Williams, Robin, and Paul Johnson

2008 *Genetic Policing: The Use of DNA in Criminal Investigations.* Cullompton:
Willan Publishing.

INDEX

abstraction, 90, 94, 100–105, 149, 150

Actor-Network Theory, 9

agential realism, 10

Amsterdam, Anthony, 23, 24, 35, 58

Appadurai, Arjun, 11–12, 148, 156, 160, 175n1

articulation work, 115–16, 118

artifacts, 7; black-boxed, 165; fluidity of, 10; moving, 165; producing, 111; as social beings, 9

Barad, Karen, 10, 163

Bayesian approach, 78–80, 81, 84, 174nn11,20; compared to other approaches, 119–20; consistency across specializations, 86–89; criticism of, 86; distribution of responsibility, 80, 112–16; and economic value, 89, 169–70n5; and limitations of knowledge, 84; perceived accessibility of, 119–20; propositions in, 78–79; and quantification, 84, 86; shaping epistemic culture, 86, 89; underlying philosophy of, 78

Bennett, Lance, 19–20, 22–24, 41, 64, 136, 138, 141, 142, 143, 144

bias: in court, 143–44; in laboratory, 85–86, 88, 164; in legal storytelling, 23, 143–45, 164; in witness accounts, 25–26, 29

biography of forensic evidence, 12, 33, 51, 69, 89, 92, 131, 148–49, 154, 156, 160, 161; expectations, 159; sequentiality, 158–59

black box, 115, 128, 165–67, 176n6 (ch 6)

boundary object, 111–12, 116–17, 128, 129, 166

boundary work, 110, 166

Bruner, Jerome, 19, 23, 24, 35, 58

buccal swab, 1, 2, 55, 66–67, 69, 75, 90, 171n2, 172n13

burden of proof, 17, 18, 47, 141

calibration talks, 86–89

certainty: absolute, 70, 89; beyond a reasonable doubt, 132–33, 146, 163; forensic evidence and, 26; in laboratory, 70, 76, 80, 83, 84, 120, 122, 175n5 (ch 6); sufficient, 43–47; sufficient for indictment, 39–48; unattainable, 6. See also uncertainty

classification of crime, 35–38, 47, 49, 55, 170n1 (ch 2)

Cole, Simon, 8, 74, 84, 86, 90, 108, 113, 164, 175n5 (ch 5), 177n3

confessions: acceptance of, 41, 135; false, 41–42, 43, 135, 171n4; and forensic evidence, 42–43, 67–68; and supportive evidence, 41

contamination, 75, 115; prevention of, 71–72, 106; uncertainty associated with, 70, 75

coordination, 115, 116, 118, 130, 156–57, 158, 162, 166

counter-expertise, 9, 27, 126–27, 147

court, 5, 16–33, 131–47, 148; hearing, 16–19; importance of spoken word in, 50; responsibility for forensic evidence, 3, 80, 90, 109, 112–15, 148, 150, 165 crime: classification of, 35–38, 47, 49, 55, 170n1 (ch 2); differentiations of, 37; making, 34; normal, 36; plaintiffless, 30; police solved, 60, 172n6; prerequisites of, 37, 44–45; solved, 6, 60, 93, 131, 152, 163

crime scene: examination of, 1, 91, 96–100; feeling of, 102; luck at, 104; normal, 102; requiring imagination, 101–5; uncertainty, 104–5

crime scene division, 3–6, 91–108, 173n2

Crime Scene Investigation (TV series), 43, 70, 103, 108

crime scene report, 92–96

crime scene technician, 2–4, 12, 15, 91–108, 121, 148–50, 155; legal storytelling of, 105; mediating by, 105–8, 117, 122–28, 175n3 (ch 6)

criminal investigation division, 3, 11, 12, 53–69, 90, 93, 112, 124

criminal justice system, Swedish, 17, 19, 123, 133, 170nn1,2 (ch 1), 176n6 (ch 6); cooperation of, 108, 109–30, 162, 164; epistemic cultures in, 107, 111, 112, 118, 125, 128, 148, 149, 156–58, 160; limitations of, 146; moving forensic evidence through, 12, 108, 109–30, 148, 157, 161; producing forensic evidence, 1–2, 8, 9, 10

CSI. See Crime Scene Investigation (TV series)

CSI effect, 108

culpability, 3, 7, 27, 33, 90, 95, 113, 131, 132, 146, 148, 156

Daston, Lorraine, 26, 84–85, 88

databases: criminal/police, 64–65; elimination, 173n6; fingerprint, 72–73; forensic DNA, 8, 66, 71, 73, 173n7; producing suspects, 8, 164, 173n7; reference, 81–82, 174n13

defense lawyer, 1, 8–9, 27, 51, 144, 148, 166, 171n9; access to, 13; in court, 18–19; and forensic evidence, 26–29, 68, 113–16, 118; and translation work, 121, 125–29

Dugdale, Anni, 161, 162

epistemic cultures, 53, 61–65, 67–69, 89, 105–8, 109–112, 116, 118, 128–31, 148–50, 152, 156–58, 160, 160–67

equivalence in translation, 117, 122–23

ethnographic fieldwork, 12–15, 170n6; "at home," 13; limits, 150–51; restrictions, 13; at SKL, 71

evaluation of evidence, 113, 134–45, 147, 157, 160–61; legal storytelling in, 136–45; risk evaluation in, 135

evaluation of laboratory results, 77–89, 165; consistency in, 87–89; responsibility for, 112; scale of conclusions for, 79, 83; transparency of, 87–89

everyday discursive skills and knowledge, 18, 20, 22–23, 142–44, 148

evidence: admissibility of, 18; assembling, 39–43; assessing, 24, 39–43; centrality in court, 132; collecting, 35–36; evaluating, 133–45, 160–61; freedom of, 18; of intent, 32, 44–45; main and supportive, 28–33, 41; uncertain, 80. *See also* forensic evidence; verbal evidence; witness evidence

exchange: of commodities, 11, 116, 156, 175n1; of forensic data, 8; of knowledge, 110, 116, 167

expert statements, 5, 71, 77, 111, 117, 118, 128, 149; conveying uncertainty, 114–15, 120; in court, 18, 51, 75; in crime scene reports, 95, 107; distribution of responsibility in, 80, 109; moving, 109–30, 166; nuances in, 25, 107, 109, 113, 114, 116, 124; and translation work, 117–24, 128, 175n3 (ch 6)

expert witness, 9, 18–19, 27, 51, 108, 113–14, 118, 125, 129

facts, 3, 7; forensic evidence and, 24, 25–26, 112; making, 7–8, 9, 10, 111, 145–46, 164; moving, 165–67; as social beings, 9

Feldman, Martha, 19, 22–23, 136, 138, 141–44

fieldwork, ethnographic, 12–15, 170n6; "at home," 13; limits, 150–51; restrictions, 13; at SKL, 71

flexibility. *See* multiplicity

flora of fiber, 42, 74

forensic analyses: commissioning, 5, 43, 58, 126; comparison in, 66, 72–77; and confessions, 42–43; DNA, 73; drug,

legal storytelling *(continued)*
19–24, 138–45; pretrial, 34–52, 53, 58,
64, 67; reasonableness in, 138–45. *See
also* stock scripts; story, legal

likelihood ratio, 78, 80, 87, 174n11; estima-
tion of, 82–84; expressed through scale,
79, 120, 175n4; intervals of, 81–84; and
populations, 81; propositions in, 78–79.
See also Bayesian approach

Lynch, Michael, 8, 18, 74, 76, 84, 90, 95, 113,
115, 164, 165

match: accuracy of, 77, 79, 115; being evaluation, 82–84; DNA, 2–2, 29, 30, 82, 112,
122, 147; fingerprint, 14, 73, 78; requiring evaluation, 76–80

M'charek, Amade, 8, 81

mechanical objectivity, 26, 84–89

mediation: between civilians and investigation, 107–8; between crime scene and
laboratory, 105–6; by crime scene technicians, 92, 105–8, 122, 128; between epistemic cultures, 105–8; between laboratory and prosecution/police, 106–7, 122

Mol, Annemarie, 9, 155–57, 158, 162, 164,
165, 169n4

motive, 23, 141, 176n4

moving: expert statements, 109–30, 166;
knowledge, 110–12, 116–18, 164–65

multiplicity, 9, 111, 155–59, 161, 162; of
forensic evidence, 129, 131, 151, 154–59,
161, 165; of knowledge, 164; of legal
stories, 35, 39, 41, 43, 105, 150, 154

narrative, 19, 22–24, 32, 63–64; and forensic evidence, 32, 155; in statements,
28–32, 43, 137, 143–44. *See also* legal
storytelling; story, legal

objectivity: mechanical, 26, 84–89; organic,
88–89, 129

obligations: of impartiality, 4, 18–19, 35; to
people, 19, 59, 128, 135, 171n3 (ch 3);
personal vs. abstract, 59–60; to society,
47–48, 107, 135; to suspects, 38, 60, 107;
to victims, 60, 171n1 (ch 3)

organic objectivity, 88–89, 129

Orr, Julian, 63–64

personal identification number, 173n9

phenomena, 10, 163

plaintiff, 12, 13, 15, 146, 169nn1,2; in court,
17–19, 50–51; at crime scene, 96–100,
102, 105, 107–8

plasticity: of forensic evidence, 154–58; of
knowledge, 110–12, 117, 165. *See also*
multiplicity; stability

police humor, 63, 69, 172n9

police investigator, 4–5, 15, 43, 53–69, 90,
93, 99, 106–7, 121, 149, 155, 160; identity
work by, 68–69; personal relationships,
54, 58–69, 149, 160; perspective, 59, 129,
152; in prosecutor's office, 34, 50–52,
60–61, 109, 172n8

police patrol, 4, 5, 13, 57–59, 92, 96–97, 99,
151–52, 177n2 (ch 2)

police slang, 14, 170n9, 172n4

police-solved crimes, 60, 172n6

police work, 53–69; and forensic technologies, 68–69; of making suspects, 65,
172n11; "real," 55, 68–69

population, reference, 70, 81–82;
suspect, 8

prerequisites of a crime, 37; proving, 37,
44–46, 49, 142–43

pretrial investigation, 34–52, 94, 106, 132,
154, 159, 162; concluding, 43–48; leader,
4, 5, 94, 106, 121, 126, 150, 151; leading,
34–36; report, 5, 17, 118, 124, 171n9; and
uncertainty, 6, 39, 43–48, 56, 146

professional pride: of crime scene technicians, 93, 103; of prosecutors, 48

professional vision, 75, 112, 149; at crime
scene, 92, 101–5, 149, 155; in laboratory,
75–76, 83, 86, 88, 89, 149

proof, burden of, 17, 18, 47, 141

propositions in likelihood ratios, 78–80,
86, 112, 113, 115, 118, 146–47, 150, 166,
174n21; levels of, 79

prosecutor, 4–5, 15, 25–26, 34–52, 53–54,
107, 109, 113–30, 132, 145, 149–51; in
court, 16–22, 24; perspective, 153, 156,
160, 162; and police investigators,
59–62

public opinion on police work, 55

quantification, 84–89

uncertainty *(continued)*
146; at crime scene, 104–5; distribution
of, 90, 112, 114, 115; and forensic evidence,
25–28, 71–72; friction about sources of,
112–16; in forensic analyses, 74–75, 81;
judges on, 6, 133; managing, 70, 72, 76,
89, 90; in pretrial investigation, 6, 39,
43–48, 56, 146; and reasonable doubt, 6,
133, 163; resolving in court, 146; and
verbal evidence, 25–28. *See also* certainty

verbal evidence: as main evidence, 28–33;
and narrative, 32; and uncertainty, 25–28

verdict: gaining legal effect, 146, 176n8 (ch
7); making, 132–36
view from nowhere, 143

witnesses, 4, 12, 13, 15, 17–18, 29–31, 33, 34,
36, 39–42, 44–45, 53, 55, 67, 136, 139,
144–45; anticipated performance in
court, 50–51; expert, 9, 18–19, 27, 51, 108,
113–114, 118, 125, 129. *See also* expert
witness
witness evidence, 18, 25, 29, 31. *See also*
statements; verbal evidence
Woolgar, Steve, 71, 92, 94

www.ingramcontent.com/pod-product-compliance
Lightning Source LLC
Chambersburg PA
CBHW031134270326
41929CB00011B/1618